"This volume provides a great entry point into the vast and growing psychological literature on one of the defining problems of the early 21st century – fake news and its dissemination. The chapters by leading scientists first focus on how (false) information spreads online and then examine the cognitive processes involved in accepting and sharing (false) information. The volume concludes by reviewing some of the available countermeasures. Anyone new to this area will find much here to satisfy their curiosity."

– **Stephan Lewandowsky**, *Cognitive Science,*
University of Bristol, UK

"Fake news is a serious problem for politics, for science, for journalism, for consumers, and, really, for all of us. We now live in a world where fact and fiction are intentionally blurred by people who hope to deceive us. In this tremendous collection, four scientists have gathered together some of the finest minds to help us understand the problem, and to guide our thinking about what can be done about it. *The Psychology of Fake News* is an important and inspirational contribution to one of society's most vexing problem."

– **Elizabeth F Loftus**, *Distinguished Professor,*
University of California, Irvine, USA

"This is an interesting, innovative and important book on a very significant social issue. Fake news has been the focus of intense public debate in recent years, but a proper scientific analysis of this phenomenon has been sorely lacking. Contributors to this excellent volume are world-class researchers who offer a detailed analysis of the psychological processes involved in the production, dissemination, interpretation, sharing, and acceptance of fake news. This book should be essential reading to anyone interested in public affairs, and especially to students, researchers, applied professionals in the social sciences."

– **Joseph P Forgas**, *Scientia Professor,*
University of New South Wales, Sydney, Australia

D1457438

THE PSYCHOLOGY OF FAKE NEWS

This volume examines the phenomenon of fake news by bringing together leading experts from different fields within psychology and related areas, and explores what has become a prominent feature of public discourse since the first Brexit referendum and the 2016 US election campaign.

Dealing with misinformation is important in many areas of daily life, including politics, the marketplace, health communication, journalism, education, and science. In a general climate where facts and misinformation blur, and are intentionally blurred, this book asks what determines whether people accept and share (mis)information, and what can be done to counter misinformation? All three of these aspects need to be understood in the context of online social networks, which have fundamentally changed the way information is produced, consumed, and transmitted. The contributions within this volume summarize the most up-to-date empirical findings, theories, and applications and discuss cutting-edge ideas and future directions of interventions to counter fake news.

Also providing guidance on how to handle misinformation in an age of "alternative facts", this is a fascinating and vital reading for students and academics in psychology, communication, and political science and for professionals including policy makers and journalists.

Rainer Greifeneder is Professor of Social Psychology at the University of Basel, Switzerland. His research focuses on the impact of feelings on judgment, individuals' experiences and perceptions of being socially excluded, and the way individuals construe truth.

Mariela E. Jaffé is Postdoctoral Researcher in Social Psychology at the University of Basel, Switzerland. Her research interests focus on the construal of truth, individuals' preferences regarding diversity, and the use of decision-making aids.

Eryn J. Newman is Lecturer at the Australian National University. Her research focuses on how people come to believe and remember things are true and how tangential information or "pseudo-evidence" can bias people's assessments of information they encounter.

Norbert Schwarz is Provost Professor of Psychology and Marketing and Co-director of the Mind & Society Center at the University of Southern California. His research addresses the context sensitive and embodied nature of judgment and decision making and its implications for public opinion, consumer behavior, and social science research.

THE PSYCHOLOGY OF FAKE NEWS

Accepting, Sharing, and Correcting Misinformation

Edited by Rainer Greifeneder, Mariela E. Jaffé, Eryn J. Newman, and Norbert Schwarz

Routledge
Taylor & Francis Group

LONDON AND NEW YORK

First published 2021
by Routledge
2 Park Square, Milton Park, Abingdon, Oxon OX14 4RN

and by Routledge
52 Vanderbilt Avenue, New York, NY 10017

Routledge is an imprint of the Taylor & Francis Group, an informa business

British Library Cataloguing-in-Publication Data
A catalogue record for this book is available from the British Library

Library of Congress Cataloging-in-Publication Data
A catalog record for this book has been requested

ISBN: 978-0-367-27181-7 (hbk)
ISBN: 978-0-367-27183-1 (pbk)
ISBN: 978-0-429-29537-9 (ebk)

Typeset in Bembo
by Apex CoVantage, LLC

Published with the generous support of the Swiss National Science Foundation (10.13039/501100001711), Grant #10BP12_193570.

CONTENTS

CONTRIBUTORS

Robert Ackland
Australian National University, Australia

Dolores Albarracín
University of Illinois at Urbana-Champaign, USA

Jordan R. Axt
McGill University, Canada

Judit Bar-Ilan
Bar-Ilan University, Israel

Andrew Dawson
University of Southern California, USA

Rainer Greifeneder
University of Basel, Switzerland

Karl Gwynn
Australian National University, Australia

Gali Halevi
Icahn School of Medicine at Mount Sinai, USA

Mariela E. Jaffé
University of Basel, Switzerland

Madeline Jalbert
University of Southern California, USA

Aaron C. Kay
Duke University, USA

Mark J. Landau
University of Kansas, USA

Benjamin A. Lyons
University of Utah, USA

Elizabeth J. Marsh
Duke University, USA

Vittorio Merola
Stony Brook University, USA

Eryn J. Newman
Australian National University, Australia

Daphna Oyserman
University of Southern California, USA

Jason Reifler
University of Exeter, UK

Jon Roozenbeek
University of Cambridge, UK

Norbert Schwarz
University of Southern California, USA

Matthew L. Stanley
Duke University, USA

Sander van der Linden
University of Cambridge, UK

Lynn Zhang
University of Southern California, USA

ACKNOWLEDGEMENTS

Numerous people have helped to put together this volume. We are extremely grateful for their support. We thank all reviewers for taking part in the peer-review process and for providing editors and authors with tremendously useful feedback and suggestions. We thank Saskia Bollin for her invaluable assistance in all phases of the project. We thank all at Routledge who were part of the process, from the first proposal to the book's publication, especially Eleanor Taylor. And we thank the Swiss National Science Foundation for its generous support (grant #IZSEZ0_180211 and grant # 10BP12_193570).

1

WHAT IS NEW AND TRUE[1] ABOUT FAKE NEWS?

Rainer Greifeneder, Mariela E. Jaffé, Eryn J. Newman, and Norbert Schwarz

Following Brexit and the 2016 US presidential campaign, the Oxford Dictionary selected "post-truth" as the Word of the Year 2016, which the dictionary defined as "relating to or denoting circumstances in which objective facts are less influential in shaping public opinion than appeals to emotion and personal belief" (Oxford-Dictionary, 2016). A year later, the Collins Dictionary designated "fake news" as the Collins Word of the Year 2017 in response to a 365% increase in its usage in the Collins corpus of the English language (Collins-Dictionary, 2017). As the dissemination of fake news flourished and became a topic of public discourse and concern, designating something as fake news became another tool in the repertoire of political propaganda. From US president Donald Trump accusing journalists and mainstream media of spreading fake news about him (e.g., Pengelly, 2017) to the mainstream media tracking fake news spread by Donald Trump (Kessler, Rizzo, & Kelly, 2019), and the German party AFD (Alternative für Deutschland) returning to the Nazi term *Lügenpresse* (lying press) to describe mainstream media, accusations of spreading fake news has become a daily occurrence. Against the background of this general climate, the present volume presents insights into fake news from multiple scientific disciplines and perspectives.

What is fake news and what is misinformation?

Fake news can be defined as "false, often sensational, information disseminated under the guise of news reporting" (Collins-Dictionary, 2017). Analyses of Google searches indicate that, prior to 2016, the term was used to locate satirical news, as offered by the satirical print magazine *The Onion* and the satirical television show *The Daily Show*. By the end of 2016, the use had shifted to searches pertaining to the US presidential election, Donald Trump, Twitter, and CNN

(Cunha, Magno, Caetano, Teixeira, & Almeida, 2018). The dissemination of false information under the guise of news reporting had become serious business.

What sets fake news apart from news reports that are merely false is the intention to deceive. As the Council of Europe (Wardle & Derakhshan, 2017) noted, the public discussion of fake news often subsumes disinformation, misinformation, and mal-information. The term "disinformation" refers to false information that is created to harm a person, social group, organization, or country, whereas "misinformation" is merely false but not intended to harm. Because intention to harm is often difficult to determine, the term "misinformation" is also used for false information in general and the contributions to this volume follow this usage. Of course, harm can also be achieved by spreading factually correct information with harmful implications – for example, by leaking factually true private information that should not have any bearing on public issues – a type of information that is sometimes referred to as "mal-information". All of these classes of information are more influential when the information is accepted as true and is shared with others. Once accepted, false information is very difficult to correct and can continue to influence related beliefs even when people no longer endorse the false information that gave rise to those beliefs (for a review, see Lewandowsky, Ecker, Seifert, Schwarz, & Cook, 2012). The contributions to the present volume focus on the processes involved in accepting, sharing, and correcting false information.

In the public discourse, the term "fake news" is usually associated with the political realm, but fake news stories are not confined to it; fabricated information is disseminated in all areas, perhaps most prominently in the domains of consumer products, health, and finances. But even reputable scientific journals are not free of fake news in the form of deliberately deceptive reports based on manipulated or freely invented data (Bar-Ilan & Halevi, 2020).

Fake news has gained public attention for several reasons. *First*, misinformation has become part of everyday life (see Lyons, Merola, & Reifler, 2020). For instance, Allcott and Gentzkow (2017) estimated that the average US-American adult has consumed one to three pieces of fake news in the months prior to the 2016 US presidential election and the fact checkers of the *Washington Post* reported that President Trump made 10,796 false or misleading claims in the first 869 days of his presidency (Kessler et al., 2019). Furthermore, Vosoughi, Roy, and Aral (2018) found in analyses of Twitter data that false information is retweeted more rapidly and more often than true information, particularly news on politics.

Second, to the extent that people believe misinformation and act upon it, fake news can have serious consequences. To illustrate, during what has become known as Pizzagate (Wikipedia, n.d.), a piece of fake news about an alleged connection among officials of the US Democratic party, a pizza restaurant in Washington, D.C., and human trafficking instigated a young man to "investigate" the cause himself by firing a rifle inside the restaurant. Not all direct consequences of fake news are as dramatic; but, when individuals or groups act upon disinformation, consequences may often not be to their individual, or societies-at-large, advantage.

Third, peaceful human interaction and individual as well as societal prosperity strongly depend on interpersonal trust (e.g., Greifeneder, Müller, Stahlberg, Van den Bos, & Bless, 2011). Division of labor, trade between persons and countries, as well as democracies all necessitate shared beliefs that some things are true and that agents can be relied upon. Individuals found guilty of lying are not (or to a lesser extent) believed, and companies or countries known to have violated financial promises face serious backlash. Fake news about a government has the potential to erode society's trust and therefore constitute a threat, especially to democracies. Moreover, denouncing established newspapers, broadcasters, and journals has the potential to erode trust in those organizations that take on the role of fact checkers in modern societies. In the United States, trust in mainstream news sources showed a pronounced partisan divide at the time of the 2016 election, with 51% of Democrats but only 14% of Republicans reporting "a fair amount" or "a great deal" of trust in mainstream news source (Swift, 2016).

Brief history of fake news dissemination

The intention to deceive is as old as humankind, and systematic fake news campaigns have been documented throughout history (see Posetti & Matthews, 2018). What changed is the ability to spread misinformation quickly and efficiently to ever larger audiences. When Ramses II pretended in 1274 BC that his attempt to capture the city of Kadesch was successful, word of his fake victory had to be spread by mouth and via wall paintings. When Octavian waged a propaganda campaign against Antony in Roman times, he could smear him as a womanizer and drunk in short slogans written upon coins that allowed for a wider distribution (Kaminska, 2017). Gutenberg's invention of the printing press in 1493 enabled one-to-many communication on a larger scale and with it the broad dissemination of true as well as false information. In 1835, a then New York based newspaper, *The Sun*, published a series of articles on the discovery of humanoid life on the moon that became known as the Great Moon Hoax (Thornton, 2000). The introduction of the radio further facilitated the dissemination of any news, including extended disinformation campaigns in the lead-up to World War II (Herzstein, 1978; Kallis, 2005).

However, the systematic use of print and broadcast media, and broad dissemination of their products, required considerable resources, which limited the range of actors who could take advantage of these technologies. On the negative side, this allowed actors who enjoyed access to spread disinformation without much opposition; on the positive side, it also gave attempts to implement ethical norms of journalism a chance to shape reporting (Ward, 2015; see also the contributions in Bertrand, 2018). The introduction of the internet, followed by the development of social media, reduced the existing access barriers to the extent that most individuals are now able to participate in large-scale dissemination.

With modern smartphone technology and online social networks, every internet user can be a broadcaster. To illustrate, the average Twitter user has 707 followers (Smith, 2019) to whom information can be broadcasted within split seconds. This level of reach was previously impossible for individuals, creating a fundamentally new era, where news dissemination is no longer an access-restricted privilege but available to all (internet users). Although this change has the potential to empower citizens, it also enables the uncontrolled spread of misinformation and calls for the development of new social norms of careful information evaluation and sharing.

Today, social media sites decide the newsfeed for their users by way of algorithms. In particular, companies like Facebook filter the stream of available news and present their users with a curated feed. The details of the curation algorithm are unknown to users and undergo frequent changes. What is known is that the algorithm favors information that fits the user's profile of preferences and withholds information that does not. The resulting filter bubble (Pariser, 2011) presents largely consistent information that reinforces the user's worldview and presents few challenges, leaving users confident that their own views are correct and the views of others at best mistaken and at worst malevolent (for a discussion, see Schwarz & Jalbert, 2020). Many observers suspect that such filter bubbles contributed to the outcome of the 2016 Brexit vote (see Oyserman & Dawson, 2020). Combined with the natural homophily of human social networks, where individuals are usually befriended with likeminded and similar others, filter mechanisms can create powerful homogeneous networks in which content that fits the members' values and norms stands a higher chance of being communicated. Critically, information shared within such bubbles may travel like a piece of sound in an echo chamber, allowing isolated voices to sound like a chorus.

Further adding to the dissemination efficiency of social media is that agents in the information sharing game no longer need to be human. Social bots can generate, share, redistribute, and like content with little or no human guidance or interaction. This affects the content, amount, and qualification (liking) of information, and may strongly alter information ecologies within specific bubbles. Although Twitter, Facebook, and other networks are aiming to reduce automated accounts, this is an arms race, where those who want to deceive adapt their behavior to bypass or override the latest technology developed by those who wish to restrict the network to human agents. In the very near future, the increasing perfection of deep fakes – fake videos or photos that are enormously difficult to identify as misleading fabrications – will add further challenges to the maintenance of a credible information environment.

This volume

In a climate where facts and misinformation blur, and are intentionally blurred, the present volume asks what determines whether people accept and share (mis-) information, and what can be done to counter misinformation. All three aspects need to be understood in the context of online social networks, which have fundamentally changed the way information is produced, consumed, and transmitted. To address this set of questions, the volume brings together leading experts from different fields within psychology and related areas such as information sciences and political science.

This volume is divided into three sections. The first section focuses on the origins and aftermath of fake news, in online social networks and academia. Lyons, Merola, and Reifler (2020) ask "How Bad Is the Fake News Problem?" and present data on perceived fake news consumption after the 2016 presidential campaign in the United States. Ackland and Gwynn (2020) provide a data-driven report on news diffusion on Twitter as a function of truth status, that is, whether the news was true or false. The authors also provide an overview on the literature of fact checking. Finally, Bar-Ilan and Halevi (2020) investigate the aftermath of retracted research contributions, especially those that originated in scientific misconduct, including data fabrication and falsification. They focus on examples from medical and biomedical sciences, given their potentially disastrous impact on public health.

The volume's second and third sections are primarily informed by psychological research. Communication serves fundamental informational and social human needs. The ingeniousness of online social networks rests in catering to these needs, allowing humans to pass on information, to learn, to be surprised, informed, and to be in a position to evaluate content and others. In satisfying these needs, however, many motivational and cognitive processes may act like filters and distortions themselves, affecting what kind of information individuals selectively search, perceive, believe to be true, or retrieve from memory. It remains an enormous challenge in combating fake news that humans are most gullible when it comes to things they wish to be true or believe to be true (for the power of confirmation biases, e.g., Nickerson, 1998).

At the heart of the volume's second section are cognitive processes underlying the acceptance, sharing, and correction of misinformation. Schwarz and Jalbert (2020) review the major criteria people use to determine whether something is likely to be true. They highlight that a message is most likely to be accepted when it is compatible with other things the person knows, internally coherent, presented by a credible source, accepted by similar others, and supported by evidence. Each of these criteria can be addressed on the basis of substantive information; however, these criteria can also be addressed by probing the metacognitive experience of fluency, that is, the ease or difficulty with which the message can be processed. Drawing on experimental research, Schwarz and Jalbert show how fluency operates and discuss its implications for the acceptance of fake news.

A picture tells more than a thousand words. It also influences what we believe, surprisingly, even if the picture carries no (or no additional) probative information, as Newman and Zhang (2020) report. The authors review experimental research into the truth-coating power of pictures and discuss the implications for belief construction and memory. They also address and rigorously examine why pictures have the power to mislead and offer conclusions about the boundary conditions for the biasing effect of photos.

Moving from pictures to sentence structures, Jaffé and Greifeneder (2020) show that the mere conceptual framing of information in negative terms may increase perceived truth. They further develop a framework of antecedents to this effect, showing, for instance, that expectations play a vital role.

Marsh and Stanley (2020) put the spotlight on memory processes, especially the construction, representation, and updating of knowledge. Guided by the question of whether false beliefs are a natural product of an adaptive knowledge system, they offer cognitive science insights into which strategies for combatting fake news are likely to prove successful, and which are not.

Individuals generally associate inoculation with medical treatment. But the concept of inoculation has also been applied to beliefs, based on the assumption that a small attack that is successfully combatted may increase the odds of successfully combatting later larger attacks (McGuire, 1964). Applying this notion to fake news, van der Linden and Roozenbeek (2020) offer insights into how fake news can be combatted by a psychological vaccine in the form of media education that prepares recipients for what they may encounter.

In the volume's third section, researchers turn to motivational processes. Oyserman and Dawson (2020) offer substantive evidence on how identity-based motivation shapes what individuals believe, share, and accept. Their approach highlights one of the fundamental pillars of social psychology: individuals do not react to the objective environment but to its subjective construction, which is heavily tainted by how individuals see themselves and what they aspire to.

Motivational processes are also at the heart of the insights offered by Albarracín (2020), who reviews research into conspiracy beliefs. She explains which processes increase conspiracy beliefs and highlights the role of ego-defensive motivations.

Finally, Axt, Landau, and Kay (2020) focus on the propaganda aspect of fake news, which is directed to discrediting traditional news sources, perhaps best captured in the Nazi term *Lügenpresse* (lying press) reintroduced by the German party AFD and reflected in Donald Trump's references to the "fake" and "lying" mainstream media. The authors discuss that the notion of intentionally deceiving media may be particularly appealing to individuals with a high need for structure, as a world in which media are deceptive by intent is more structured than a world in which the media are simply sloppy.

Note

1 As far as we know today.

References

Ackland, R., & Gwynn, K. (2020). Truth and the dynamics of news diffusion on twitter. In R. Greifeneder, M. Jaffé, E. J. Newman, & N. Schwarz (Eds.), *The psychology of fake news: Accepting, sharing, and correcting misinformation* (pp. 27–46). London: Routledge.

Albarracín, D. (2020). Conspiracy beliefs: Knowledge, ego-defense, and social integration. In R. Greifeneder, M. Jaffé, E. J. Newman, & N. Schwarz (Eds.), *The psychology of fake news: Accepting, sharing, and correcting misinformation* (pp. 196–219). London: Routledge.

Allcott, H., & Gentzkow, M. (2017). Social media and fake news in the 2016 election. *Journal of Economic Perspectives, 31*, 211–236. doi: 10.1257/jep.31.2.211

Axt, J. R., Landau, M. J., & Kay, A. C. (2020). Fake news attributions as a source of non-specific structure. In R. Greifeneder, M. Jaffé, E. J. Newman, & N. Schwarz (Eds.), *The psychology of fake news: Accepting, sharing, and correcting misinformation* (pp. 220–234). London: Routledge.

Bar-Ilan, J., & Halevi, G. (2020). Retracted articles: The scientific version of fake news. In R. Greifeneder, M. Jaffé, E. J. Newman, & N. Schwarz (Eds.), *The psychology of fake news: Accepting, sharing, and correcting misinformation* (pp. 47–70). London: Routledge.

Bertrand, C.-J. (2018). *Media ethics and accountability systems.* New York: Routledge.

Collins-Dictionary. (2017). Collins 2017 word of the year shortlist. Retrieved November 2, 2019, from www.collinsdictionary.com/word-lovers-blog/new/collins-2017-word-of-the-year-shortlist,396,HCB.html

Cunha, E., Magno, G., Caetano, J., Teixeira, D., & Almeida, V. (2018). Fake news as we feel it: Perception and conceptualization of the term "fake news" in the media. In S. Staab, O. Koltsova, & D. Ignatov (Eds.), *Social informatics: SocInfo 2018: Lecture notes in computer science* (Vol. 11185, pp. 151–166). Heidelberg: Springer.

Greifeneder, R., Müller, P., Stahlberg, D., Van den Bos, K., & Bless, H. (2011). Guiding trustful behavior: The role of accessible content and accessibility experiences. *Journal of Behavioral Decision Making, 24*, 498–514. doi: 10.1002/bdm.705

Herzstein, R. E. (1978). *The war that Hitler won: The most infamous propaganda campaign in history* (Vol. 1977). New York: Putnam Publishing Group.

Jaffé, M. E., & Greifeneder, R. (2020). Can that be true or is it fake news? New perspectives on the negativity bias in judgments of truth. In R. Greifeneder, M. Jaffé, E. J. Newman, & N. Schwarz (Eds.), *The psychology of fake news: Accepting, sharing, and correcting misinformation* (pp. 115–130). London: Routledge.

Kallis, A. (2005). *Nazi propaganda and the second world war.* New York: Palgrave Macmillan.

Kaminska, I. (2017). A lesson in fake news from the info-wars of ancient Rome. *Financial Times.* Retrieved from https://www.ft.com/content/aaf2bb08-dca2-11e6-86ac-f253db7791c6

Kessler, G., Rizzo, S., & Kelly, M. (2019). President Trump has made 10,796 false or misleading claims over 869 days. *Washington Post.* Retrieved from https://www.washingtonpost.com/politics/2019/06/10/president-trump-has-made-false-or-misleading-claims-over-days/

Lewandowsky, S., Ecker, U. K. H., Seifert, C. M., Schwarz, N., & Cook, J. (2012). Misinformation and its correction continued influence and successful debiasing. *Psychological Science in the Public Interest, 13*, 106–131. doi: 10.1177/1529100612451018

Lyons, B., Merola, V., & Reifler, J. (2020). How bad is the fake news problem? The role of baseline information in public perceptions. In R. Greifeneder, M. Jaffé, E. J. Newman, & N. Schwarz (Eds.), *The psychology of fake news: Accepting, sharing, and correcting misinformation* (pp. 11–26). London: Routledge.

Marsh, E. J., & Stanley, M. (2020). False beliefs: Byproducts of an adaptive knowledge base? In R. Greifeneder, M. Jaffé, E. J. Newman, & N. Schwarz (Eds.), *The psychology of fake news: Accepting, sharing, and correcting misinformation* (pp. 131–146). London: Routledge.

McGuire, W. J. (1964). Inducing resistance to persuasion: Some contemporary approaches. *Advances in Experimental Social Psychology, 1*, 191–229.

Newman, E. J., & Zhang, L. (2020). Truthiness: How non-probative photos shape belief. In R. Greifeneder, M. Jaffé, E. J. Newman, & N. Schwarz (Eds.), *The psychology of fake news: Accepting, sharing, and correcting misinformation* (pp. 90–114). London: Routledge.

Nickerson, R. S. (1998). Confirmation bias: A ubiquitous phenomenon in many guises. *Review of General Psychology*, 2, 175. doi: 10.1037/1089–2680.2.2.175

Oxford-Dictionary. (2016). Word of the year 2016 is . . . Retrieved November 2, 2019, from https://languages.oup.com/word-of-the-year/word-of-the-year-2016## targetText=After%20much%20discussion%2C%20debate%2C%20and,to%20 emotion%20and%20personal%20belief

Oyserman, D., & Dawson, A. (2020). Your fake news, our fakes: Identity-based motivation shapes what we believe, share, and accept. In R. Greifeneder, M. Jaffé, E. J. Newman, & N. Schwarz (Eds.), *The psychology of fake news: Accepting, sharing, and correcting misinformation* (pp. 173–195). London: Routledge.

Pariser, E. (2011). *The filter bubble: How the new personalized web is changing what we read and how we think*. New York: Penguin.

Pengelly, M. (2017). Trump accuses CNN of "fake news" over reported celebrity apprentice plans. Retrieved July 30, 2019, from www.theguardian.com/us-news/2016/dec/10/trump-celebrity-apprentice-cnn-fake-news

Posetti, J., & Matthews, A. (2018). A short guide to the history of "fake news" and disinformation: A new ICFJ learning module. Retrieved November 2, 2019, from www.icfj.org/news/short-guide-history-fake-news-and-disinformation-new-icfj-learning-module

Schwarz, N., & Jalbert, M. (2020). When news feels true: Intuitions of truth and the acceptance and correction of misinformation. In R. Greifeneder, M. Jaffé, E. J. Newman, & N. Schwarz (Eds.), *The psychology of fake news: Accepting, sharing, and correcting misinformation* (pp. 73–89). London: Routledge.

Smith, K. (2019). 58 incredible and interesting twitter stats and statistics. Retrieved July 31, 2019, from www.brandwatch.com/blog/twitter-stats-and-statistics/

Swift, A. (2016). Americans' trust in mass media sinks to new low. Retrieved November 2, 2019, from https://news.gallup.com/poll/195542/americanstrust-mass-media-sinks-new-low.aspx

Thornton, B. (2000). The moon hoax: Debates about ethics in 1835 New York newspapers. *Journal of Mass Media Ethics*, 15, 89–100. doi: 10.1207/S15327728JMME1502_3

van der Linden, S., & Roozenbeek, J. (2020). A psychological vaccine against fake news. In R. Greifeneder, M. Jaffé, E. J. Newman, & N. Schwarz (Eds.), *The psychology of fake news: Accepting, sharing, and correcting misinformation* (pp. 147–169). London: Routledge.

Vosoughi, S., Roy, D., & Aral, S. (2018). The spread of true and false news online. *Science*, 359, 1146–1151. doi: 10.1126/science.aap9559

Ward, S. J. A. (2015). *The invention of journalism ethics: The path to objectivity and beyond*. Montreal: McGill-Queen's Press.

Wardle, C., & Derakhshan, H. (2017). *Information disorder: Toward an interdisciplinary framework for research and policy making*. Strasbourg: Council of Europe.

Wikipedia. (n.d.). Pizzagate conspiracy theory. Retrieved July, 30, 2019, from https://en.wikipedia.org/wiki/Pizzagate_conspiracy_theory

PART I

The journey and aftermath of (false) information in networks

2

HOW BAD IS THE FAKE NEWS PROBLEM?

The role of baseline information in public perceptions

Benjamin A. Lyons, Vittorio Merola, and Jason Reifler

In February 2019, the UK Parliament released a scathing report likening Facebook executives to "digital gangsters" for how they treat user data. The damning report grew out of a larger effort to understand the role of social media in elections specifically and in undermining democratic institutions more generally. Of particular concern was how social media platforms help spread "fake news" and other forms of disinformation. It is understandable why the UK Parliament might express an interest in how digital media could negatively affect democracy. After all, the British firm Cambridge Analytica was caught up in scandals for the role it may have played in two elections with surprising outcomes – the UK Brexit referendum and Donald Trump's shocking victory in the 2016 US presidential election.

As these campaigns were unfolding – especially the US presidential election – the novel form of political content "fake news" was beginning to be noticed. Fake news produced content that was false and showed no regard to accuracy or journalistic standards. These sites would often pass themselves as real news sites. Some of the more infamous claimed that Pope Francis endorsed Donald Trump for president (he did not), that an FBI agent involved in the release of Clinton emails was involved in a murder-suicide (no such event happened), and that those protesting the outcome of the election were being paid by George Soros (also not true). Some of these articles were shared on Facebook hundreds of thousands – if not millions – of times. The combination of a novel form of media with some outrageously large engagement metrics occurring at the same time as unexpected election results leads to a natural, if naive, inference – lots of people consumed fake news, and this consumption has had an effect on these election outcomes.

However, anecdotal news coverage is now being replaced by coverage of empirical research into fake news (Grinberg, Joseph, Friedland, Swire-Thompson, &

Lazer, 2019; Guess, Nyhan, & Reifler, 2018; Guess, Nagler, & Tucker, 2019). Contrary to the despair of popular narratives, fake news accounted for limited amounts of news consumption during the 2016 election. Specifically, this research finds that about one in four (27%) American adults visited a fake news website in the lead-up to the 2016 election, visiting an average of 5.5 articles each, and "fake news websites represented an average of approximately 2.6% of all the articles Americans read on sites focusing on hard news topics" during this time (Guess et al., 2018). Exposure to fake news has further declined between 2016 and 2018 (Guess et al., 2019).

News headlines may simplify these findings, giving readers a contextualized summation such as "'Fake News': Wide Reach but Little Impact, Study Suggests" (Carey, 2018) or "Majority of Americans Were Not Exposed to 'Fake News' in 2016 U.S. Election, Twitter Study Suggests" (Fox, 2019). Readers are heavily influenced by the headline of a news article (e.g., Ecker, Lewandowsky, Chang, & Pillai, 2014). However, it is less clear how the statistical baselines established in the research themselves might influence public views about fake news (e.g., Kessler, Levine, Opitz, & Reynolds, 1987) – in the absence of a summative headline, how does the public make sense of information about how much of the public was exposed to fake news, and how much they read, on average?

Theory

Potential effects of statistical baselines

Research shows fake news consumption during the 2016 election was less than the popular imagination held, and limited to a small segment of the population (Grinberg et al., 2019; Guess et al., 2018; Guess, Lyons, Montgomery, Nyhan, & Reifler, 2019). However, this academic research is unlikely to captivate the public as fully as the original introduction to the problem of fake news. The public is likely unaware of the actual prevalence of fake news consumption, instead making inferential errors (e.g., Ahler & Sood, 2018) based on salient cases. As such, public opinion surveys show generally high rates of concern. Pew Research Center (Barthel, Mitchell, & Holcomb, 2016), for example, found that 64% of Americans thought fake news was sowing "a great deal of confusion" following the election, and 71% said they often or sometimes saw "completely made-up" political news online.

Providing baseline statistical information about consumption may influence subjective judgments about fake news consumption's prevalence, its prevalence over time, its prevalence among select demographic subgroups, and overall concern about the problem and support for solutions. However, it is unclear which direction such statistical baselines, on their own, may influence these perceptions and attitudes. It is possible the information may contrast with an assumed widespread prevalence and drive down subjective sense of prevalence and concern. On the other hand, the public may struggle to place the baselines in an appropriate context, and the presentation of the information about consumption, regardless of its size, may act as a cue raising the salience of the fake news problem, leading to greater subjective assessments of prevalence and concern. The effects of statistical information may also depend on individual characteristics, such as familiarity (e.g., Facebook use) and interest in and knowledge about politics, as well as cognitive traits such as cognitive reflection, need for evidence, and reliance on intuition.

Decreasing perceived prevalence and concern

One way statistical baselines about fake news consumption may reduce perceived consumption and concern is by providing a descriptive norm (e.g., Rimal & Real, 2005). Based on public opinion data (Barthel et al., 2016), the public's existing perceptions of fake news consumption may be seen as a normative misperception (Neighbors, Dillard, Lewis, Bergstrom, & Neil, 2006). As such, providing actual baseline information may bring perceptions in line with reality. The statistical baselines of actual 2016 election consumption – 27% of all Americans exposed to at least one fake news article, an average of 5.5 articles each – may contrast with more extreme existing inferences derived from anecdotal experience, and serve to drive down subjective assessments of public consumption (e.g., "very little"? "A lot"?) and concern about the issue going forward.

Increasing perceived prevalence and concern

On the other hand, people are notoriously bad at making sense of statistical information (Hoffrage, Lindsey, Hertwig, & Gigerenzer, 2000). Providing statistical baselines, then, may actually increase subjective assessments of fake news' reach and personal concern. Importantly, "[i]t is the personal meaning of information not the objective details which is stored and made available for recall in decision making" (Kessler et al., 1987, p. 367; Neisser, 1978). Any baseline may only serve to concretize a previously vague problem.

The availability heuristic (e.g., An, 2008; Tversky & Kahneman, 1974) may account for such an outcome. The ease with which individuals bring exemplars for events to mind influences downstream perceptions and judgments about the probability or prevalence of such events (Folkes, 1988; MacLeod & Campbell, 1992). Providing baseline statistics could serve as a sort of exemplar, making the problem of fake news consumption more available at the top of the reader's mind, resulting in greater subjective assessments of prevalence and concern. In other words, by raising the salience of fake news, baseline consumption information could increase the intensity of subjective assessments (Carroll, 1978).

Effects on group-centric biases

In addition to generalized overestimation of fake news consumption (Barthel et al., 2016), individuals likely exhibit group-centric biases in beliefs about who consumes fake news (e.g., Ahler & Sood, 2018; Turner, Brown, & Tajfel, 1979). Voters who supported Hillary Clinton likely estimate that Trump voters consumed fake news at greater rates than other Clinton voters did, and vice versa. Voters over 60 may assume that younger voters consumed greater amounts of fake news than did their age group, and vice versa. College graduates may assume that those without a college degree were more susceptible to fake news, though it is not clear whether this would be a symmetric perceptual relationship due to widespread assumptions about the positive effects of higher education. Providing baseline information about overall fake news consumption may work to widen these gaps when participants are asked to assess whether various demographic groups consumed less than average, more than average, or about average amounts of fake news. If a statistical baseline treatment works to raise the salience of fake news and inflate subjective assessment of its prevalence, individuals may then project favorable biases onto the distribution of their heightened assessments of general consumption. If fake news looms as a larger problem in the reader's mind, they may then account for this higher rate of perceived consumption by attributing it (disproportionately) to an outgroup, rather than to the social categories to which they belong (Turner et al., 1979).

Conditional effects of statistical baselines

Familiarity with social media and general political sophistication may lead individuals to disregard new information about fake news consumption during the 2016 election. With strong existing priors on the issue, heavy social media users and political sophisticates should be less likely to update their views on fake news in the face of new, briefly presented findings (e.g., Hill, 2017). In contrast, those giving the matter less previous thought may be more influenced by baseline information. Similarly, differences in cognitive traits that govern how individuals interact with new information – such as cognitive reflection (Frederick, 2005), need for evidence (Garrett & Weeks, 2017), and reliance on intuition (Garrett & Weeks, 2017) – may lead individuals to be more or less open to new statistical information about fake news consumption in forming subjective assessments. Those who are more cognitively reflective, those with a greater need for evidence in forming their beliefs, and those who rely less on intuition may be more likely to consider and be influenced by new evidence.

Effects of different statistical baselines

Different forms of statistical information such as averages and percentages may be perceived differently (Garcia-Retamero & Galesic, 2009; Schapira, Davids, McAuliffe, & Nattinger, 2004; Westwood, Messing, & Lelkes, 2019). For this reason, we vary our treatments. We test the effects of information about both the percentage of the population exposed to any fake news (about 27% in the lead-up to the 2016 election) and the average number of fake news articles each

American read during the time period (5.5 articles). We also test a treatment that includes both baselines. Combining multiple baselines may serve as a further signal-strengthening cue, raising the salience of the fake news problem.

Methods

Sample

Our data come from a sample of 981 American adults recruited via Amazon Mechanical Turk in January 2019. Participants were compensated $.55 for the study, which they completed in an average of 5.92 minutes (SD = 6.42). Our sample had an average age of 36.57 (SD = 11.03). Just over half of the sample was male (55%) and approximately three-quarters were white (76%). The median respondent reported possessing a four-year degree (46% had less than a four-year degree).

We measure party identification using the standard American National Election Study branching format, where respondents are first asked which party they identify with. Those who say either Republican or Democrat are asked a follow-up question assessing the strength of their partisanship (either "strong" or "not strong"). Those who do not initially identify with a party are asked a different follow-up question about whether they "lean" toward one party or the other; we code these "leaners" as partisans. (While these measures are often used to construct a seven-point scale ranging from "strong Democrat" to "strong Republican", we create dummy variables for Democrat and Republican identifiers.) Just over half identify as Democrats (56%) and about a third as Republicans (33%), with the remainder identifying with neither party. Ideology is nearly identical (51% self-report as liberals and 30% as conservatives). In terms of 2016 presidential candidate support, 29% report they supported Trump, 46% say they supported Clinton, and the remainder claim not to have supported either major party candidate.

Design and procedure

Treatments consisted of information baselines about Americans' exposure to fake news during the 2016 presidential election. Estimates come from Guess and colleagues (2018). Participants were randomly assigned to one of four groups. All groups were informed that we would "ask you about your thoughts about the prevalence of fake news in the lead-up to the 2016 U.S. presidential election (October 7 to November 14, 2016)". The first group (n = 244) were then exposed to baseline consumption information in terms of the average number of fake news articles each American saw during the lead-up to the 2016 presidential election, worded as follows: "For your reference, researchers estimate that each voting-age American saw an *average of about five and half fake news articles* during this time". The second group (n = 251) saw baseline consumption information in terms of the percent of Americans exposed to any fake news articles in the lead-up to the election, worded as follows: "For your reference, researchers estimate that *27% of voting-age Americans visited a fake news article* during this time". A third group (*n* = 232) saw both baseline information treatments. A fourth group (*n* = 254) served as a control and saw no baseline information.

Participants first provided pre-treatment measures of demographics and moderator variables. Next, they were exposed to the information treatments, before providing outcome measures of their perception of fake news' reach and influence, and their attitudes toward fake news and steps to mitigate it.

Measures

Dependent variables

Participants provided a series of estimates about fake news exposure and its influence, as well as attitudes toward fake news.

Perceived overall consumption was measured by asking "How much fake news do you think Americans consumed during the 2016 election?" on a 5-point scale, ranging from "none" (1) to "a great deal" (5), M = 3.45, SD = .96. *Perceived consumption trend (2016–present)* was measured on a 3-point scale (1 = decreased, 2 = stayed the same, 3 = increased), M = 2.49, SD = .64.

Perceived group consumption was gauged for a number of salient demographic groups (see Grinberg et al., 2019; Guess et al., 2018; Guess et al., 2019). Participants were asked to "Use your best estimate. How much fake news did individuals in the following groups" consume during the time period in question. Responses were recorded on a 5-point scale ranging from "much less than average" to "much more than average". Target groups included Trump supporters (M = 3.88, SD = 1.03), Clinton supporters (M = 3.24, SD = 1.02), ages 18–34 (M = 3.44 SD = 1.04), ages 34–59 (M = 3.52, SD = .91), ages 60+ (M = 3.62, SD = 1.17), college graduates (M = 3.02, SD = 1.06), and non-college graduates (M = 3.68, SD = .97).

Participants also provided "downstream" outcomes that may be influenced by shifting perception of the prevalence of fake news using 7-point Likert scales. These included concern about the effects of fake news (M = 5.54, SD = 1.47), belief that "fake news is why Donald Trump won the 2016 presidential election" (M = 4.17, SD = 2.07), belief that "Facebook has taken significant action to limit fake news on its platform" (M = 3.56, SD = 1.71), "support [for] increased regulation of fake news by the U.S. government" (M = 4.81, SD = 1.84), and "support [for] public spending on digital media literacy initiatives" (M = 4.90, SD = 1.68). These items formed a scale with only middling reliability (alpha = .63). Therefore, we examine each outcome individually.

Moderators

The following measures were considered as potential moderators of baseline consumption information treatment effects.

Facebook use (M = 6.02, SD = 2.57) was measured on a 9-point scale ranging from "never" to "almost constantly". Political knowledge (M = 2.80, SD = 1.14) was an additive index of correct responses to five questions: how many years a US senator is elected for, how many years a US House representative is elected for, how many senators come from each state, how many times an individual can be elected president, and the current UK prime minister. Political interest (M = 3.35, SD = 1.08) was measured on a 5-point scale ranging from "not at all interested" to "extremely interested".

Cognitive reflection was an additive index of correct responses to three items, using alternate question wording (Patel, 2017) to reduce prior exposure effects (M = 1.61, SD = 1.20). Need for evidence (M = 5.77, SD = 1.06) was the average of three items on a 7-point Likert scale, and reliance on intuition (M = 4.11, SD = 1.45) was the average of four items on a 7-point Likert scale (Garrett & Weeks, 2017).

Results

Effects on perceived consumption and concern

We initially modeled treatment effects on perceived overall consumption, perceived consumption trend (2016–present), and each of the concern/perceived influence outcome measures individually, using OLS regression with each treatment entered as an indicator variable and the control group serving as the reference category. These results are shown in Table 2.1.

This analysis shows no effect of the information baselines on perceived overall consumption (Column 1). However, simultaneous exposure to both information baselines (Treatment 3) increased perception that fake news consumption has increased since 2016 (Column 2), b = .14, p = .017. Similarly, simultaneous exposure to both baselines increased concern about fake news (Column 3), b = .26, p = .049.

Our results show no baseline information effects on belief that fake news spurred Trump to victory, belief that Facebook has taken significant steps to address fake news, or support for government regulation of fake news (Columns 4–6). We find that exposure to the percent of Americans exposed to fake news in 2016 decreases support for publicly funded media literacy programs (Column 7), b = −.34, p = .024.

In examination of potential moderators of these treatment effects, we find that the effect of simultaneous exposure to both baselines on increasing concern about fake news was significantly stronger among Trump supporters, b = .83, p = .006. The other political and cognitive measures did not moderate the treatment effects.

Effects on group-centric bias

Next, we examined perceptions of consumption among different demographic groups. First, we present the means of each group's perceived consumption

TABLE 2.1 Treatment effects on perceived consumption and concern

	Overall consumption			2016–2018 trend			Concern			Helped Trump			Facebook actions			Support regulation			Support literacy		
	b	SE	p	b	SE	p	b	SE	p	b	SE	p	b	SE	p	b	SE	p	b	SE	p
5.5 article baseline	0.06	0.09	0.472	0.04	0.06	0.480	0.15	0.13	0.270	−0.14	0.19	0.456	−0.07	0.15	0.656	−0.18	0.17	0.288	−0.22	0.15	0.146
27% baseline	−0.03	0.09	0.743	0.08	0.06	0.162	0.19	0.13	0.138	−0.11	0.18	0.567	−0.03	0.15	0.838	−0.10	0.16	0.525	−0.34	0.15	0.024
Both baselines	−0.10	0.09	0.275	0.14	0.06	0.017	0.26	0.13	0.049	−0.08	0.19	0.684	0.00	0.16	0.984	−0.09	0.17	0.607	−0.09	0.15	0.577
Constant	3.47	0.06	0.000	2.42	0.04	0.000	5.39	0.09	0.000	4.25	0.13	0.000	3.58	0.11	0.000	4.91	0.12	0.000	5.06	0.11	0.000
R2	0.00			0.01			0.00			0.00			0.00			0.00			0.01		

Note: N = 980

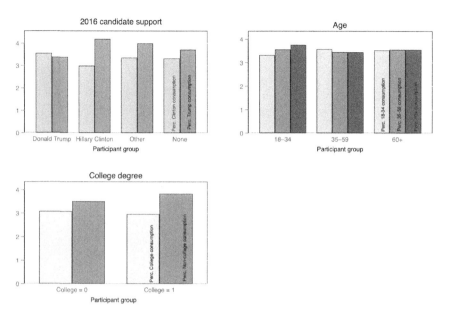

FIGURE 2.1 Perceived consumption of fake news among demographic groups, across participant demographic group

among the in-group and out-groups in Figure 2.1. As shown in this figure, Clinton supporters estimated significantly more fake news consumption among Trump supporters than among their in-group. Trump supporters, meanwhile, estimated that Clinton supporters consumed slightly more fake news than their in-group. College graduates likewise estimated significantly more fake news consumption among non-college graduates than among their in-group. Non-college graduates, however, also estimated more fake news consumption among non-college graduates, though to a lesser degree. Finally, participants 18–34 years old estimated more fake news consumption among Americans age 60+ than among their in-group, but participants age 60+ did not exhibit the reverse perception (note that our sample age skewed young: 18–34, $n = 513$; 35–59, $n = 422$; 60+, $n = 45$).

We then computed the difference score for these group perceptions (i.e., perceived Trump supporters' consumption – perceived Clinton supports' consumption), shown across participants' own demographic groups in Figure 2.2.

Next, we modeled perceived consumption of demographic groups using OLS regression. We included our informational baseline treatments and group-membership categories as predictors. Results are shown in Table 2.2. In each case, relevant group memberships predicted perceived consumption. Trump support (versus those who did not support a candidate) predicted lower perception of Trump supporter fake news consumption ($b = -.49$, $p < .001$) and higher perception of Clinton support consumption ($b = .21$, $p = .013$). Clinton support (versus those who did not support a candidate) predicted lower perception

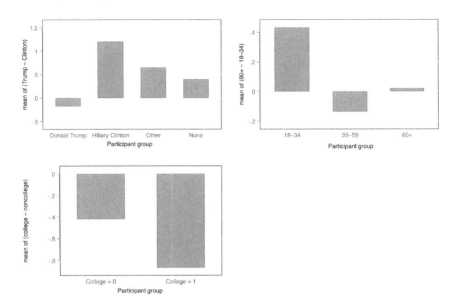

FIGURE 2.2 Mean difference in perceived consumption of fake news, across participant demographic group

of Clinton support consumption (b = −.35, p < .001) and higher perception of Trump supporter consumption (b = .32, p < .001). Belonging to the 18–34 age group (compared to the 35–59 age group) predicted greater perceived fake news consumption among ages 60+ (b = .31, p < .001) and less perceived consumption among the 18–34 age group (b = −.24, p < .001). A college degree (versus having a high school degree or less) predicted greater perceived consumption among those without a college degree (b = .33, p < .001), and less perceived consumption among those with a degree (b = −.13, p = .064).

When adding the full set of group memberships, we see that non-relevant group memberships – specifically, vote support – also predicted perceived consumption of the other target groups. Trump support predicted more perceived consumption among the 18–34 age group (b = .44, p < .001), and less perceived consumption among the 60+ age group (b = −.34, p < .001) after accounting for age, while Clinton support predicted the reverse – more consumption among both the 60+ (b = .34, p < .001) and 35–59 age groups (b = .23, p = .002). Trump support likewise predicted more perceived consumption among those with a college degree (b = .54, p < .001), whereas Clinton support predicted more perceived consumption among those without a degree (b = .24, p = .002) and less consumption among those with a degree (b = −.19, p = .019), after accounting for educational attainment. In this way, perceived consumption of differing demographic groups may reflect differing conceptions of what "fake news" is among Clinton and Trump supporters.

TABLE 2.2 Perceived consumption of demographic groups, by treatment and participant demographics

	Age								
	60+			*35–59*			*18–34*		
	b	*SE*	*p*	*b*	*SE*	*p*	*b*	*SE*	*p*
5.5 article baseline	−0.11	0.10	0.31	0.04	0.08	0.61	0.12	0.09	0.21
27% baseline	−0.11	0.10	0.28	−0.05	0.08	0.57	−0.03	0.09	0.73
Both baselines	−0.14	0.11	0.18	0.05	0.08	0.56	0.08	0.09	0.39
18–34	0.31	0.08	0.00	0.11	0.06	0.07	−0.24	0.07	0.00
60+	0.11	0.18	0.54	0.11	0.14	0.45	−0.03	0.16	0.83
Constant	3.54	0.08	0.00	3.44	0.07	0.00	3.53	0.08	0.00
N			980			980			979
R2			0.02			0.01			0.03
	Candidate support								
	Clinton			*Trump*					
	b	*SE*	*p*	*b*	*SE*	*p*			
5.5 article baseline	0.01	0.09	0.91	−0.04	0.09	0.61			
27% baseline	−0.14	0.09	0.11	0.06	0.09	0.47			
Both baselines	−0.05	0.09	0.62	−0.01	0.09	0.89			
Trump support	0.21	0.09	0.01	−0.49	0.08	0.00			
Clinton support	−0.35	0.08	0.00	0.32	0.08	0.00			
Constant	3.39	0.08	0.00	3.87	0.08	0.00			
N			980			979			
R2			0.06			0.11			
	Education								
	College			*No college*					
	b	*SE*	*p*	*b*	*SE*	*p*			
5.5 article baseline	0.20	0.09	0.04	−0.18	0.09	0.04			
27% baseline	−0.22	0.09	0.02	−0.16	0.09	0.06			
Both baselines	0.04	0.10	0.64	−0.07	0.09	0.44			
College	−0.13	0.07	0.06	0.33	0.06	0.00			
Constant	3.09	0.08	0.00	3.61	0.07	0.00			
N			980			980			
R2			0.02			0.03			

TABLE 2.3 Perceived consumption difference scores, by treatment and participant demographics

	Trump–Clinton			Old–young			Non-college–college		
	b	SE	p	b	SE	p	b	SE	p
5.5 article baseline	−0.06	0.13	0.664	−0.22	0.15	0.150	−0.37	0.12	0.003
27% baseline	0.20	0.13	0.132	−0.09	0.15	0.574	0.06	0.12	0.624
Both baselines	0.03	0.14	0.829	−0.22	0.16	0.157	−0.11	0.13	0.378
Trump support	−0.71	0.13	0.000						
Clinton support	0.68	0.12	0.000						
18–34				0.56	0.11	0.000			
60+				0.15	0.27	0.575			
College							0.45	0.09	0.000
Constant	0.49	0.13	0.000	0.01	0.12	0.968	0.52	0.10	0.000
N		979			979			980	
R 2		0.14			0.03			0.04	

We then modeled difference scores using the same procedure. Results are shown in Table 2.3. Group membership also predicted these difference scores: Clinton support (b = .68, p < .001) and Trump support (b = −.71, p < .001) each predicted the Trump–Clinton difference score; age 18–34 (b = .56, p < .001) predicted the old-young difference score; and college degree (b = .45, p < .001) predicted the education difference score. In terms of the treatments, only one informational baseline predicted one difference score: exposure to the average number of fake news articles consumed by Americans in 2016 decreased the perceived gap between Americans with and without college degrees in fake news consumption, b = −.37, p = .003.

Next, we included the interaction terms for each information treatment and group membership category. These results suggest that informational treatments increased the Trump–Clinton difference score for Clinton supporters, as shown in Figure 2.3. Among participants who supported Clinton in 2016, the treatment including information about the percentage of Americans exposed to fake news (b = .93, p = .004) and the treatment including both baselines (b = .77, p = .024) increased the gap between perceived Clinton supporter fake news consumption and perceived Trump supporter fake news consumption.

Discussion

Public alarm over fake news may be disproportionate to the actual prevalence of exposure and consumption of this fabricated content. How might the provision of actual consumption statistics affect subjective assessments of fake news consumption and concern about its influence? Do such information treatments serve as descriptive norms and lead to a "correction", decreasing subjective

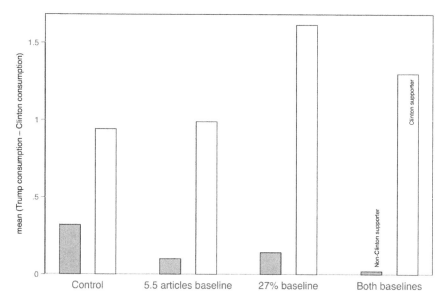

FIGURE 2.3   Mean difference in perceived consumption of fake news, across treatments and participant candidate support

assessments? Or do they serve to increase the salience of the fake news problem and inflate these assessments? We find that the effects of baseline information on fake news perceptions, at least in the format in which we deliver it, are likely small. Moreover, without the proper contextualization, this information may do more to *exacerbate* than to downplay perceived prevalence, perceived influence, and concern about fake news. Simultaneous exposure to both information baselines (the percent of all Americans exposed to fake news *and* the average number of articles consumed) increased perception that fake news consumption has increased since 2016, and increased general concern about fake news. We find little evidence that measures of political or cognitive sophistication moderate our treatment effects.

We find sizeable gaps in who the public thinks consumed the most fake news. Not surprisingly, the gaps are driven by the public's own membership in various social categories. Our data show notable in-group biases in perceived consumption across 2016 vote preference, age, and educational attainment subgroups (though these perceptual gaps are not always fully symmetric).

Moreover, non-relevant group memberships – specifically, vote support – also predicted perceived consumption of other target groups. Trump supporters assumed the young and the educated were consuming more fake news, even after accounting for their age and education, whereas Clinton supporters assumed the old and those without a college degree were consuming more fake news. These spillover relationships may reflect that the public has a good handle on the differing demographic bases of electoral support of Clinton and Trump, or it may reflect differing conceptions of what constitutes "fake news" (or both). Clinton supporters may use a definition closer to academics' definitions of fake news (e.g., Guess et al., 2018), whereas Trump supporters, following his rhetorical cues, may see news outlets such as *The New York Times* and *The Washington Post* as "fake news". In some cases (i.e., among Clinton supporters), information about the rate of fake news consumption may widen the perceived gap in consumption between Trump and Clinton supporters.

It is important to note several limitations of this research. First, as the sample of participants was drawn from Amazon Mechanical Turk, which skews young, educated, and liberal, we are limited in making broader generalizations about our findings (but see, e.g., Coppock, 2019; Coppock, Leeper, & Mullinix, 2018; Mullinix, Leeper, Druckman, & Freese, 2015). This should be kept in mind particularly when considering the group-differences results that reflect observed (untreated) group difference. Future work should replicate these tests among a nationally representative sample of voters. Next, our manipulations were quite subtle. We did not include a manipulation check in order to simulate the effects of such statistical baselines in limited-attention media browsing environments (e.g., Twitter). This may have resulted in weaker effects on our outcomes of interest. Also in regard to our treatments, it is important to note that not all baselines are created equal (Westwood et al., 2019). There are likely limits to the sort of salience-inducing effect we speculate occurred by way of our treatments. For example, a baseline that stated some event occurred among 5% of the population may be less likely to drive up concern than a 27% baseline, so it may be that the availability heuristic is not the only mechanism of baseline effects, instead depending on context. Future studies should manipulate baseline rates to determine whether anchoring plays a role in these effects, and test mechanisms more formally.

Regardless, our findings shed additional light on how the public thinks about and perceives fake news. Empirical estimates derived from social scientific research are unlikely to dramatically reshape public perceptions of fake news as a social issue all on their own. The public's social identities likely shape who they see as the prototypical fake news consumer, and in that sense, what they define as fake news itself. Toward that end, media literacy initiatives may focus on communicating the basics of what constitutes legitimate journalism.

Fake news is seen by many as a real and present danger to democracy. The European Union organized a high-level group to study the problem, and several national governments have held hearings or formed committees to examine the problem. At the same time, the accumulating academic evidence is that fake news consumption is fairly limited, and there is little evidence to suggest it is changing election outcomes. The results in this chapter suggest that it may be hard to sway beliefs about fake news consumption. This finding may be a problem.

As misinformation researchers, we are acutely aware of the corrosive effects that misinformation can have on politics and society. Nonetheless, the deleterious effects of fake news, specifically, must be appropriately calibrated. While misinformation is indeed a serious problem facing society, it is important not to be distracted by these potentially more niche forms while letting misinformation spread unabated by other means. For example, misinformation communicated by elites – especially when they have direct access to much larger audiences via social media – is likely a more severe problem than fake news websites. It would be a shame if efforts to constrain misinformation solved the problem of fake news, but in so doing gave a free pass to other forms of deception and dissembling.

References

Ahler, D. J., & Sood, G. (2018). The parties in our heads: Misperceptions about party composition and their consequences. *The Journal of Politics*, *80*(3), 964–981.

An, S. (2008). Antidepressant direct-to-consumer advertising and social perception of the prevalence of depression: Application of the availability heuristic. *Health Communication*, *23*(6), 499–505.

Barthel, M., Mitchell, A., & Holcomb, J. (2016). Many Americans believe fake news is sowing confusion. *Pew Research*. Retrieved from www.journalism.org/2016/12/15/many-americans-believe-fake-news-is-sowing-confusion/

Carey, B. (2018, January 2). "Fake news": Wide reach but little impact, study suggests. *The New York Times*. Retrieved from www.nytimes.com/2018/01/02/health/fake-news-conservative-liberal.html

Carroll, J. S. (1978). The effect of imagining an event on expectations for the event: An interpretation in terms of the availability heuristic. *Journal of Experimental Social Psychology*, *14*(1), 88–96.

Coppock, A. (2019). Generalizing from survey experiments conducted on Mechanical Turk: A replication approach. *Political Science Research and Methods*, *7*(3), 613–628.

Coppock, A., Leeper, T. J., & Mullinix, K. J. (2018). Generalizability of heterogeneous treatment effect estimates across samples. *Proceedings of the National Academy of Sciences*, *115*(49), 12441–12446.

Ecker, U. K., Lewandowsky, S., Chang, E. P., & Pillai, R. (2014). The effects of subtle misinformation in news headlines. *Journal of Experimental Psychology: Applied*, *20*(4), 323.

Folkes, V. S. (1988). The availability heuristic and perceived risk. *Journal of Consumer Research*, *15*(1), 13–23.

Fox, A. (2019, January). Majority of Americans were not exposed to "fake news" in 2016 U.S. election, Twitter study suggests. Retrieved from www.sciencemag.org/news/2019/01/majority-americans-were-not-exposed-fake-news-2016-us-election-twitter-study-suggests

Frederick, S. (2005). Cognitive reflection and decision making. *Journal of Economic Perspectives*, *19*(4), 25–42.

Garcia-Retamero, R., & Galesic, M. (2009). Communicating treatment risk reduction to people with low numeracy skills: A cross-cultural comparison. *American Journal of Public Health*, *99*(12), 2196–2202.

Garrett, R. K., & Weeks, B. E. (2017). Epistemic beliefs' role in promoting misperceptions and conspiracist ideation. *PloS One*, *12*(9), e0184733.

Grinberg, N., Joseph, K., Friedland, L., Swire-Thompson, B., & Lazer, D. (2019). Fake news on Twitter during the 2016 US presidential election. *Science*, *363*(6425), 374–378.

Guess, A., Lyons, B. A., Montgomery, J., Nyhan, B., & Reifler, J. (2019). Fake news, Facebook ads, and misperceptions: Assessing information quality in the 2018 U.S.

midterm election campaign. Retrieved from www.dartmouth.edu/~nyhan/fake-news-2018.pdf

Guess, A., Nagler, J., & Tucker, J. (2019). Less than you think: Prevalence and predictors of fake news dissemination on Facebook. *Science Advances, 5*(1), eaau4586.

Guess, A., Nyhan, B., & Reifler, J. (2018). Selective exposure to misinformation: Evidence from the consumption of fake news during the 2016 US presidential campaign. Retrieved from www.dartmouth.edu/~nyhan/fake-news-2016.pdf

Hill, S. J. (2017). Learning together slowly: Bayesian learning about political facts. *The Journal of Politics, 79*(4), 1403–1418.

Hoffrage, U., Lindsey, S., Hertwig, R., & Gigerenzer, G. (2000). Communicating statistical information. *Science, 290*, 2261–2262. doi: 10.1126/science.290.5500.2261

Kessler, S., Levine, E. K., Opitz, J. M., & Reynolds, J. F. (1987). Psychological aspects of genetic counseling: IV. The subjective assessment of probability. *American Journal of Medical Genetics, 28*(2), 361–370.

MacLeod, C., & Campbell, L. (1992). Memory accessibility and probability judgments: An experimental evaluation of the availability heuristic. *Journal of Personality and Social Psychology, 63*(6), 890.

Mullinix, K. J., Leeper, T. J., Druckman, J. N., & Freese, J. (2015). The generalizability of survey experiments. *Journal of Experimental Political Science, 2*(2), 109–138.

Neighbors, C., Dillard, A. J., Lewis, M. A., Bergstrom, R. L., & Neil, T. A. (2006). Normative misperceptions and temporal precedence of perceived norms and drinking. *Journal of Studies on Alcohol, 67*(2), 290–299.

Neisser, U. (1978). Memory: What are the important questions? In M. M. Gruneberg, P. E. Morris, & H. N. Sykes (Eds.), *Practical aspects of memory* (pp. 3–24). London: Academic Press. [Reprinted in Neisser, U. (1982). Memory: What are the important questions. *Memory Observed: Remembering in Natural Contexts, 3*–19].

Patel, N. (2017). *The cognitive reflection test: A measure of intuition/reflection, numeracy, and insight problem solving, and the implications for understanding real-world judgments and beliefs.* (Unpublished doctoral dissertation). Columbia, MO: University of Missouri.

Rimal, R. N., & Real, K. (2005). How behaviors are influenced by perceived norms: A test of the theory of normative social behavior. *Communication Research, 32*(3), 389–414.

Schapira, M. M., Davids, S. L., McAuliffe, T. L., & Nattinger, A. B. (2004). Agreement between scales in the measurement of breast cancer risk perceptions. *Risk Analysis: An International Journal, 24*(3), 665–673.

Turner, J. C., Brown, R. J., & Tajfel, H. (1979). Social comparison and group interest in ingroup favouritism. *European Journal of Social Psychology, 9*(2), 187–204.

Tversky, A., & Kahneman, D. (1974). Judgment under uncertainty: Heuristics and biases. *Science, 185*(4157), 1124–1131.

Westwood, S., Messing, S., & Lelkes, Y. (2019). Projecting confidence: How the probabilistic horse race confuses and demobilizes the public. Retrieved from https://papers.ssrn.com/sol3/papers.cfm?abstract_id=3117054

3

TRUTH AND THE DYNAMICS OF NEWS DIFFUSION ON TWITTER

Robert Ackland and Karl Gwynn

Introduction

This chapter investigates two aspects of misinformation: how to determine whether information (such as a news story) is true, and how the truthfulness of information affects its diffusion or spread. The chapter has a particular focus on the significance of social media for misinformation (in particular fake news): its prevalence, impact, and methods for identifying and studying the phenomenon. We review recent literature on how computational methods and "big data" sources (e.g., social media) are being used for identifying misinformation and understanding how people engage with and spread misinformation.

Our empirical application involves a new approach for manually checking the truthfulness of news stories, and we apply this method to a sample of Australian political news stories from 2017. We then explore how the veracity of news affects its diffusion (via retweets) on Twitter, focusing on the following key measures of diffusion: reach (how many people are involved in the diffusion), speed, and breadth (how far into the network does the news spread, and how diverse are the actors involved in the diffusion).

Background

In this section, we first review existing definitions of misinformation and fake news and then summarize the reasons why people contribute to spreading misinformation. We then summarize research on how social media potentially exacerbates the problem of fake news. Approaches to checking the veracity of news are then outlined and assessed in their ability to accurately determine measurements of truthfulness, with a particular focus on manual approaches (truthfulness checked by domain experts) and computational approaches. We also summarize some key research that uses computational methods and big data to understand the phenomenon of misinformation.

Definition of misinformation and fake news

Misinformation refers to false information that has the capacity to spread through society and influence public opinion. Examples of misinformation are satire news (designed for humor and not intended to deceive), rumors (pieces of information that have not yet been confirmed as true or false), conspiracy theories (which by definition are not verifiable, and tend to be spread by people who believe them to be true), and hoaxes (which are designed to deceive, may be humorous or malicious, and often involve citing a trusted source). Misinformation, like all information, is *piecemeal* and subject to revision when newer knowledge becomes available.

Contemporary usage of the term "misinformation" has become politicized, following misinformation scandals such as the "Obama's birth certificate" and "Clinton's child sex ring" incidents. While misinformation can refer to any publicly accessible erroneous information, the use of the term today generally implies malintent and deception.[1] For the purpose of this chapter, misinformation will refer to all instances where information can be verified as containing clear falsehoods.

Fake news is a type of misinformation where the information relates to a news event, and malintent is present on behalf of the person(s) creating the news, but not necessarily on behalf of the person(s) spreading the news. Allcott and Gentzkow (2017) define fake news as news articles that are "intentionally and verifiably false". Production of fake news is generally motivated by financial or ideological gain as it can mislead readers into believing that false news content is true. However, the term fake news is also sometimes used in reference to legitimate publications as a method of discreditation and defamation (this is a notable tactic by the US president Donald Trump); this is suggestive of the sensitivity of the topic and capacity for the word to be misapplied.[2]

Motivations for spreading misinformation

Why do people spread inaccurate information? Often, they believe information to be truthful due to heuristic biases. Heuristics are the tendencies of individuals to rely on simplistic patterns to reduce the expenditure of critical thought. This is evident in the reliance on prior beliefs and opinions: if the information confirms these priors, it is more likely to be believed (confirmation bias) and hence potentially spread (e.g., Ecker, Lewandowsky, Fenton, & Martin, 2014). Lewandowsky, Ecker, Seifert, Schwarz, and Cook (2012) have identified four factors that influence whether a person believes information: consistency of message (is it consistent with prior beliefs?), coherency of message (is it internally coherent and plausible?), credibility of source, and general acceptability (how many other people appear to believe it?). Another reason for spreading misinformation relates to normative pressures whereby people spread misinformation in order to gain social affirmation and acceptance: this relates to social identity theory (e.g., Tajfel & Turner, 2001, 2004). Once someone believes misinformation, it is difficult to change these beliefs (Lewandowsky et al., 2012), and attempts to correct falsifications may even perpetuate misinformation spread, particularly within ideological groups (Nyhan & Reifler, 2010). This supports the need for accurate and timely detection of false information, and has motivated the building of systems for detecting misinformation.

Fake news in the digital age

Although fake news is not a new phenomenon, there are several reasons why it is of growing importance and concern in the digital age (see, e.g., Allcott & Gentzkow, 2017; Shu, Sliva, Wang, Tang, & Liu, 2017).

First, barriers to entry in news media have dropped significantly as websites can be easily set up and monetized via advertising. Regarding the process of spreading of fake news, the fixed costs associated with getting on social media are very small – this increases the viability of short-term strategies involving establishing a social media presence for a particular fake news campaign, and reduces incentive for establishing long-term presence associated with quality journalism. Second, social media are well suited to dissemination of fake news; the format of social media is such that information tends to be distributed in short snippets of text, which makes it harder for users to assess veracity. Third, there has been a continued decline in public trust and confidence in mainstream media. Fourth, in many western countries there has been a rise in political polarization (degree of negative feelings oriented to the other side of the political spectrum) and this can increase the likelihood of fake news being believed.

The increase in political polarization is related to another important aspect of social media that may be affecting the extent to which people are exposed to fake news. In early research into political communication, Katz and Lazarsfeld (1955) contended that media-savvy individuals ("opinion leaders") were intermediaries between mass media and the public (the "two-step flow of communication"). However, social media has led to a reduction in the presence or importance of intermediaries between producers and consumers of information (this is referred to as "disintermediation") with people now able to create and share information via online social networks. It is much easier to have fine-grained control over particular information sources (e.g., follow users on Twitter who share your political beliefs) and this "narrowcasting" can lead to the creation of so-called echo chambers: groups of like-minded users who are not subject to outside views, which can lead to greater polarization (difference in attitudes). Related to this is the phenomenon of "filter bubbles": algorithms used by social media companies select new content for users based on their previous engagement with content, thus reinforcing information consumption patterns and making it less likely that users are exposed to new information.[3]

Echo chambers and filter bubbles are relevant to the fake news problem because they can affect the likelihood of a person transmitting fake news in the following ways. First, one is more likely to be connected to other people who evidently believe the news (this leads to social credibility and reinforcement). Second, one is more likely to be exposed to the fake news story, and increased exposure has been found to increase the likelihood of belief (Hasher, Goldstein, & Toppino, 1977), and less likely to be exposed to information that would counter an ideologically aligned but fake news story. Finally, there is increased normative pressure to spread fake news (even if one does not believe it).

Allcot and Gentzkow (2017) found that fake news was heavily tilted in favor of Donald Trump in 2016; their database contains 115 pro-Trump fake news stories that were shared on Facebook 30 million times, and 41 pro-Clinton fake news stories that were shared 7.6 million times on Facebook. Guess, Nyhan, and Reifler (2018) study how political identity affected consumption of fake news during the 2016 US presidential election. The authors found that Trump supporters were disproportionately inclined to visit websites hosting fake news, and that this was due to the fact that fake news was largely targeted at Trump supporters, and hence was attitude-consistent (and thus likely to be consumed).[4]

The dangers of fake news are that it can lower trust in democratic institutions, reduce social cohesion, and contribute to the rise of populist leaders (some commentators have attributed a significant role to fake news in the election of Donald Trump in 2016). However, Vargo, Guo, and Amazeen (2018) look at another potential impact of fake news – its potential for shaping the online news landscape. The authors used the Network Agenda-Setting (NAS) conceptual framework, which posits that the news media can influence how the public connects or relates issues to one another (e.g., energy crisis is related to foreign-relation problems) and also the salience or popularity of issues. Fake news could have an agenda-setting impact on news media (particularly partisan news media) simply by generating misinformation that needs to be responded to by journalists (e.g., through fact checking). They test the agenda-setting potential of fake news using the GDELT Global Knowledge Graph, a network of people, locations, themes, and events computationally constructed from global news (Leetaru & Schrodt, 2013). Using Granger causality tests,[5] the authors found that fake news was successful in transferring issue salience to online media for particular issues (e.g., international relations) during the period 2014–2016. They also distinguished partisan news media outlets and found that conservative media transferred issue salience to fake news media, and this in turn drove the agenda of liberal media (who were responding to fake news).

Overview of approaches for verifying news

There are two broad approaches to establishing the veracity of news.[6] The first approach involves the news content itself – features of the text (and images, if present) of the news item, and also its source. The news content approach to assessing the veracity of news can be further delineated by knowledge-based and style-based approaches.

Knowledge-based approaches involve using external sources to check the claims made in the news item ("fact checking"), and there are three main variants of fact checking.

(1) Fact checking by domain experts (the present chapter involves an implementation of expert-oriented fact checking and so we provide a summary of relevant literature in the next section).
(2) Crowdsourcing is fact checking involving an aggregated consensus of members of the general public. Applications such as Fiskkit and the LINE account "For real" allow user suggestion and comment to provide an indication of news truthfulness, and there is considerable interest in the use of distributed ledger technology (blockchain) for crowdsourcing fact checking.
(3) Knowledge graphs such as DBpedia or Google Knowledge Graph are networks showing the connection between real-world entities (people, places, things). Fact checking can be automatically performed by comparing the content of news stories (and in particular, relationship between entities mentioned in the news story) with content existing within the knowledge graph. The primary issue with this method is that while it is fast and accurate, it relies on information sources that cannot incorporate all knowledge.

Style-based approaches to checking news veracity involves linguistic analysis of text content in the news itself. This includes lexical features (e.g., number of words, average word length, number of unique words) and syntactic features (e.g., n-grams, parts of speech). Domain-specific linguistic features, such as external links and the presence of tables and graphs, may also be useful. Images can also be used to evoke particular emotional responses (anger, shock), which increase the likelihood of believing the news, and so features extracted from images are also used in detecting fake news.

The second approach for checking veracity of news involves using data on the social context of news, that is, how it is consumed and shared. This is where social media has had a major impact, because it allows for fine-grained data on the social context in which news is being consumed and spread. First, features relating to the users who have engaged with news may be used in detecting fake news. In the case of Twitter, such features may include the number of friends/followers, age of user account, and the number of tweets authored. Second, with social media it is also possible to collect post-level data – the reactions that people have to news items (e.g., quoted retweets when forwarding news URLs, comments on Facebook posts) – and these can provide useful information for detecting fake news. These reactions can be mined for linguistic features as discussed previously, but there is also the possibility of making use of social media data on the debate or contestation surrounding particular news items. Third, there are network features that can be used to detect fake news, for example, networks of the diffusion of news on Twitter via retweets (retweet cascades).

Fact checking by domain experts

Fact checking is frequently employed as a method of determining the reliability of statements and news, especially when there is a perceived risk of misinformation. Fact checking has risen to prominence over the past decade as websites such as Politifact.com and Factcheck.org have become established political fact verifiers. The recent inclusion of fact checking during media coverage of the 2016 US presidential election and the Trump presidency highlights the ability of fact checking to confront misinformation and fake news. The Australian political system has its own fact-checking outlets, such as RMIT University-ABC Fact Check and The Conversation's FactCheck.

The fact-checking industry has grown from a minor attraction during election cycles to a prominent element of the political sphere. Young, Jamieson, Poulsen, and Goldring (2018) identify the 1988 presidential election as the first example of contemporary fact checking being used to monitor the behavior of potential presidential candidates. This was framed as "adwatches" where fact checking was televised drawing on the combined knowledge of academics and media professionals. What started as a footnote gained traction as the American political environment adopted rhetorical techniques designed to mislead and misinform the public.

The spread of political misinformation was a prominent area of academic debate during the 2000s, particularly regarding the US invasion of Iraq and supposed stockpiling of weapons of mass destruction (WMDs). The revelation of government-coordinated misinformation spurred research into how individuals determine true from false and the ease in which politicians deceive the public.

Nyhan and Reifler (2010) make a binary distinction between the "uninformed" and "misinformed" subject: uninformed subjects react through heuristic biases whereas misinformed subjects have received false information through a political affiliation. Reversing misinformation through "corrective information" is generally unsuccessful because subjects have embedded knowledge within their political identity. This is a far more challenging issue than an uninformed public whose lack of knowledge is not embedded in conceptions of political and social identity.

Coinciding with the rapid growth of the internet, fact checking became increasingly prevalent online as it could quickly produce responses to political misinformation. Factcheck.org was launched in 2003 by the Annenberg Public Policy Center with the goal of confronting misinformation through the combined ability of journalism and scholarship. Following the success of Factcheck. org, websites like Politifact and Fact Checker (*Washington Post*) were established with similar methods of detecting misinformation.

Up until this point, fact checking had remained a relatively well-regarded source of information that increased accountability in politics. While the effectiveness of fact checking in terms of audience engagement has been looked at by authors such as Nyhan and Reifler (2010), the epistemological and methodological foundations of fact checking have not been explored extensively. Uscinski and Butler (2013) provide a critique of fact-checking practices, stating that "These practices share the tacit presupposition that there cannot be genuine political debate about facts" (p. 163).

Uscinski and Butler (2013) contend that fact checking takes a complex inter-relationship between politics, policy, society, economics, and history, reducing it to the most simplistic of metrics that assigns truth across a unidimensional spectrum. If a radically interpretative epistemology is adopted, truth cannot be dictated by a politician or a fact checker when a complex reality allows for varying conceptions of the truth. The authors outline key methodological failings of fact checking that are defined by a simplistic objectivist epistemology. These include selections effects (where the selection of facts is usually based on sensationalist or headlining stories), multiple fact/part of a fact concerns (defining the measurable parameters of a single fact), casual claims (assertion of an unknown relationship between facts), future predictions, and selection criteria (What constitutes truth? How true does something need to be?). The authors refrain from providing a simple answer to the failures of the fact-checking methodology. Instead they re-emphasize the interpretative nature of facts and the complex nature of political rhetoric and information.

Amazeen (2015) is critical of the generalizations and sampling used in Uscinski and Butler's (2013) critique of fact checking. While acknowledging the interpretive nature of fact checking, Amazeen (2015) suggests that Uscinski and Butler (2013) selected examples of fact checks that most clearly support their opinion. Amazeen (2015) claims that many facts are beyond debate and that interpretative facts are actually a small minority of the overall facts analyzed, and highlights the consistency across separate agencies in their fact check of common stories. However, for Uscinski (2015) the consistency across fact-checking agencies is simply a reflection of fact checkers sharing political biases and access to information. Uscinski (2015) argues that fact-checker consistency merely indicates their collective approach to fact checking rather than an empirical validation of inter-agency consistency. Uscinski (2015) further questions the very role of the "fact checker", as such actors lack qualifications, or are "epistemologically naïve" to believe that no qualification are needed and that the truth is easily accessible (p. 247).

Wu, Agarwal, Li, Yang, and Yu (2017) attempt to overcome some of the methodological failings of fact checking by introducing computational methods. The authors propose "query perturbations" as a way of avoiding issues of "cherry-picking" within fact checking – a problem highlighted by Uscinski (2015) as a key failing of fact checking given its reliance on unjustified selection criteria. What query perturbations aim to do is extend the parameters of the fact to see if the claimed truth still holds up under different levels of measurement. The example used by Wu et al. (2017) is the claim by New York's former mayor

Rudy Giuliani that adoption rates grew by 65–70% during his time in power. This is true given a very particular measurement (1990–1995, 1996–2001 as two grouped sets of data) but when adjusted for the actual time Giuliani was mayor (1994–2001), there was in fact a 1% decrease in adoptions during his term. This indicates the ways in which data can be manipulated to present truths that are statistically correct but contextually inaccurate.

Computational approaches to studying misinformation

This section summarizes recent studies that use computational approaches to either identify misinformation or study its spread and impact.

Most computational approaches for detection of misinformation such as fake news on social media use machine learning classification to predict whether a news article is true or not. The first automated approaches to detecting misinformation on the internet were in the context of detection of problematic emails and website text content (e.g., spam and hoaxes). These approaches generally involved applying supervised machine learning approaches to text. For detection of spam emails, for example, this involves constructing a training dataset consisting of emails that have been manually coded as spam and non-spam, and a classifier (e.g., logistic regression, neural network) is used to predict the likelihood of an email being problematic, based on extracted features, for example, keywords, or patterns in sentence structure.

Castillo, Mendoza, and Poblete (2011) investigate the use of automated methods to assess the credibility ("offering reasonable grounds to be believed", p. 675) of news-related tweets. Human coders first identified a set of tweets relating to news events and a second set of coders labeled the tweets as to whether they believed they were true or false. The authors extracted a set of features from tweets that are related to the preceding social context approach: *post-based features* (e.g., length of tweet, use of punctuation such as exclamation marks, positive/ negative sentiment of the tweet, whether it is a retweet, whether it contains a hashtag); *user-based features* (age of account, number of followers and following, number of tweets authored); and *propagation-based features* (number of retweets). It was found that credible information was more likely to be spread by users with newer accounts, who are more active (in terms of tweets) and with many followers and followees. Positive sentiment, as well as the presence of question marks and smiley emoticons, in the tweets spreading the story were associated with less credible news stories, while the presence of a URL in the tweet was associated with higher credibility. Regarding propagation-related features, tweets having many retweets are more likely to be judged as credible.

Tacchini, Ballarin, Della Vedova, Moret, and Alfaro (2017) developed an approach to classify posts on public Facebook pages as containing valid science or conspiracy theory science, using data on which Facebook users had "liked" the different posts.[7] Their approach relies on an assumption of assortativity in behavior of Facebook users; the users will tend to group or cluster by liking similar posts, based on their preferences toward consuming information containing scientific fact or conspiracy theory. However, as noted by the authors, this approach requires as input some information from the content of the post since *a priori* it is not known whether a set of Facebook users liking the same post are doing it because they value the science or the conspiracy.

Vosoughi, Mohsenvand, and Roy (2017) investigated supervised learning approaches to automatically verify rumors on Twitter. Their dataset consisted of 209 manually selected and annotated rumors relating to real-world events, and they focused on features related to linguistic style of the tweets, the users spreading the rumors, and the dynamics of propagation. They were motivated to build a system that could be used for real-time rumor identification, and their system correctly predicted the veracity of 75% of rumors faster than trusted public sources (e.g., journalists, law enforcement officials). To measure propagation, they devised an approach to reconstruct the retweet cascade networks (the Twitter API does not provide retweet cascades, instead connecting all retweet events to the original tweet, regardless of the actual chain of retweets) using data on timestamps of retweets and following relationships between people who retweeted.[8] They found that the temporal dynamics of features had significant predictive power, and since these dynamics are generally invariant to the size of a rumor (e.g., the total amount of attention it garnered), this allows their approach to generalize to events and rumors of various sizes.

A key finding was that propagation features did most of the "heavy lifting" in terms of prediction of veracity of rumor, and they found that rumors that were eventually found to be true tended to propagate by high-influence users (in terms of number of followers) retweeting low-influence users. A justification for this finding was that a high influence person would not risk retweeting a tweet from a lesser-known person, unless confident that the rumor was in fact true. Another key finding was that tweets of rumors subsequently found to be false tended to exhibit a bi-modal distribution in terms of language sophistication (compared to other tweets in their corpus) and the authors related this to intent of the spreaders; spreaders of malicious rumors tend to use sophisticated language to make the rumor more legitimate and believable, whereas spreaders of rumors that were non-malicious tended to be careless in their language and hence lacking in linguistic sophistication. Finally, they found that false rumors tend to be spread by users who are influential and controversial (where the controversiality of users is computed by first measuring the sentiment of up to 1,000 replies to the user and then constructing a score whereby users with many replies and an even mix of negative and positive replies are rated as more controversial), whereas spreaders of rumors subsequently found to be true tend to be influential and less controversial.

Vosoughi, Roy, and Aral (2018) studied the propagation behavior of true and false news on Twitter (as noted previously, they eschewed the use of the term "fake news"), using the approach for reconstructing retweet cascade trees used in Vosoughi et al. (2017). They found that false news spreads deeper (measured as the length of the longest sub-tree within a retweet cascade), farther (the unique number of retweeters of a story, which is a measure of how many people consumed the news), and more broadly (the maximum width of a sub-tree). They also found that false news diffused faster, with the truth taking about six times as long as falsehood to reach 1,500 people. These patterns were especially pronounced for fake political news, compared with news regarding, for example, terrorism, natural disasters, or other topics.

The authors found that network and user characteristics did not explain the markedly different diffusion profiles of true and false news. The people spreading false news were less connected (fewer followers and followees), less active on Twitter, and had been on Twitter for shorter periods of time; falsehood was 70% more likely to be retweeted, compared with truth, even after controlling for these factors. They therefore investigated the impact (on diffusion) of a particular characteristic of the news itself: novelty. They measured novelty of news by comparing the topic distribution (identified using a Latent Dirichelet Allocation topic model) of the news stories in their sample with the tweets that users were exposed to in the 60 days prior to their retweeting of sample news stories. They found that false news is more novel than true news, and suggested that the differential diffusion patterns could be due to people preferring to share novel information (regardless of its veracity) because novelty attracts attention (it allows us to update our understanding of the world) and also there may be social benefits to spreading novel information (one is "in the know").

Shin, Jian, Driscoll, and Bar (2018) studied the dynamic process of misinformation on social media by tracking the life cycle of 17 political rumors that circulated on Twitter during the 2012 US presidential election. Consistent with the findings of Vosoughi et al. (2018), Shin et al. (2018) found that false rumors tended to re-emerge on Twitter (often with "mutations", i.e., textual changes) exhibiting multiple spikes in attention over time, whereas true rumors did not, tending to have a single prominent pike of attention. The authors proposed three potential reasons for these different temporal patterns. First, rumor spreaders may feel that false rumors needed more "help" in gaining wider acceptance and hence require repeated attempts at spreading. Second, since true rumors tend to originate from mainstream media outlets, rumor spreaders may feel that they've "exhausted" their potential readership and hence not allocate resources to their further spread. Finally, spreading false rumors may be for the purpose of identity signaling, rather than persuasion, and repeated attempts at spreading false rumors reflects people "participating in a common epistemological sphere" (p. 285) thus promoting group bonding.

In addition to examining propagation features as signatures for identifying fake news, researchers have also modeled the spread of misinformation using formal models of contagion processes. For example, Tambuscio, Ruffo, Flammini, and Menczer (2015) use stochastic epidemic models to model the spread of a hoax as a virus. This approach implicitly views the spread of misinformation as a simple contagion process (only requires one contact between "adopter/infected" and "non-adopter/non-infected" person for there to be adoption or transmission), but Törnberg (2018) instead draws on the concept of "complex contagion" (multiple sources of reinforcement may be required to induce adoption), which is useful for describing the spread of behaviors such as social movements and avant-garde fashion (Centola & Macy, 2007). Törnberg (2018) contends that the spread of fake news involves complex contagion since a person's decision whether to spread or not can involve group identity processes. The simulation models directly address the potential contribution of echo chambers (which as noted earlier can reinforce group identity) to the spread of fake news.

Some researchers have focused specifically on the role of social bots in spreading misinformation. For example, Ferrara (2017) analyzed activity of social bots during a disinformation campaign relating to the 2017 French presidential election. Contrary to expectations, Vosoughi et al. (2018) found that Twitter social bots and humans exhibit similar behavior in terms of sharing true and false news. However, even if social bots do not have a greater direct impact on the spread of fake news (compared with humans), their contribution to the spread of fake news can indirectly influence more humans to believe and hence spread the fake news. By propagating falsehoods, social bots make it more likely that people will encounter this fake news, contributing to the perception that the fake news is endorsed by many people, and thus promoting further circulation of fake news.

Application: how does truthfulness of news affect the dynamics of its diffusion?

This section presents an analysis of the diffusion on Twitter (via retweets) of a sample of Australian news stories, with an objective of assessing how the truthfulness of a news story affects the dynamics of its diffusion.

Twitter retweet and following network data

The dataset is a collection of retweets of news stories published by three Australian media sources on three randomly selected days during 2017, from Ackland, O'Neil, and Park (2019).[9]

The steps for collecting the data were:

(1) Randomly select one weekday from three consecutive months in 2017 (we checked the sampled day was not dominated by a particular news event): May 22, June 16, and July 4.
(2) Collect all of the news stories tweeted by the brands on the sampled days.
(3) Collect all of the retweets of the news stories, over the next seven days.
(4) Collect the following edges (or ties) among the retweeters of political stories (we label these people "political retweeters").
(5) Collect the following edges from political retweeters to Australian federal politicians.

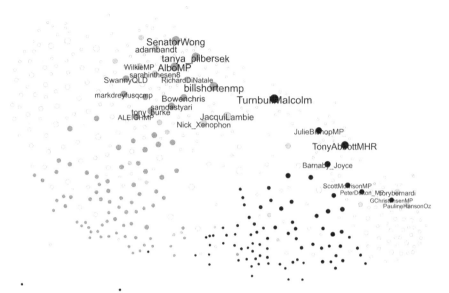

FIGURE 3.1 Twitter following network: political news story retweeters and Australian federal politicians

Note: Dark gray – Labor (political left), black – Liberal-National Coalition (political right), gray – other parties, white – political retweeters. To improve the readability of the network, edges are not displayed.

The giant component of the Twitter following network (political retweeters and Australian federal politicians) is shown in Figure 3.1; this is the network over which diffusion (via retweets) of news stories is measured. The number of nodes (edges) is 495 (12,467) and node size is proportional to indegree. The nodes in the network have been positioned using a force-directed algorithm whereby nodes that are connected (via following edges) are drawn closer together (as if the edges were springs), and nodes that are not connected are pushed apart (as if the nodes have electrostatic charges and repulse one another). Force-directed algorithms can reveal clustering in networks, and there is a marked "Divided They Follow" phenomenon displayed here with strong evidence of clustering on the basis of political ideology.

Selection of news stories

We initially planned to select news stories that contained at least one fact or statistic that is capable of being verified. However, a pilot test of the fact-checking approach indicated that we needed a further selection criteria because traditional news coverage relies heavily on quotes and observed facts, and the capacity to include misinformation is therefore relatively low. Impartiality in news content is a product of twentieth-century norm shifts following the Second World War. In response to propaganda during the war, media outlets and government sought to realign the medium of news presentation. The Commission on the Freedom of the Press (1947) developed a norm of analytical news with opinion pieces forming a separate area in newspapers (Metzgar & Hornaday, 2013). We therefore decided to focus our fact checking on opinion pieces, since these are spaces in which individualism and partiality are expected. Finally, another factor influenced our selection of news stories for fact checking: since our intention was to analyze the diffusion (via retweets) of news stories on Twitter, we also chose articles with a large number of retweets.

Fourteen articles were analyzed in total, with five from the *Sydney Morning Herald*, five from the *Huffington Post*, and four from *The Australian* (Table 3.1). Opinion pieces were the primary focus, although traditional news analysis was included to expand the sample size, as well as for comparative purposes: eight

TABLE 3.1 Sampled news stories with truth score and diffusion measures

Story id	Article	Brand	Date	Format	Truth score	Reach	Speed	Breadth
1	ALP Gender Equality	Aus	16/6/2017	Opinion	4	1	n.a.	n.a.
2	Turnbull Midwinter Ball	Aus	16/6/2017	Opinion	4	10	2.5	2.67
3	Too Late for Turnbull	Aus	22/5/2017	Opinion	5	13	3.0	2.52
4	Mediscare	Aus	16/6/2017	Opinion	4	1	n.a.	n.a.
5	Scott Morrison Economy	SMH	22/5/2017	Opinion	5	1	n.a.	n.a.
6	Off the Record	SMH	16/6/2017	Opinion	4	1	n.a.	n.a.
7	Citizenship Test	SMH	16/6/2017	Opinion	2	8	64.3	2.26
8	Tony Abbott Manifesto	SMH	4/7/2017	Opinion	5	4	3.8	1.57
9	Manus Island	HP	22/5/2017	Opinion/ Traditional	4	28	6.3	2.79
10	James Ashby Denial	HP	22/5/2017	Opinion/ Traditional	4	12	1.8	2.63
11	Illegal Medicare Machines	HP	4/7/2017	Opinion/ Traditional	4	7	1.8	2.45
12	Fake Refugees	HP	22/5/2017	Opinion/ Traditional	5	14	4.0	2.00
13	Adani Mine Investment	SMH	22/5/2017	Traditional	5	47	3.5	2.90
14	Manus Settlement	HP	16/6/2017	Traditional	4	4	5.0	1.59

Note: Aus – *The Australian*, SMH – *Sydney Morning Herald*, HP – *Huffington Post*.

articles were classified as "opinion" and six articles classified as "traditional news" (the *Huffington Post* articles were classified as a hybrid).

Fact checking of news stories

We devised and implemented an original fact-checking methodology that attempts to code news stories according to their adherence to the truth. The primary consideration of the methodology was how to fit an interpretative model of analysis within a largely quantitative framework. If fact checking was truly objective or at least had proven consistency, then this would be less of a concern. However, as indicated by Uscinski and Butler (2013), this is far from reality. To avoid, or at least mitigate, some of the inherent problems with current fact-checking approaches, we used the following work flow (Figure 3.2) to assign each news article a score on a Likert scale ranging from 1 (very untruthful) to 5 (very truthful):

(1)   Are any of the statistics or facts not supported by evidence or information from reliable sources?[10]
(2)   What is the significance of the statistic or fact that was not verified? Does it have minor/moderate/high impact on the validity of the article and/or the overarching discourses the article engages in?

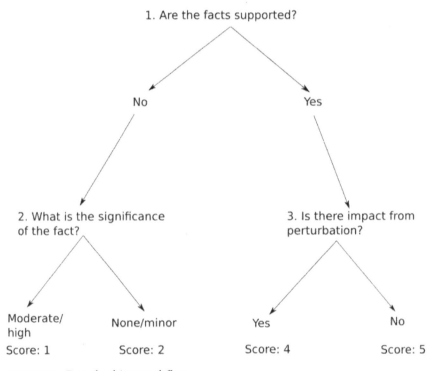

FIGURE 3.2   Fact checking workflow

(3) In the case where a fact or statistic has been verified, do reasonable perturbations to the parameters of the fact or statistic modify or compromise the underlying intent or framing of the story, in a way that is reliable and sensible?

The preceding method includes some of the foundational elements of a fact check, such as verifiability and adherence to the truth (step 1). Fact checking cannot be assumed to be an objective account of truth, and framing it in this way diminishes its legitimacy and value. Uscinski and Butler (2013) are primarily critical of fact checking because it tends to promote a voice of authority and certainty. The perspective of the fact checker is underemphasized, which implicitly suggests an empiricism in fact checking. While these points are sometimes viewed as strengths of fact checking, in the context of this research it would have diminished the applicability of the fact checks. The preceding fact-checking method highlights its interpretive limitations and avoids implying empirical truths.

Steps 2 and 3 attempt to incorporate a simplified version of query perturbation proposed by Wu et al. (2017). Step 2 assesses the impact of untrue claims by classifying facts based on their contextual relevance: if the argument relies heavily on an untrue claim then it receives a reduction in score. Step 3 perturbs the parameters of a fact to see if truthfulness is a result of statistical manipulation or cherry-picking. This is done through researcher analysis rather than computational methods so it cannot be directly compared with query perturbations proposed by Wu et al. (2017), however it is in the same spirit.[11]

The workflow can be briefly demonstrated using the "ALP Gender Equality" article that was published in *The Australian* on June 16, 2017. The statement "Bill Shorten's support for gender equality within Labor . . . is floundering at the national level of the party organisation" must pass step 1 to be considered more than an unjustified critique. The article then mentioned the existence of an "affirmative action report card obtained by The Weekend Australian": as this claim was verified, the article therefore passed step 1 in the workflow. The article then claimed "Most of the senior roles in Mr Shorten's office are filled by men". Only when considering step 3 does this article's utilization of facts become less convincing. The preceding facts have been used in a way that can be impacted by justifiable perturbations. When comparing the Labor Party to its competitor the Liberal/National Coalition, gender imbalances are relatively minor. The article bases its argumentation on a normative critique of gender levels in a party whose representation is better than its closest comparison. For this reason, the article fails step 3 and receives an overall score of 4.

Table 3.1 shows the "truthfulness" rating for the 14 news articles (the complete fact checks are available from the authors on request). There is a reasonably strong adherence to the truth, with an average score of 4.2. As anticipated, traditional news stories adhered closer to the truth, compared with opinion pieces; the latter are often written by politicians, who self-monitor misinformation to a lesser degree than media, whose reputations lie in their ability to provide the truth. The average score was quite similar across the news platforms: *The Australian* had an average of 4.3, while *The Sydney Morning Herald* and *Huffington Post* both had an average score of 4.2. Given the interpretative nature of analysis, a close look at the outliers can give an indication of what news containing substantial misinformation looks like. The "Citizenship Test" article received the lowest fact check score of 2 out of 5. This is due to a clear manipulation of facts and context, and sensationalistic rhetoric. Based on this sample of news articles, we conclude that although there are some examples of misinformation spread by new media outlets, it is not common, at least among these news brands.

Diffusion of news stories on Twitter

As noted previously, Vosoughi et al. (2018) reconstructed retweet cascade trees and then measured diffusion of true and false news stories across these trees. We take a different approach here by instead looking at how the news stories diffused (via retweets) across the network of following edges shown in Figure 3.1. For a given story, we do not know the exact pathway of diffusion (because we have not reconstructed the retweet cascade trees), but we do know exactly who in the following network retweeted the story, and when. Figure 3.3 shows the following network, with black nodes indicating those Twitter users who retweeted

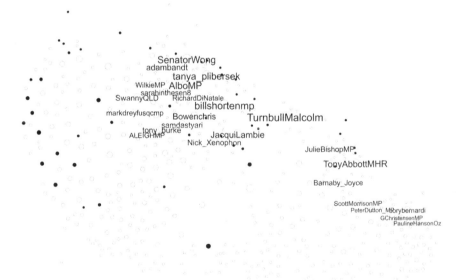

FIGURE 3.3 Twitter following network – black nodes indicate users who retweeted the "Adani Mine Investment" story

the "Adani Mine Investment" story (this was the story with the highest number of tweets – 47). It is apparent that this story was mainly retweeted by Twitter users who are located in the political left part of the map (they predominantly following Labor Party politicians), although there is a small number of retweeters of the story who are located close to prominent Liberal-National Coalition (right-wing) politicians.

We assessed how the truthfulness of the story affects its diffusion in terms of the following measures:

(1)   Reach: Total number of retweets of the story
(2)   Speed: Number of hours taken for 50% of total retweets to be achieved
(3)   Breadth: Mean geodesic distance, or average shortest path length calculated across all of the pairs of retweeters of the story

A challenge for our analysis is the fact that we do not have many data points: we only coded 14 news stories because of the time-consuming nature of fact-checking, but also because we only collected news stories from three sampled days, there was a limited supply of potential stories that fit our selection criteria stated earlier. Further, there was not much variation in the truthfulness rating of the stories: all but one story were coded 4 or 5.

The three diffusion measures (reach, speed, and breadth) are reported in Table 3.1, and it is immediately apparent that despite our best intentions in selecting news stories that had received significant retweets, four stories were retweeted only once by Twitter users in our sample. In reality, these stories were retweeted more than this, but our sample only includes those Twitter users who have (1) retweeted at least one of the political stories and (2) are connected by a following edge to at least one other political retweeter or else to an Australian federal politician. These four stories were excluded from the following analysis.

Based on the research summarized previously (especially Vosoughi et al., 2018) our expectation was that false stories would have greater diffusion (more retweets), diffuse faster, and have greater breadth of diffusion. The preceding data issues mean we cannot provide a rigorous analysis of the diffusion patterns of true versus false news stories; the intention here is to illustrate the approach, rather than provide conclusive evidence. The one story that was given a score of 2 (untruthful) – "Citizenship Test" – had a reach of eight retweets (lower than the average for all stories of 15 retweets), took 64 hours to achieve 50% of the total number of retweets (much higher than the average of ten hours), and by the end of the period the average length of the shortest path (in the following network) between those people who had retweeted the story was 2.26 (lower than the average breadth for all stories of 2.34). Thus, on all three measures, the pattern of diffusion for the one untruthful story in the sample, in comparison to the average, was the opposite of what we expected. However, as already noted, data limitations are such that we are presenting our application as a methodological contribution rather than a definitive test of the diffusion behavior of true and false news.

Conclusion

In this chapter, we reviewed the state-of-the-art research in the area of misinformation and social media, focusing on approaches for identifying misinformation (and its most topical or newsworthy form today, fake news), and also research that aims to further understanding about how misinformation spreads and its consequences. Although our emphasis has been on computational approaches involving social media data, we also reviewed current research into manual fact checking of news stories.

We then provided an empirical application aimed at characterizing the diffusion patterns of true and false Australian political news stories. The application demonstrated a new approach for fact checking news stories and we also attempted to demonstrate that it is possible to study diffusion of news stories even in the absence of retweet cascade trees (which are not provided by Twitter, and are computationally challenging to reconstruct). However, our empirical application was challenged by the fact that we had few data points (coded stories), and there was not a lot of variation in the truthfulness ratings. We offer our empirical application as a demonstration of a new approach to studying fake news using Twitter data.

Notes

1 Some authors distinguish misinformation and disinformation, where the former may involve an actor spreading inaccurate information that they believe is true, and the latter involves a conscious attempt to deceive. In practical applications, disinformation is generally treated as a subset of misinformation, as it is more difficult to ascertain the motives of actors transmitting inaccurate information.

2 Noting the current politicization of the term "fake news", Vosoughi et al. (2018) eschew its use in favor of the term "false news".

3 Bakshy, Messing, and Adamic (2015) compare the relative effects of echo chambers and filter bubbles on a person's exposure to politically diverse content on Facebook.

4 To our knowledge, it has not been tested whether Trump supporters were on a per story basis more inclined to consume fake news, or whether it was simply that they were exposed to a greater volume of attitude-consistent fake news.

5 A time series X is said to "Granger cause" time series Y if lagged values of X are statistically significant in a regression predicting future values of Y.

6 The following draws from Shu et al. (2017).

7 Vosoughi et al. (2018) argue that research into diffusion of science and conspiracy science stories does not allow understanding of factors affecting spread of true versus false news, since by definition, a conspiracy story cannot be verified as false or true.

8 The authors note that both Castillo et al. (2011) and Kwon, Cha, Jung, Chen, and Wang (2013) investigated the use of propagation features in predicting veracity of tweets, but these authors did not impute the retweet cascade tree and so were unable to use propagation features as sophisticated as those used by Vosoughi et al. (2017).

9 The three Australia media sources were *The Australian*, the *Sydney Morning Herald*, and the *Huffington Post*. These sources aim to cover a broad range of political affiliation, with *The*

Australian being on the political right, the *Sydney Morning Herald* being on the left, and the *Huffington Post* potentially on either side.
10 Reliable sources refer to evidence that comes from either a primary source or a secondary source whose integrity can be determined based on historical evidence of their truthfulness. We assessed this based on the standing of the source, as determined through external indicators such as historical veracity, accountability, and retrospective corrections. The undertaking of fact checking with this methodology must avoid all agendas and biases as much as possible. This is impossible to completely eradicate, so the verified facts must be considered an interpretive account of true and false.
11 The coding was conducted by one of the co-authors, but in a larger-scale study it would be preferable to have multiple fact checkers, and to compute intercoder reliability.

References

Ackland, R., O'Neil, M., & Park, S. (2019). Engagement with news on Twitter: Insights from Australia and Korea. *Asian Journal of Communication, 29*(3), 235–251.

Allcott, H., & Gentzkow, M. (2017). Social media and fake news in the 2016 election. *Journal of Economic Perspectives, 31*(2), 211–235.

Amazeen, M. A. (2015). Revisiting the epistemology of fact-checking. *Critical Review, 27*(1), 1–22.

Bakshy, E., Messing, S., & Adamic, L. A. (2015). Exposure to ideologically diverse news and opinion on Facebook. *Science, 348*(6239), 1130–1132.

Castillo, C., Mendoza, M., & Poblete, B. (2011). *Information credibility on twitter.* Proceedings of the 20th International Conference on World Wide Web (WWW), Hyderabad, India.

Centola, D., & Macy, M. W. (2007). Complex contagion and the weakness of long ties. *American Journal of Sociology, 113*(3), 702–734.

Ecker, U. K., Lewandowsky, S., Fenton, O., & Martin, K. (2014). Do people keep believing because they want to? Preexisting attitudes and the continued influence of misinformation. *Memory & Cognition, 42*(2), 292–304.

Ferrara, E. (2017). Disinformation and social bot operations in the run up to the 2017 French presidential election. *First Monday, 22*(8).

Guess, A., Nyhan, B., & Reifler, J. (2018). Selective exposure to misinformation: Evidence from the consumption of fake news during the 2016 U.S. presidential campaign. Retrieved from www.ask-force.org/web/Fundamentalists/Guess-Selective-Exposure-to-Misinformation-Evidence-Presidential-Campaign-2018.pdf

Hasher, L., Goldstein, D., & Toppino, T. (1977). Frequency and the conference of referential validity. *Journal of Verbal Learning & Verbal Behavior, 16*, 107–112.

Katz, E., & Lazarsfeld, P. F. (1955). *Personal influence: The part played by people in the flow of mass communications.* Glencoe, IL: Free Press.

Kwon, S., Cha, M., Jung, K., Chen, W., & Wang, Y. (2013). *Prominent features of rumor propagation in online social media.* Proceedings of the 13th International Conference on Data Mining (ICDM), IEEE, 1103–1108.

Leetaru, K., & Schrodt, P. A. (2013). *GDELT: Global data on events, location, and tone, 1979–2012.* International Studies Association Meetings, San Francisco.

Lewandowsky, S., Ecker, U. K., Seifert, C. M., Schwarz, N., & Cook, J. (2012). Misinformation and its correction: Continued influence and successful debiasing. *Psychological Science in the Public Interest, 13*(3), 106–131.

Metzgar, E. T., & Hornaday, B. W. (2013). Leaving it there? The Hutchins commission and modern American journalism. *Journal of Mass Media Ethics, 28*(4), 255–270.

Nyhan, B., & Reifler, J. (2010). When corrections fail: The persistence of political misperceptions. *Political Behavior, 32*(2), 303–330.

Shin, J., Jian, L., Driscoll, K., & Bar, F. (2018). The diffusion of misinformation on social media: Temporal pattern, message, and source. *Computers in Human Behavior, 83*, 278–287.

Shu, K., Sliva, A., Wang, S., Tang, J., & Liu, H. (2017). Fake news detection on social media: A data mining perspective. *ACM SIGKDD Explorations Newsletter, 19*(1), 22–36.

Tacchini, E., Ballarin, G., Della Vedova, M. L., Moret, S., & Alfaro, L. (2017). *Some like it Hoax: Automated fake news detection in social networks*. Proceedings of the Second Workshop on Data Science for Social Good, Skopje, FYR Macedonia. CEUR Workshop Proceedings, Volume 1960.

Tajfel, H., & Turner, J. C. (2001). An integrative theory of intergroup conflict. In M. A. Hogg & D. Abrams (Eds.), *Key readings in social psychology: Intergroup relations: Essential readings* (pp. 94–109). New York, NY, US: Psychology Press.

Tajfel, H., & Turner, J. C. (2004). The social identity theory of intergroup behavior. In J. T. Jost & J. Sidanius (Eds.), *Key readings in social psychology: Political psychology: Key readings* (pp. 276–293). New York, NY, US: Psychology Press.

Tambuscio, M., Ruffo, G., Flammini, A., & Menczer, F. (2015). *Fact-checking effect on viral Hoaxes: A model of misinformation spread in social networks*, WWW 2015 Companion.

Törnberg, P. (2018). Echo chambers and viral misinformation: Modeling fake news as complex contagion. *PLoS One, 13*(9).

Uscinski, J. E. (2015). The epistemology of fact checking (is still naïve): Rejoinder to Amazeen. *Critical Review, 27*(2), 243–252.

Uscinski, J. E., & Butler, R. W. (2013). The epistemology of fact checking. *Critical Review, 25*(2), 162–180.

Vargo, C. J., Guo, L., & Amazeen, M. A. (2018). The agenda-setting power of fake news: A big data analysis of the online media landscape from 2014 to 2016. *New Media & Society, 20*(5), 2028–2049.

Vosoughi, S., Mohsenvand, M. N., & Roy, D. (2017). Rumor Gauge: Predicting the veracity of rumors on Twitter. *ACM Transactions on Knowledge Discovery from Data (TKDD), 11*(4), 50.

Vosoughi, S., Roy, D., & Aral, S. (2018). The spread of true and false news online. *Science, 359*(6380), 1146–1151.

Wu, Y., Agarwal, P. K., Li, C., Yang, J., & Yu, C. (2017). Computational fact checking through query perturbations'. *ACM Transactions on Database Systems, 42*(1), 1–41.

Young, D. G., Jamieson, K. H., Poulsen, S., & Goldring, A. (2018). Fact-checking effectiveness as a function of format and tone: Evaluating FactCheck.org and FlackCheck.org. *Journalism & Mass Communication Quarterly, 95*(1), 49–75.

4

RETRACTED ARTICLES – THE SCIENTIFIC VERSION OF FAKE NEWS

Judit Bar-Ilan and Gali Halevi

Introduction

Scientific advancements are gradual. "Standing on the shoulders of Giants" a well-known phrase by Newton[1] refers to the scientific process wherein each paper reporting on new findings enables the scientific community to advance knowledge further by building upon previous discoveries. The purpose of scientific journals and publishing has always been to function as a reliable, vetted source for science to be shared and advanced. As a part of this responsibility, scientific journal publishers have safeguards in place to ensure that content is indeed original, reliable, and reproducible, thus keeping the scientific integrity intact. One of the main vehicles used by the scientific publishing community to ensure scientific truthfulness is the peer review process. Peer review is a practice by which each article submitted to a journal is securitized by at least two reviewers from the same field of investigation. These reviewers are always anonymous and oftentimes do not know who the authors are. These measures are specifically taken to ensure that the review is unbiased and focused on the articles and their findings. The main task of the reviewers is to verify the originality, quality, and integrity of each and every paper and examine it for accuracy of data, analysis, findings, conclusions, and more. Although reviewers can recommend major or minor revisions, they also have the ability to reject papers if they are found to be unreliable for whatever reason (Biagioli, Kenney, Martin, & Walsh, 2018; Bozzo, Bali, Evaniew, & Ghert, 2017; Nicholas et al., 2015).

However, despite of this rigorous process, papers are regularly retracted from journals due to a variety of reasons (Budd, Sievert, Schultz, & Scoville, 1999; Cokol, Ozbay, & Rodriguez-Esteban, 2008; Fang, Steen, & Casadevall, 2012; Steen, 2010, 2011). There are times when the reason for retraction might be simple and easily correctable (Bar-Ilan & Halevi, 2018; Budd, Sievert, & Schultz,

1998; Halevi & Bar-Ilan, 2016; Williams & Wager, 2013). These types of retractions occur due to administrative errors, errors in references, or copy editing mistakes not identified in time to be corrected prior to publication that result in the paper being retracted and a retraction notice issued. In most cases, these articles are corrected and then re-published. Yet, there are much more serious types of retractions; especially those that were triggered due to data falsification, manipulation of results, unethical use of subjects, plagiarism, and more (Almeida, de Albuquerque Rocha, Catelani, Fontes-Pereira, & Vasconcelos, 2015; Corbyn, 2012; Fang & Casadevall, 2011; Inoue & Muto, 2016; Noyori & Richmond, 2013).

In the medical and biomedical arenas, scientific retractions pulled from the literature due to ethical issues and containing erroneous, or even fabricated data, analysis, and findings should be carefully examined due to the enormous negative impact they have on future medical practices and, more importantly, human lives. In this chapter, we chose to focus on retracted articles in the medical and biomedical fields and demonstrate how they impacted, and in some cases, continue to impact the medical community and society. To illustrate the gravity of retracted articles in the medical arena and the potential of putting patients at risk, a paper by G. Steen (2011) evaluated over 180 retracted primary papers and 851 secondary ones that described the results of trials conducted on over 28,000 human subjects. Primary articles were considered those that were originally retracted, whereas secondary ones were those citing the original retracted articles, basing their data collection, methods, or analysis on them. The analysis showed that 70 papers that were retracted due to fraud, treated more patients per study than those retracted because of errors. This paper also found that these articles were cited over 5,000 times and the citations were mostly research related, meaning that ideas expressed in fraudulent papers influenced consequent research and patients enrolled in their studies. Therefore, incorrect or fraudulent information reported in medical studies and publications can harm patients directly due to continuous citations, use of methods, treatments, or ideas taken from the culprit publication.

There are several very famous cases of such retractions that reached the news media and created a public stir due to their gravity. These include the 1998 article by Dr. Wakefield in the *Lancet* that suggested that the combined vaccine for measles, mumps, and rubella can cause autism in children. This article – retracted in 2010 due to faulty methods and financial conflicts of the author – still, to this day, remains very influential as parents and anti-vaccine groups are reluctant to vaccinate children, which in turn caused more cases of these diseases to be detected (Facts about the Measles Outbreak, 2015). Other famous cases include Dr. Drasee, a Harvard Medical School heart researcher who fabricated the bulk of his heart research with over 100 publications retracted due to fraudulent data (Broad, 1983) or Dr. Straus, a cancer researcher, who was accused of falsifying research results, reporting on unqualified patients, administrating falsified drug dosages (Upi, 1982), and not complying with consent rules.

In addition to these high-profile cases, retractions in the medical and biomedical fields happen regularly, and although they are mostly not life-threating, the fact that they are continuously cited in the medical literature and being shared as legitimate research can present health-related threats even years after retraction.

Data sources and collection

To examine the characteristics and impact of medical and biomedical retracted papers we used the Retraction Watch Database ('Retraction Watch Database', n.d.) curated by Adam Marcus and Ivan Oransky, the owners of "Retraction Watch" ('Retraction Watch Database', n.d.), a blog dedicated to the listing and flagging of retracted articles across scientific disciplines. Our previous work on studying retracted articles has enabled us to have access to the data curated in the database, which includes over 17,000 retracted articles, retraction notices, and reasons for retraction. The data also included valuable metadata, including author/s name/s, journal title, publisher, year, and discipline. Thanks to the disciplinary classification within the database we were able to retrieve all the medical and biomedical retracted articles published between 2010 and 2014 and retracted before 2017. Our dataset included 1,294 research articles in these areas.

The main reason for this selection was our aim to track more recent retracted articles in these fields in order to be able to monitor social media attention. The use of social media to share, discuss, or promote research is a recent phenomenon. In the early days of social media, the vast majority of its use was for personal purposes. Yet, in the past decade, more and more scientists are using social media such as Twitter and Instagram to promote their research, network with colleagues, and discuss various topics via these tools. The social media life of retracted articles was one of our main interests, because such discussions do not stay within the scientific realm – they involve lay people who follow these scientists or doctors and take an active part in sharing and discussing them. Therefore, in order to be able to track social media indicators we selected articles that were published when social media was in wide use scientists. We also collected citations counts, which are mostly scientific indicators of impact. All data, including citations, were collected in February 2019 to ensure that enough time lapsed after the retraction during which citations would appear in the scientific literature and other indicators such as readership and social media mentions would also be evident on the various platforms.

To account for both the scientific and public impact of retracted articles, we used several tools to count pre- and post-retraction citations, social media mentions, and readership counts for the retracted articles. Citations, social media and readership data were collected in February 2019. Since there is usually a time gap between the publication date and the retraction date, it is important to examine citations and attention to the article pre- and post-retraction. Although scientific citations to articles pre-retraction is an acceptable phenomenon, such citations post-retraction is worrying and bears the question why would scientists keep citing a retracted paper? In some cases, the citation is negative; meaning that the scientists cite the retraction in order to give an example of bad science or to enforce results that contradict retracted ones. Yet, often we also see valid, positive citations completely ignoring the fact that the paper was pulled out of the literature (Bar-Ilan & Halevi, 2017). Although citations are considered scientific impact, readership, for example, can be a sign of both scientific and social impact since there is no telling who precisely reads these articles. Despite publishers retracting articles and issuing an appropriate notice to that affect, preprints of articles can be found in repositories and are freely available. These versions do not include the retraction notice and their readers might not be aware of the faults that led to their retraction. In addition, we also found that retracted articles become Open Access on publishers' platforms (Bar-Ilan & Halevi, 2017; Bar-Ilan & Halevi, 2018). That means that they are free for readers who do not need paid subscriptions to read them. Despite the fact that they are clearly marked as "Retracted", their free availability means that they continue to be read and shared post-retraction, which presents a real problem relating to the truthfulness of such content.

Unlike citations, social media shares and mentions also represent the impact science has on the public. According to Pew research, Facebook and Twitter are quickly becoming major sources for scientific and medical information (Greenwood, Perrin, & Duggan, 2016). Therefore, falsified, untruthful science becomes a real threat to public health when shared online via social networks and sometimes by news media outlets. The main problem with social shares is that they are so much more difficult to track and correct. Once an article becomes the focus of positive or negative attention, a formal retraction might not have the effect it needs to have to change people's perceptions the way it does with the scientific community. Although the news media might correct themselves and announce "bad science" once it's publicized, that might not happen fast enough or in an effective way that will also change public perception accordingly.

In order to report on both facets, scientific and social impact of retracted articles, we used the citation database Scopus to track citations of retracted articles both prior and after retraction. Scopus is a comprehensive database that indexes millions of articles across numerous scientific disciplines. The main advantage of using Scopus to track citations is that its metadata provides citations by year and allows one to see citations pre-retraction and later on post-retraction. This is an important piece of the puzzle as it allows us to see how many citations a retracted article receives after it is removed from the literature.

To examine social and news media attention to retracted articles as well as readership counts, we used the PlumX platform and data from Altmetric.com – both aggregators of altmetric indicators. Altmetrics is a general term used to describe "alternative metrics" in science. The traditional scientific metrics are citations, whereas altmetrics include other indicators such as readership, downloads, social media mentions, and more. The aggregators track article mentions in a variety of social media outlets such as Twitter and Facebook, blogs, and more. In addition, they track articles that were mentioned in the news media and also count the number of times they were read on Reddit and others. In addition, we also looked at readership on Mendeley, a well-known scientific network that allows researchers to save and share scientific papers. Data aggregators track mentions by identifiers, mainly by the Digital Object Identifier (DOI) link. PlumX displays these metrics on an article dashboard on which one can read the actual comments, news articles, and blog entries. Altmetric also links to the text of blogs and displays the text of tweets. This, in turn, allowed us to examine the tone and content of these mentions for a small subset of retracted articles, thus, enabling us to judge whether the impact of these retracted articles is negatively or positively persistent post-retraction. Mendeley readership counts were collected directly from Mendeley. For data collection from Mendeley and Altmetric.com we used Mike Thelwall's free tool The Webometric Analyst (http://lexiurl.wlv.ac.uk/).

Some characteristics

Where are retractions coming from?

In order to track the geographical origin of the retracted articles we used the affiliation country of the authors. Each published article has to have the author name and his/her affiliation, which includes the country. This information was used in our analysis to track the countries from which the authors of retracted articles originate. It should be noted that each article in our dataset of 1,294 papers includes more than one author. The vast majority of scientific articles are published in collaboration where teams of scientists research and publish their results together. Many times, these are international collaborations and publications therefore include authors from several countries. Our map was constructed out of all the countries that appear in the articles; therefore, an article in the database with multiple authors from different countries is assigned to all countries. As can be seen from the map (Figure 4.1), the majority of retracted articles in our dataset originate from the United States (341), China (309), India (115), and Japan (68).

One of the strengths of the Retraction Watch Data Base is that it also extracts the reasons for retractions and categorizes them into more than 70 categories. In most cases, more than one category is assigned to each article. Our analysis showed that retracted articles originating from the United States were mostly retracted because of duplication/manipulation of images as well as falsification/fabrication of data. Chinese papers were mostly retracted due to fake peer review, which was discovered by an investigation by the journal or plagiarism of the article. Indian papers were mostly retracted because of plagiarism, whereas Japanese papers were retracted mostly because of unreliable results and data fabrication/falsification. An interesting article published in 2017 (Fanelli, Costas, Fang, Casadevall, & Bik, 2017) provides and overview of the main reasons why

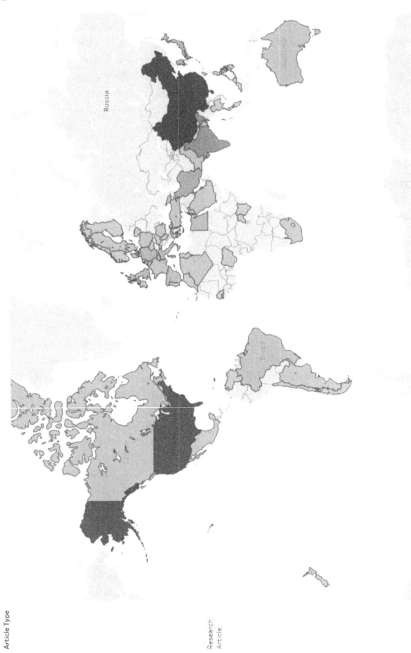

FIGURE 4.1 Geographic origins of retracted articles (powered by Tableau)

Source: Created by authors

scientists fabricate or falsify data or engage in misconduct. The main reason is the pressure to publish; scientists face enormous pressure to produce a certain number of articles every year to sustain grants or receive tenure or promotion. This is especially true in the United States and the United Kingdom where the number of publications and the number of citations they receive are the main metrics used to evaluate scientific performance. This gets more complicated in countries like China where scientists are rewarded in cash for reaching a certain number of publications. These factors along with the fact that countries vary in their misconduct policies and enforcement create environments where such conduct is more prevalent (Redman & Merz, 2008)

Publications and retractions by year

An interesting finding that we noticed in our analysis was the relative number of publications versus the amount of retractions. Whereas the annual number of publications from 2010 on that are retracted in later years stays stable, with approximately 260 publications per year (in our dataset), the number of retractions of previously published papers increases every year (see Figure 4.2). Some of the reasons for the increasing number of retractions per year can be attributed to the fact that in today's connected environment, data checking and plagiarism can be checked much faster and errors can be more easily communicated to editors who, in turn, can issue retractions that are posted to journals' online sites at increasing rates. This quicker turnaround process can be seen in the decreasing time it takes for papers to be retracted (see Table 4.1).

We also looked at the time gap between publication to retraction and calculated the average number of years that it takes. As can be seen in Table 4.1, the time gap is indeed decreasing. While in 2010 the average amount of time it took to retract articles was 2.7 years, in 2014 it went down to 1.1 year. This is a very encouraging finding that means that faulty research is taken out of circulation much faster than it used to. In the medical and biomedical arenas where discoveries can influence future studies as fast as they are reported, it is crucial to remove fraudulent research as soon as possible so as to avoid any harm to patients or the general public.

Reasons for retraction

We created a word cloud out of the text of "reasons for retraction", one of the data fields provided by Retraction Watch. In a word cloud, the size of the word or phrase is determined by the number of times it appears. The more times it appears, the bigger it becomes. In the word cloud depicted in Figure 4.3, it is evident that the most recurring reasons for retractions in our dataset of medical and biomedical articles are investigation by journal/publisher. An investigation on its own is not a reason for retraction, but looking at the phrases depicted in this word cloud we see that plagiarism, manipulation of images, errors in data, misconduct by author,

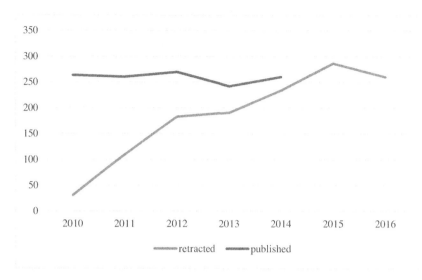

FIGURE 4.2 Yearly publication of retracted articles and retractions

Source: Created by authors

TABLE 4.1 The average number of years to retract by year of publication

Year	Number of publications	Average number of years to retract
2010	263	2.67
2011	260	2.15
2012	269	1.87
2013	242	1.51
2014	260	1.07
All years	1294	1.86

falsification of data, and fake peer review are dominant reasons. Duplication of article and image/s that are also dominant usually refers to authors that recycle their papers and submit the same materials to several journals. This is a conduct that every beginner researchers knows is not allowed. When submitting an article to a journal, one of the questions an author must confirm and testify to is the originality of the submission, which means that the paper was not submitted anywhere else. An author that recycles the same materials in order to game the publication process is deliberately breaking the ethical rules of scientific publishing.

Another interesting aspect in this word cloud is the number of times retractions due to data-related issues appear. Note the size of phrases such as "fabrication of data", "errors in data", "unreliable data", "issues about data", "duplication of data" and others. This means that there is a large number of publications that were taken out of the scientific literature due to severe issues with the reported

FIGURE 4.3 The word cloud of the reasons for retraction

Source: Created by authors

data. Now, although in other areas of scholarly communications, data-related issues are grave, in the medical and biomedical arenas these issues are more severe mainly because research in these disciplines relate directly to medical treatments, procedures, and drugs prescribed to patients. In addition, falsified medical data can mislead the public and cause real physical harm to people.

Major journals

In our dataset, there were 740 journals listed. Interestingly, 2% of them are responsible for 20% of all retractions. Table 4.2 lists the journals with the largest number of retracted articles in the medical and biomedical arena. While *PLoS One* and *The Journal of Biomedical Chemistry* are the journals with the highest retracted articles in the years we cover in our dataset, *Tumor Biology* is worth expanding on. In 2017, *Tumor Biology* retracted over 107 papers because of fake peer review, which means that the author faked the review either by inventing an external expert or providing a real expert but writing the review him/herself (McCook, 2017; Tumor Biology-Retraction Watch, n.d.). The magnitude of the amount of retractions in one journal resulted in the journal being removed from Web of Science and is no longer indexed in the database. The sheer number of retracted articles in

TABLE 4.2 List of journals with most retractions before 2017

Journal title	Number of retractions
PLoS One	40
The Journal of Biological Chemistry	40
Immunopharmacology and Immunotoxicology	19
Molecular Biology Reports	18
Proceedings of the National Academy of Sciences of the United States of America	16
The Journal of Neuroscience	16
Tumor Biology	16
Archives of Biological Sciences	12
Diagnostic Pathology	12
European Journal of Medical Research	12
Nature	11
Asian Pacific Journal of Tropical Medicine	9
BioMed Research International	8
Molecular Cell	8
Biochemical and Biophysical Research Communications	7
Cell	7

that one journal due to fake peer review indicates a systematic neglect of ethical standards that are at the core of any reputable journal. In this case, a large journal such as *Tumor Biology* completely neglected their responsibility while allowing over 100 papers to be published based on fraudulent peer review.

Major publishers

Our specific dataset contains articles published by 136 publishers (see Figure 4.4). Out of those, 13 publishers (or 10%) are responsible for more than 69% of the retractions. Figure 4.4 features the top publishers, among them are Elsevier, Springer, Wiley, and Taylor & Francis. Although *Nature* merged with Springer, in our dataset they are listed separately because of the timing of the merger. It is not surprising that these publishers are at the top of the list since these are publishers that specialize in the medical and biomedical fields. Despite Elsevier showing as the top of publishers retracting articles in these scientific areas it should be mentioned that Elsevier is the largest publisher in the medical and biomedical arenas with over 2,000 journals dedicated to these disciplines. Springer *Nature* has 1,446 journals, Wiley 822, and Taylor & Francis 812 journals in these disciplines (data from Scopus).

Citations

Citations are considered the gold standard of scientific impact. Tenures, promotions, and funding are based on the number of publications and the number of

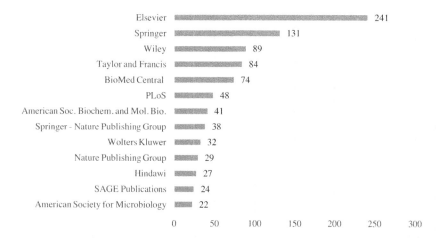

FIGURE 4.4 Publishers with the highest numbers of retracted articles

Source: Created by authors

citations they receive coupled with the prestige of the journal in which they are published. Therefore, for any researcher, they are by far the most important metrics since they determine the fate of one's career and reputation. It is therefore understandable that the pressure to publish is great and researchers are aware of the number of citations their articles receive. Anyone who heard the phrase "Publish or Perish" (attributed in the academic context to Logan Wilson (Garfield, 1996) knows that researchers are under an enormous pressure to publish (Neill, 2008, 2008; Nygaard, 2017). This pressure was also blamed for the increasing amount of plagiarism and other misconduct in the academic arena (Nygaard, 2017; Rawat & Meena, 2014). Our dataset allowed us to use Scopus to track pre- and post-retraction citations because we had the dates of the original article publication and the retraction notice. While pre-retraction citations are acceptable, post-retraction citations are disturbing since they indicate that an article that has been pulled out of the literature still receives citations, i.e., academic acknowledgment after it was flagged as fraudulent. Table 4.3 illustrates the pre- and post-retraction citations by publication year. The citations data in this chapter were collected in February 2019. It should be noted that according to citations regulations, even if an article mentions a retracted paper in a negative way it still has to cite it, which means that the faulty paper continues to accumulate academic impact despite its retraction status.

Readership

The ability to track the number of times an article is read is relatively new. "Readership" is a part of a group of metrics called "altmetrics" (alternative metrics)

TABLE 4.3 Pre- and post-retraction citations per publication year

Year of publication	Pre- and post-retraction citations	Citations before retraction	Citations after retraction
2010	6,819	4,587	2,232
2011	6,104	3,650	2,454
2012	4,063	2,266	1,797
2013	2,858	1,570	1,288
2014	2,145	986	1,159
All years	21,989	13,059	8,930

TABLE 4.4 Mendeley reader counts of the retracted articles

Year of publication	Number of publications	Number of readers	Average number of readers	Article with most readers
2010	263	7,790	29.6	328
2011	260	8,896	34.2	388
2012	269	8,226	30.6	752
2013	242	12,414	51.3	4,130
2014	260	4,814	18.5	265
All years	1,294	42,140	32.6	4,130

aimed to examine the manner by which scientific literature is used beyond citations. Readership counts are available on a number of platforms, among which is Mendeley, a hybrid platform that serves as a reference manager and also a social network where scholars can save and share articles. The readership count in Mendeley can relate to citations in some ways. First, users on Mendeley are mostly scholars and students and therefore the network is an academic one rather than an open social one, although anyone can join. Significant, medium-strength correlations were found by several studies (Costas, Zahedi, & Wouters, 2015; Haustein, 2016; Li & Thelwall, 2012) between readership and citation counts, indicating there is a partial overlap between readers and citers. The correlations are even stronger for medical fields (Thelwall, 2016).

In our dataset, 91% of retracted articles (1,178) had Mendeley reader counts. We also found that 1,091 (84%) of all retracted articles in the dataset had both Scopus citations and Mendeley reader counts. Table 4.4 displays the total and average reader counts per year of publication. Overall, the number of readers is quite high but the most noticeable year is 2013 where we see a significant rise in the number of reads. The reason lies in two articles published that year in *Nature* (see case of Haruko Obokata) that were retracted due to falsification and misconduct and created quite a stir in the scientific world. These two papers alone were the two most read articles, with 4,130 and 2,066 readers, and have been cited 166 and 85 times respectively. Both these articles also received 78 and 40 citations post-retraction and despite the scandal that led to the suicide of one of the authors.

Social media

In order to account for the social impact of retracted articles, we used two platforms that track social media mentions: Altmetric.com and PlumX. When an article is published, it is given a unique number (DOI), that can be searched for and discovered in search engines. Both PlumX and Altmetric.com platforms are well known for tracking social media mentions of academic publications through a unique number called DOI (Distinct Object Identifier) and are able to point to mentions on social media channels such as Twitter, Facebook, Wikipedia, and others. Altmetric.com and PlumX track social media mentions in slightly different ways. For example, when scanning blogs and news, Altmetric.com tracks Wikipedia in English only, while PlumX tracks Wikipedia in Swedish as well, or when counting Facebook mentions Altmetric.com scans posts on public Facebook pages, while PlumX reports likes, shares, and comments combined. Other research found that Twitter mentions of scientific publications is usually the most meaningful compared to other social media outlets (Thelwall, Haustein, Larivière, & Sugimoto, 2013). However, tracking overall social media mentions is still considered one of the best ways to gauge public reactions to scientific literature. Table 4.5 summarizes the number of times retracted articles where showing on social and news media. As can be seen from the table, Altmetric.com was able to identify 456 articles that were mentioned on Twitter while PlumX identified 305 articles. It is clear that Twitter is by far the most dominant social media channel used to share and comment on articles, with over 7,000 mentions identified by Altmetric.com and close to 6,000 on PlumX. Facebook is the second most popular platform on which these retracted articles were shared, discussed, and commented on, with over 10,000 appearances on PlumX. In addition, since we were examining retracted medical and biomedical papers it is not surprising that news media covered quite a few of them as well. Altmetric.com was able to identify 81 retracted articles in the news media. These numbers are very much in line with other research that has shown that most people in the United States consume medical and scientific information from social media (Greenwood et al., 2016; NW, Washington, & Inquiries, 2018). The highest number of social and news media mentions was tracked for the 2013 article "Primary Prevention of Cardiovascular Disease with a Mediterranean Diet", which was published in the *New England Journal of Medicine* in 2013. This article was retracted due to the study design and the fact that a significant amount of people dropped off the control groups, which basically skewed the results. Although the same article was re-published later with a new analysis, the impact of the retraction continues to steer controversy today. So far (August 2019), this retracted article gained 195 news articles; over 47,000 shares, likes, and comments on

TABLE 4.5 Major altmetrics by Altmetric.com and PlumX

	Coverage Altmetric	Sum of mentions Altmetric	Average mentions Altmetric	Article mentioned most Altmetric	Coverage PlumX	Sum of mentions PlumX	Average mentions PlumX	Article mentioned most PlumX
Twitter	456	7,094	15.6	2,305	305	5,891	19.3	2,392
Facebook	104	675	6.5	272	133	10,355	77.9	7,689
News	81	468	5.8	97	12	49	4.1	15
Blogs	68	1,210	17.8	65	56	100	1.8	11
Wikipedia	39	49	1.3	3	51	64	1.3	6

Facebook; and over 1,600 tweets and retweets, and the debate continues. To view this article dashboard with the social media comments, please visit https://plu.mx/judit/a/--LPrDZbZGFIxEcIgDOzjbhPj1--P4QGWWC7IKS-Um0/.

Most impactful retracted articles

In this section, we discuss the articles in our dataset that were cited the most (pre- and post-retraction), the ones that were read the most, and those that received the most tweets as tracked by Altmetric.com and PlumX.

Most cited retracted article before and after retraction

Estruch, R., Ros, E., Salas-Salvadó, J., Covas, M. I., Corella, D., Arós, F., . . . & Lamuela-Raventos, R. M. (2013). Primary prevention of cardiovascular disease with a Mediterranean diet. *New England Journal of Medicine, 368*(14), 1279–1290.

This article was considered a breakthrough in cardiovascular research pointing to the benefits of an olive oil–based diet to improve cardiovascular conditions. However, faults in the study design and reported findings by the authors who wrote "Because of irregularities in the randomization procedures, we wish to retract the article" (see retraction notice). Although the data was reanalyzed and the article later republished, the debate around the actual benefits of the Mediterranean Diet continues to this day.

Most cited article before retraction

Dunoyer, P., Schott, G., Himber, C., Meyer, D., Takeda, A., Carrington, J. C., & Voinnet, O. (2010). Small RNA duplexes function as mobile silencing signals between plant cells. *Science*, 1185880.

This article was considered groundbreaking due to its claim that small RNAs found in plants can function as a defense against viral attacks. The article was retracted six years after publication due to image duplication and manipulations that the editors deemed as deliberate and that could not have been a result of a mistake. Interestingly, all the authors except the main author agreed to retract the article (Berg, 2016). Since the time gap between publication and retraction was six years, the article gained a large number of citations pre-retraction.

Most cited post-retraction

Séralini, G. E., Clair, E., Mesnage, R., Gress, S., Defarge, N., Malatesta, M., . . . & De Vendômois, J. S. (2012). Long term toxicity of a Roundup herbicide and a Roundup-tolerant genetically modified maize. *Food and Chemical Toxicology, 50*(11), 4221–4231.

This article was the first to point to GMO (genetically modified organisms) food as being toxic to human health and the source of several cancer types. The study was attacked by scientists who pointed to several crucial points in the study design and analytics and was retracted that same year. However, the study sparked serious political debate by groups of anti-GMO activists who claimed that the retraction was invalid and driven by politics rather than science. To this day, the debate continues, with several recent news media articles published on the issue of GMO food safety. To see all news and other discussions, please visit https://plu.mx/judit/a/-BV5QqinvoXUlWNq7GKRdJQgWyZMb1bGDBtTn ZaZRVU/.

Most read and most tweeted (Altmetric.com and PlumX)

Obokata, H., Wakayama, T., Sasai, Y., Kojima, K., Vacanti, M. P., Niwa, H., . . . & Vacanti, C. A. (2014). Stimulus-triggered fate conversion of somatic cells into pluripotency. *Nature*, *505*(7485), 641.

This article was the center of a scandal that resulted in the suicide of one of the authors. A group of Japanese researchers claimed that they found a way to create pluripotent stem cells, which are able to give rise to almost any other cell type by using physical stimulus. As can be imagined, the impact of such a discovery, if it was true, would have been universally life changing as a potential cure for any disease known to mankind. However, this study was a result of falsified experiments and data. This article was retracted that same year but still read and shared over 12,000 times and mentioned on social media over 2,400 times. To see a complete overview of this article, including social and news media mentions, please visit https://plu.mx/judit/a/-XiygtWNXexZCjaHt_l6yDTcT9zIKiNbPqUL4-3V-Tw/.

Highly impactful retracted articles – some recent examples

Data analytics and study design issues

Séralini, G. E., Clair, E., Mesnage, R., Gress, S., Defarge, N., Malatesta, M., . . . & De Vendômois, J. S. (2012). Long term toxicity of a Roundup herbicide and a Roundup-tolerant genetically modified maize. *Food and Chemical Toxicology*, *50*(11), 4221–4231.

In 2012, a group of French scientists published an article regarding the harmfulness of genetically modified maize. The article's conclusions suggested that GMO foods could cause all types of cancer, proving it through a two-year experiment in mice. The article titled "Long term toxicity of a Roundup herbicide and a Roundup-tolerant genetically modified maize" created a media storm, calling all GMO foods to be avoided due to serious health hazards, which quickly turned into thousands of international social media shares and heated discussions. The article was retracted after a series of letters to the editors pointed out the inadequacy of the study design, the data analysis and interpretation of results pointing out its invalidity, and that it should not be used to inform health policy or public health recommendations. However, this article and the results reported in it prevail in both the scientific literature and in the social media and public news arenas. Despite the 2012 retraction, our data shows that high citation rate to this article still persists through 2018 (see Table 4.6, third row). According to Scopus metrics, this article is in the 99th percentile of citations in its field, with a total of 181 citations tracked in Scopus until very recently. The social and news media attention to this article and its results are much higher. PlumX tracked nearly 8,000 likes, shares, and comments on Facebook; over 1,100 mentions on Twitter; and more than ten mentions in the news and in blogs. We found that the article is mentioned, despite its flaws, in contexts of health and nutrition recommendations (see for example Templeton, 2019; Ten Scientific Studies Prove that Genetically Modified Food Can Be Harmful To Human Health, 2018). It should be noted that the retracted article was republished as-is (without another round of peer review) in *Environmental Sciences Europe* in 2014. The republished article also received considerable news and social media attention, readers on Mendeley and citations on Scopus.

Misconduct, fraudulent reporting

Obokata, H., Wakayama, T., Sasai, Y., Kojima, K., Vacanti, M. P., Niwa, H., . . . & Vacanti, C. A. (2014). Stimulus-triggered fate conversion of somatic cells into pluripotency. *Nature, 505*(7485), 641.

In 2014, a group of Japanese scientists published two related high-profile research papers on a breakthrough in stem cell research that was published in *Nature*. The main discovery, according to them was that they managed to prove that physical stimulus could transform adult cells into pluripotent stem cells that are able to give rise to almost any other cell type. The acronym STAP (stimulus-triggered acquisition of pluripotency), which was coined by this group, became instantly famous. The significance of this research is that before this research was published, scientists assumed that this could only be achieved by genetic manipulation. If this research was true, the consequence would have been a gigantic step toward the elimination of genetically inherited diseases for example. However, five months after the publication of the paper and following an investigation of the scientists by their institution, it was retracted due to misconduct. The scientists involved were accused of poor data management and record-keeping, manipulation of images and figures, and more. Because of the enormity of the so-called discovery, the retraction gained an enormous amount of scientific and public attention (see last row in Table 4.6) to the point where in 2014 a co-author of these papers committed suicide, another suffered a stroke, and a third was hospitalized for depression (Goodyear, 2016). Despite the fact that this article was relatively quickly retracted, the social media attention to this article persisted years after. There are over 2,000 shares on Twitter and numerous shares on Facebook, most of which just link to the article without mentioning the scandal behind it or the fact that it was retracted years prior. That said, some claim that it was social media that had a major role in exposing this article (Diaz, 2018). The

TABLE 4.6 Citations, readers, and tweets of the most cited, read, and tweeted retracted articles

	Publication year	Retraction year	Cits. overall	Pre-retraction cits,	Post-retraction cits.	Readers	Tweets A	Tweets P
Most cited overall	2011	2014	388	246	92	323	1	0
Most cited pre-retraction	2010	2016	262	250	12	288	1	1
Most cited post-retraction	2012	2013	181	56	125	752	1,277	1,136
Most read & tweeted (A and P)	2013	2014	166	88	78	4,130	2,305	2,392

Note: A for Altmetric.com and P for PlumX

scientific impact viewed through 167 citations tracked by Scopus are mostly negative. Many of the articles discuss aspects of scientific misconduct, reproducibility
issues, and ethics in genetic research. The same lead author, with a large number
of overlapping co-authors, published another paper in *Nature* in the same year:
"Bidirectional Developmental Potential in Reprogrammed Cells with Acquired
Pluripotency", which was retracted for similar reasons in 2014. She also set up a
website after the two articles were retracted (STAP HOPE PAGE, n.d.) trying
to convince the public of her methods. The website has not been updated since
2016. She also published a book in Japanese in 2016 on the STAP-cell scandal
(Knoepfler, 2016).

Reproducibility issues

Yi, P., Park, J. S., & Melton, D. A. (2013). Betatrophin: A Hormone that Con-
trols Pancreatic β Cell Proliferation. *Cell 53*(4), 747–757.

In 2013, a group of Harvard scientists published a high-profile paper that suggested that they found a new hormone that could increase the amount of beta
cells, which in turn can cure type 1 diabetes. The article was published in one of
the most prestigious scientific journals *Cell* and retracted in 2017 due to the fact
that no one, including the scientists themselves, could reproduce the results of
their experiments. Although no ethical issues rose in the review and retraction
processes, the topic of reproducibility should be paid attention. The progress of
science depends on the ability to reproduce experimental results and, through that,
find ways to build upon them and advance to the next level of discovery. This
article is a good example of a scientific breakthrough that never was due to the
growing problem of reproducibility, and although not mentioned as much in the
news or social media outlets, was and still is heavily cited, with 30 citations in
2018 alone. If results cannot be reproduced, the science ends there. According to
a *Nature* survey (Baker, 2016), 70% of researchers have tried and failed to reproduce another scientist's experiments and more than 50% failed to reproduce their
own experiments. This is an enormous challenge to the overall trust in the entire
scientific process. The survey found that the main reason these experiments cannot be reproduced is that scientists selectively report on results that support their
hypothesis in order to publish faster and secure funding for example. Yet the
crisis of reproducibility (as named by the article) is heightened because journals
are reluctant to make this problem public by publishing negative replications and
"In fact, several respondents who had published a failed replication said that editors and reviewers demanded that they play down comparisons with the original
study" (p. 454).

Conclusions

In 2012, the National Academy of Sciences in the United States published a
review of 1,047 articles in biomedical and life sciences indexed in PubMed (Fang

et al., 2012). This study found that only 21.3% of these articles were retracted because of honest mistakes (as opposed to deliberate fraud), whereas 67.4% of retractions were due to misconduct, including fraud, plagiarism, and duplications. Named the "retraction epidemic", the study points to the fact that the number of retractions in these fields have increased tenfold since 1975. On the one hand, this is a positive development since it does demonstrate the self-regulation of the scientific publication process in which articles do not cease to be scrutinized after publication and once found to be fraudulent are removed from the literature. On the other hand, it is still worrying that such articles manage to escape the watchful eye of reviewers and get published in highly reputable journals such as *Nature*, *The Lancet*, *Cell*, and more.

In this chapter, we examined a dataset of retracted articles in the medical and biomedical fields published between 2010 to 2014 and retracted due to numerous reasons but mainly because of fraud and misconduct. Data and images manipulations, unethical experiments, and misleading analysis and conclusions have led to massive retractions across journals. As demonstrated, the time gap between publication and retraction remains problematic. Although this time gap is seen to get shorter in time, averaging a little over a year now as opposed to ten years in the past, it is still enough for these articles to influence the medical and biomedical scientific process on many levels. First, these articles are cited in the scientific literature, which means that their findings are being applied in studies. One should not forget that in this area, studies mean patients, enrolled in clinical trials or being administered procedures or drugs. Second, these articles, and especially those that claim some type of breakthrough, are heavily mentioned in the social and news media, which reaches hundreds of thousands of people quickly and without barriers.

After being retracted, these articles are seen to be cited and publicly discussed on these channels. This is the most concerning phenomenon of retracted articles. This is probably due to their availability as Open Access content, free for all to read, or due to versions of the articles such as pre- or post-print versions that circulate in freely available repositories. And while public sharing and discussion of retracted articles might not raise a brow, considering the fact that people might misinterpret or not even know a certain article was retracted, continuous citations are certainly worrying. Despite the fact that some citations may prove to be negative ones, meaning that the authors mention the article to demonstrate its fraudulence, our previous research showed that many of the citations are positive and cite retracted research as valid (Bar-Ilan & Halevi, 2018).

So, what can be done? Readers must be alert. Whether scientific or lay persons, anyone who relies on published articles or news regarding studies in the medical and biomedical arenas must scrutinize their content. For the lay person things to watch for are sponsorship or funding source. Every researcher must reveal his/her funding source or study sponsor. If an organization or company is the study sponsor, one should carefully and cautiously assess the study to discover whether or not it was written to support certain economic interests. Scientists, who are well versed in the terminology, the study design, and data collection method should scrutinize the article for data and image integrity as well as analysis and conclusions.

According to COPE (Promoting integrity in research and its publication | Committee on Publication Ethics: COPE, n.d.) guidelines, retracted articles should not be removed but be clearly labeled as retracted. However, the guidelines do not say that retracted articles should be freely available on the publisher's website. We found many retracted articles to be freely accessible, whereas other articles in the same journal and issue are behind paywall. Allowing these to be open and freely available increases the chances of people who do not have access to paid-for content to read, save, share, and promote them on social media.

In addition, we recommend that publishers remove all retracted articles from their journals' websites so readers will not have access to their full text. The fact that retracted articles can be found in their full text for free aggravates the problem. Retracted research should not be found anywhere on journals' sites. Although it is clear that publishers cannot address preprints available on repositories, they can and should address faculty publications' availability on their own sites.

Just like with other forms of fake news, apply caution and do your own investigation. One newly available comprehensive and searchable source is the Retraction Watch Database. Acting on fraudulent, false medical and biomedical literature can cost you your health.

Note

1 Newton, "Letter from Sir Isaac Newton to Robert Hooke"

References

Almeida, R. M. V., de Albuquerque Rocha, K., Catelani, F., Fontes-Pereira, A. J., & Vasconcelos, S. M. (2015). Plagiarism allegations account for most retractions in major Latin American/Caribbean databases. *Science and Engineering Ethics*, 1–10.

Baker, M. (2016). 1,500 scientists lift the lid on reproducibility. *Nature News*, *533*(7604), 452. https://doi.org/10.1038/533452a

Bar-Ilan, J., & Halevi, G. (2017). *Temporal characteristics of retracted articles: Research in progress.* ISSI 2017–16th International Conference on Scientometrics and Informetrics, Conference Proceedings, 650–655. Retrieved from www.scopus.com/inward/record.uri?eid=2-s2.0-85036606736&partnerID=40&md5=7be4a5ef9ec4266667ff48734340dd63

Bar-Ilan, J., & Halevi, G. (2018). Temporal characteristics of retracted articles. *Scientometrics*, *116*(3), 1771–1783.

Berg, J. M. (2016). Retraction. *Science*, *354*(6309), 190–190. https://doi.org/10.1126/science.aai9397

Biagioli, M., Kenney, M., Martin, B., & Walsh, J. P. (2018). Academic misconduct, misrepresentation and gaming: A reassessment. *Research Policy*, *48*(2), 401–413

Bozzo, A., Bali, K., Evaniew, N., & Ghert, M. (2017). Retractions in cancer research: A systematic survey. *Research Integrity and Peer Review*, *2*(1), 5.

Broad, W. J. (1983, June 14). Notorious darsee case shakes assumptions about science. *The New York Times*. Retrieved from www.nytimes.com/1983/06/14/science/notorious-darsee-case-shakes-assumptions-about-science.html

Budd, J. M., Sievert, M., & Schultz, T. R. (1998). Phenomena of retraction: Reasons for retraction and citations to the publications. *Journal of the American Medical Association*, *280*(3), 296–297. https://doi.org/10.1001/jama.280.3.296

Budd, J. M., Sievert, M., Schultz, T. R., & Scoville, C. (1999). Effects of article retraction on citation and practice in medicine. *Bulletin of the Medical Library Association*, *87*(4), 437–443.

Cokol, M., Ozbay, F., & Rodriguez-Esteban, R. (2008). Retraction rates are on the rise. *EMBO Reports*, *9*(1), 2–2. https://doi.org/10.1038/sj.embor.7401143

Corbyn, Z. (2012). Misconduct is the main cause of life-sciences retractions. *Nature*, *490*(7418), 21.

Costas, R., Zahedi, Z., & Wouters, P. (2015). Do "altmetrics" correlate with citations? Extensive comparison of altmetric indicators with citations from a multidisciplinary perspective. *Journal of the Association for Information Science and Technology*, *66*(10), 2003–2019. https://doi.org/10.1002/asi.23309

Diaz, A. (2018, March 3). Science and social media. Retrieved January 22, 2019, from Northwest Jammin website: https://medium.com/northwest-jammin/science-and-social-media-9e33ba90e04d

Facts about the Measles Outbreak. (2015, February 2). *The New York Times*. Retrieved from www.nytimes.com/interactive/2015/02/02/us/measles-facts.html

Fanelli, D., Costas, R., Fang, F. C., Casadevall, A., & Bik, E. M. (2017). Why do scientists fabricate and falsify data? A matched-control analysis of papers containing problematic image duplications. *BioRxiv*, 126805. https://doi.org/10.1101/126805

Fang, F. C., & Casadevall, A. (2011). Retracted science and the retraction index. *Infection and Immunity*, *79*(10), 3855–3859.

Fang, F. C., Steen, R. G., & Casadevall, A. (2012). Misconduct accounts for the majority of retracted scientific publications. *Proceedings of the National Academy of Sciences*, *109*(42), 17028–17033.

Garfield, E. (1996). What is the primordial reference for the phrase "publish or perish". *The Scientist*, *10*(12), 11.

Goodyear, D. (2016, February 22). The stem-cell scandal. Retrieved from www.newyorker.com/magazine/2016/02/29/the-stem-cell-scandal

Greenwood, S., Perrin, A., & Duggan, M. (2016, November 11). Social media update 2016. Retrieved March 5, 2017, from Pew Research Center: Internet, Science & Tech website: www.pewinternet.org/2016/11/11/social-media-update-2016/

Halevi, G., & Bar-Ilan, J. (2016). *Post retraction citations in context*. Proceedings of the Joint Workshop on Bibliometric-Enhanced Information Retrieval and Natural Language Processing for Digital Libraries (BIRNDL), Newark, NJ, 23–29.

Haustein, S. (2016). Grand challenges in altmetrics: Heterogeneity, data quality and dependencies. *Scientometrics*, *108*(1), 413–423. https://doi.org/10.1007/s11192-016-1910-9

Inoue, Y., & Muto, K. (2016). Noncompliance with human subjects' protection requirements as a reason for retracting papers: Survey of retraction notices on medical papers published from 1981 to 2011. *Accountability in Research*, *23*(2), 123–135. https://doi.org/10.1080/08989621.2015.1069713

Knoepfler, P. (2016, March 31). Haruko Obokata (小保方 晴子) launches new website with STAP claims. Retrieved July 11, 2019, from The Niche website: https://ipscell.com/2016/03/haruko-obokata-%e5%b0%8f%e4%bf%9d%e6%96%b9-%e6%99%b4%e5%ad%90-launches-new-website-with-stap-claims/

Li, X., & Thelwall, M. (2012). F1000, Mendeley and traditional bibliometric indicators. *Proceedings of the 17th International Conference on Science and Technology Indicators, 2*, 451–551. Science-Metrix and OST Montréal, Canada.

McCook, A. A. (2017, April 20). A new record: Major publisher retracting more than 100 studies from cancer journal over fake peer reviews. Retrieved February 2, 2019, from Retraction Watch website: https://retractionwatch.com/2017/04/20/new-record-major-publisher-retracting-100-studies-cancer-journal-fake-peer-reviews/

Neill, U. S. (2008). Publish or perish, but at what cost? *The Journal of Clinical Investigation, 118*(7), 2368–2368.

Nicholas, D., Watkinson, A., Jamali, H. R., Herman, E., Tenopir, C., Volentine, R., . . . Levine, K. (2015). Peer review: Still king in the digital age. *Learned Publishing, 28*(1), 15–21.

Noyori, R., & Richmond, J. P. (2013). Ethical conduct in chemical research and publishing. *Advanced Synthesis & Catalysis, 355*(1), 3–9.

NW, 1615 L. St, Washington, S. 800, & Inquiries, D. 20036 U.-419–4300 | M.-419–4372 | M. (2018, March 20). Science-related Facebook pages draw millions of followers, but only about three-in-ten posts feature new scientific discoveries. Retrieved August 27, 2018, from Pew Research Center: Internet, Science & Tech website: www.pewinternet.org/2018/03/21/the-science-people-see-on-social-media/ps_2018-03-21_facebook-and-science_0-01/

Nygaard, L. P. (2017). Publishing and perishing: An academic literacies framework for investigating research productivity. *Studies in Higher Education, 42*(3), 519–532.

Promoting integrity in research and its publication | Committee on Publication Ethics: COPE. (n.d.). Retrieved July 11, 2019, from https://publicationethics.org/

Rawat, S., & Meena, S. (2014). Publish or perish: Where are we heading? *Journal of Research in Medical Sciences: The Official Journal of Isfahan University of Medical Sciences, 19*(2), 87.

Redman, B. K., & Merz, J. F. (2008). Scientific misconduct: Do the punishments fit the crime? American Association for the Advancement of Science. *Science, 321*(5890), 775.

Retraction Watch Database. (n.d.). Retrieved January 18, 2019, from http://retractiondatabase.org/RetractionSearch.aspx?

STAP HOPE PAGE. (n.d.). Retrieved July 11, 2019, from STAP HOPE PAGE website: https://stap-hope-page.com/

Steen, R. G. (2010). Retractions in the scientific literature: Is the incidence of research fraud increasing? *Journal of Medical Ethics, 37*(4), 249–253.

Steen, R. G. (2011). Retractions in the scientific literature: Do authors deliberately commit research fraud? *Journal of Medical Ethics, 37*(2), 113–117.

Templeton, B. (2019, February 22). Templeton times: Cancer-linked monsanto chemical discovered in five major orange juice brands from collective evolution. Retrieved July 29, 2019, from Templeton Times website: http://templeton01436.blogspot.com/2019/02/cancer-linked-monsanto-chemical.html

Ten Scientific Studies Prove that Genetically Modified Food Can Be Harmful To Human Health. (2018, March 13). Retrieved July 29, 2019, from Global Research website: www.globalresearch.ca/ten-scientific-studies-proving-gmos-can-be-harmful-to-human-health/5377054

Thelwall, M. (2016). Interpreting correlations between citation counts and other indicators. *Scientometrics, 108*(1), 337–347. https://doi.org/10.1007/s11192-016-1973-7

Thelwall, M., Haustein, S., Larivière, V., & Sugimoto, C. R. (2013). Do Altmetrics Work? Twitter and Ten Other Social Web Services. *PLoS One, 8*(5). https://doi.org/10.1371/journal.pone.0064841

Tumor Biology-Retraction Watch. (n.d.). Retrieved February 2, 2019, from https://retractionwatch.com/category/by-journal/tumor-biology/

Upi. (1982, May 20). Doctor admits filing false data and is barred from U.S. support. *The New York Times*. Retrieved from www.nytimes.com/1982/05/20/us/doctor-admits-filing-false-data-and-is-barred-from-us-support.html

Williams, P., & Wager, E. (2013). Exploring why and how journal editors retract articles: Findings from a qualitative study. *Science and Engineering Ethics*, *19*(1), 1–11.

PART II

Cognitive processes in accepting, sharing, and correcting misinformation

5

WHEN (FAKE) NEWS FEELS TRUE

Intuitions of truth and the acceptance and correction of misinformation

Norbert Schwarz and Madeline Jalbert

An analysis of 2.8 million episodes of news sharing on Twitter found that 59% of the news items were shared without having been opened (Gabielkov, Ramachandran, Chaintreau, & Legout, 2016). Apparently, six out of ten readers found the headline compelling enough to share the piece without reading it. In this chapter, we review what makes a message "feel" true, even before we have considered its content in any detail. We first discuss the basic psychological processes involved in assessing the truth of a message and illustrate them with select experiments. Subsequently, we address the implications of these processes for information sharing on social media and the correction of misinformation.

Evaluating truth

While retweeting something without reading it may strike many readers as surprising and irresponsible, it is not distinctly different from how we communicate in everyday life. In daily conversations, we proceed on the tacit assumption that the speaker is a cooperative communicator whose contributions are relevant to the ongoing conversation, truthful, informative, and clear (Grice, 1975; Sperber & Wilson, 1986). Unless we have reason to doubt that the speaker observes these tacit rules of conversational conduct, we accept the content of the utterance without much questioning and treat it as part of the common ground of the conversation. These conversational processes contribute to many errors in human judgment (for reviews, see Schwarz, 1994, 1996). Some research even suggests that comprehension of a statement requires at least temporary acceptance of its truth (Gilbert, 1991) before it can be checked against relevant evidence.

While suspension of belief is possible (Hasson, Simmons, & Todorov, 2005; Schul, Mayo, & Burnstein, 2008), it requires implausibility of the message or distrust at the time it is received. Hence, the deck is usually stacked in favor of accepting information rather than rejecting it, provided there are no salient markers that call the speaker's cooperativeness into question. Going beyond the default of information acceptance requires motivation and cognitive resources, which we are most likely to invest when the topic is important to us and there are few competing demands and distractions. In the absence of these conditions, information is likely to be accepted – and sometimes passed on – without much scrutiny.

When people do evaluate whether information is likely to be true, they typically consider some (but rarely all) of the five criteria shown in Table 5.1 (Schwarz, 2015). Is the claim compatible with other things they know? Is it internally consistent and coherent? Does it come from a trustworthy source? Do other people agree with it? Is there much evidence to support it? Each of these criteria is sensible and does, indeed, bear on the likely truth of a message. These criteria can be assessed by considering relevant knowledge, which is a relatively slow and effortful process and may require extensive information search. The same criteria can also be assessed by relying on one's intuitive response, which is faster and less taxing. When the initial intuitive response suggests that something may be wrong, people are likely to turn to the more effortful analysis, provided time and circumstances allow for it. This makes initial intuitive assessments of truth a key gatekeeper for whether people will further engage with the message using a critical eye or just nod along in agreement. These assumptions are compatible with a long history of research in social (e.g., Petty & Cacioppo, 1986) and cognitive (e.g., Kahneman, 2011; Stanovich, 1999) psychology, where the slow and effortful strategy is often referred to as "analytic", "systematic", or "system 2"

TABLE 5.1 Truth criteria

Criterion	Analytic evaluation	Intuitive evaluation
Compatibility: Is it compatible with other things I know?	Is this compatible with knowledge retrieved from memory or obtained from trusted sources?	Does this make me stumble or does it flow smoothly?
Coherence: Is it internally coherent?	Do the elements fit together in a logical way? Do the conclusions follow from what is presented?	Does this make me stumble or does it flow smoothly?
Credibility: Does it come from a credible source?	Does the source have the relevant expertise? Does the source have a vested interest? Is the source trustworthy?	Does the source feel familiar and trustworthy?
Consensus: Do other people believe it?	What do my friends say? What do the opinion polls say?	Does it feel familiar?
Evidence: Is there supporting evidence?	Is there supportive evidence in peer-reviewed scientific articles or credible news reports? Do I remember relevant evidence?	Does some evidence easily come to mind?

processing and the fast and intuitive strategy as "intuitive", "heuristic", or "system 1" processing.

Key to intuitive assessments of truth is the ease with which the message can be processed. For example, when something is incompatible with other things we know or the story we are told is incoherent, we stumble and backtrack to make sure we understood it correctly (Johnson-Laird, 2012; Winkielman, Huber, Kavanagh, & Schwarz, 2012). This makes the subjective experience of ease of processing, often referred to as processing fluency, a (fallible) indicator of whether the message may have a problem that needs closer attention. Similar considerations apply to the other truth criteria, as discussed later in the chapter. Throughout, difficult processing marks the message for closer scrutiny, whereas easy processing favors message acceptance.

If ease or difficulty of processing was solely determined by attributes substantively associated with whether a message is likely to be true, relying on one's processing experience would not pose a major problem. However, messages can be easy or difficult to process for many reasons – reading may be slow because the message is incoherent (a relevant criterion) or because the print font is hard to read (which is unrelated to truth). Because people are more sensitive to their subjective experiences than to the source of those experiences (Schwarz, 2012), many incidental influences that have no bearing on the substance of the message can influence its perceived truth. We discuss these incidental influences and their role in media consumption after reviewing the five dominant truth criteria. As will become apparent, when thoughts flow smoothly, people are likely to agree without much critical analysis (see also Oyserman & Dawson, this volume).

The "big five" of truth judgment: analytic and intuitive processes

A claim is more likely to be accepted as true when it is *compatible* with other things one knows than when it is at odds with other knowledge. Compatibility can be assessed analytically by checking the information against one's knowledge, which requires motivation and time (Petty & Cacioppo, 1986). A less demanding indicator is provided by one's metacognitive experiences and affective responses. When something is inconsistent with existing beliefs, people tend to stumble – they take longer to read it, and have trouble processing it (e.g., Taber & Lodge, 2006; Winkielman et al., 2012). Moreover, information that is inconsistent with one's beliefs produces a negative affective response, as shown in research on cognitive consistency (Festinger, 1957; Gawronski & Strack, 2012). Accordingly, one's processing experiences and affective responses can serve as (fallible) indicators of whether a proposition is consistent with other things one believes.

A given claim is also more likely to be accepted as true when it fits a broader story that lends *coherence* to its individual elements, as observed in research on mental models (for a review, see Johnson-Laird, 2012) and analyses of jury decision making (Pennington & Hastie, 1993). Coherence can be determined through a systematic analysis of the relationships between different pieces of declarative information. Alternatively, it can be assessed by attending to one's processing experience: coherent stories are easier to process than stories with internal contradictions (Johnson-Laird, 2012), which makes ease of processing a (fallible) indicator of coherence. Indeed, people draw on their fluency experience when they evaluate how well things "go together" (Topolinski, 2012), as observed in judgments of semantic coherence (Topolinski & Strack, 2008, 2009) and syllogistic reasoning (Morsanyi & Handley, 2012).

Information is also more likely to be accepted as true when it comes from a credible and trustworthy source. As decades of persuasion research illustrates, evaluations of *source credibility* can be based on declarative information that bears, for example, on the communicator's expertise, education, achievement, or institutional affiliation and the presence or absence of conflicting interests (for reviews, see Eagly & Chaiken, 1993; Petty & Cacioppo, 1986). However, credibility judgments can also be based on feelings of familiarity. In daily life, people trust familiar others more than strangers (Luhmann, 1979), from personal interactions to e-commerce (Gefen, 2000). Familiarity resulting from previous encounters or even just repeatedly seeing pictures of a face is sufficient to increase perceptions of honesty and sincerity as well as agreement with what the person says (Brown, Brown, & Zoccoli, 2002; Weisbuch & Mackie, 2009). Similarly, the mere repetition of a name can make an unknown name seem familiar, making its bearer "famous overnight" (Jacoby, Woloshyn, & Kelley, 1989), which may also increase perceived expertise. Familiar people are also easier to recognize and remember, and their names become easier to pronounce with repeated encounters. Variables that influence the ease with which source information can be processed can therefore enhance the perceived credibility of the source. Indeed, a given claim is more likely to be judged true when the name of its source is easy to pronounce (Newman et al., 2014).

To assess the likely truth of a claim, people also consider whether others believe it – if many people agree, there's probably something to it. This *social consensus* (Festinger, 1954) criterion is central to many social influence processes and is sometimes referred to as the principle of "social proof" (Cialdini, 2009). As numerous studies indicated, people are more confident in their beliefs if they are shared by others (Newcomb, 1943; Visser & Mirabile, 2004), more likely to endorse a message if many others have done so as well (Cialdini, 2009), and place more trust in what they remember if others remember it similarly (Harris & Hahn, 2009; Ross, Buehler, & Karr, 1998). Conversely, perceiving dissent reliably undermines message acceptance, which makes reports on real or fabricated controversies an efficient strategy for swaying public opinion (Lewandowsky, Ecker, Seifert, Schwarz, & Cook, 2012; Lewandowsky, Gignac, & Vaughan, 2013). To assess the extent of consensus, people may consult public opinion polls or ask their friends. Alternatively, they may rely on how "familiar" the belief feels – after all, one should have encountered popular beliefs, shared by many, more frequently than unpopular beliefs, held by few. Empirically, familiar information is easier to read, understand, and remember than unfamiliar information, which makes ease of processing a (fallible) indicator of familiarity and popularity. Accordingly, incidental changes in ease of processing can influence perceived consensus.

Finally, people's confidence in a belief increases with the *amount of supporting evidence*. Support can be assessed through an external search, as in a scientific literature review or through recall of pertinent information from memory; in either case, confidence increases with the amount of supportive information. Alternatively, support can be gauged from how easy it is to find supportive evidence – the more evidence there is, the easier it should be to find some (in memory or in the literature). This lay theory is at the heart of Tversky and Kahneman's (1973) availability heuristic. Unfortunately, this heuristic can be misleading. If the only supportive piece of information comes to mind easily because it has been endlessly repeated or is very vivid and memorable, we may erroneously conclude that support is strong. Moreover, attention to *what* comes to mind and attention to the *ease* with which it does so will often lead to different conclusions. On the one hand, reliance on the substantive arguments brought to mind results in higher confidence the more arguments one retrieves or generates. On the other hand, reliance on ease of recall results in lower confidence the more arguments one tries to come up with because finding many arguments is difficult, which suggests that there probably aren't many (Haddock, Rothman, Reber, & Schwarz, 1999; for reviews, see Schwarz, 1998; Schwarz & Vaughn, 2002).

Regardless of which truth criteria people draw on, easily processed information enjoys an advantage over information that is difficult to process: it feels more familiar, more compatible with one's beliefs, more internally consistent, more widely held, better supported, and more likely to have come from a credible source. These inferences reflect that familiar, frequently encountered information and information that is coherent and compatible with one's knowledge is indeed easier to process than information that is not. Hence, ease of processing provides heuristically useful – but fallible – information for assessing how well a claim meets major truth criteria.

Making claims "feel" true

So far, our discussion highlighted that ease or difficulty of processing can result both from variables that are meaningfully related to key criteria of truth or from incidental influences. This is important for two reasons. From a research perspective, it allows researchers to manipulate processing fluency in ways that are independent of substantive characteristics of a message and its source. From an applied perspective, it highlights that claims can "feel" true merely because they are easy to process, which provides many opportunities for manipulation. Next, we review some of the most important variables that influence the ease or difficulty of message processing.

Repetition

Demagogues have known for millennia that truth can be created through frequent repetition of a lie – as Hitler put it, "Propaganda must confine itself to a few points and repeat them over and over again" (cited in Toland, 1976, p. 221). Empirical research supports demagogues' intuition. Studying wartime rumors, Allport and Lepkin (1945) found that the best predictor of whether people believed a rumor was the number of times they were exposed to it. Testing this observation in the laboratory, Hasher, Goldstein, and Toppino (1977) asked participants to rate their confidence that each of 60 statements was true. Some statements were factually correct (e.g., "Lithium is the lightest of all metals"), whereas others were not (e.g., "The People's Republic of China was founded in 1947"). Participants provided their ratings on three occasions, each two weeks apart. Across these sessions, some statements were repeated once or twice, whereas others were not, resulting in one, two, or three exposures. As expected, participants were more confident that a given statement was true the more often they had seen it, independent of whether it was factually true or false. Numerous follow-up studies confirmed the power of repetition across many content domains, from trivia statements (e.g., Bacon, 1979) to marketing claims (e.g., Hawkins & Hoch, 1992) and political beliefs (e.g., Arkes, Hackett, & Boehm, 1989), with the time delay between exposure and judgment ranging from minutes (e.g., Begg & Armour, 1991) to months (Brown & Nix, 1996). Dechêne, Stahl, Hansen, and Wänke (2010) provide a comprehensive meta-analysis of this "illusory truth" effect.

The influence of repetition is most pronounced for claims that people feel uncertain about, but is also observed when more diagnostic information about the claims is available (Fazio, Rand, & Pennycook, 2019; Unkelbach & Greifeneder, 2018). Worse, repetition even increases agreement among people who actually know that the claim is false – if only they thought about it (Fazio, Brashier, Payne, & Marsh, 2015). For example, repeating the statement "The Atlantic Ocean is the largest ocean on Earth" increased its acceptance even among people who knew that the Pacific is larger. When the repeated statement felt familiar, they nodded along without checking it against their knowledge. Even warning people that some of the claims they will be shown are false does not eliminate the effect, although it attenuates its size. More importantly, warnings only attenuate the influence of repetition when they *precede* exposure to the claims – warning people *after* they have seen the claims has no discernable influence (Jalbert, Newman, & Schwarz, 2019).

Repetition also increases perceived social consensus, that is, the perception that a belief is shared by many others. Weaver, Garcia, Schwarz, and Miller (2007) had participants read opinion statements purportedly taken from a group discussion in which a given opinion was presented once or thrice. Each opinion statement was attributed to a group member. Not surprisingly, participants assumed that more people shared the opinion when they read it three times from three different group members (72%) than when they read it only once (57%). However, reading the opinion three times from the *same* group member was almost as influential, resulting in a consensus estimate of 67% – apparently, the single repetitive source sounded like a chorus. Later studies showed that people trust an eyewitness report more the more often it is repeated, even when all repetitions come from the same single witness (Foster, Huthwaite, Yesberg, Garry, & Loftus, 2012). Similarly, newspaper readers are more confident in the accuracy of a report when the same message is presented in several newspapers, even if all newspapers solely rely on the same single interview with the same speaker (Yousif, Aboody, & Keil, 2019). Such findings suggest that frequent repetition of the same soundbite in TV news can give the message a familiarity that increases its perceived popularity and truth. This concern also applies to social media, where the same message keeps showing up as friends and friends of friends like it and repost it, resulting in many exposures within a network.

Beyond repetition

Despite its popularity with past and present demagogues, repetition is just one of many variables that can facilitate easy processing of a statement, making the statement appear more popular, credible, and true. Next, we review some of these other variables.

Reber and Schwarz (1999) manipulated the ease of reading through the *color contrast* of the print font. Depending on condition, some statements (e.g., 'Orsono is a city in Chile') were easy to read due to high color contrast (e.g., dark blue print on a white background), whereas others were difficult to read due to low color contrast (e.g., light blue print on a white background). As predicted, the same statement was more likely to be judged true when it was easy rather than difficult to read. Similarly, the readability of *print fonts* can influence intuitive assessments of truthfulness and the extent to which we closely scrutinize a message. For example, when asked, "How many animals of each kind did Moses take on the Ark?" most people answer "two" even though they know that the biblical actor was Noah, not Moses. Song and Schwarz (2008) presented this Moses question (taken from Erickson & Mattson, 1981) in one of the fonts shown in Figure 5.1. They warned participants that some of the questions may be misleading, in which case they should answer "Can't say". When the Moses question was presented in the easy to read black Arial font, 88% failed to notice a problem and answered "two", whereas only 53% did so when the question was presented in the more difficult to read gray Brush font.

Other variables that influence ease of processing have similar effects. For example, handwritten essays are more compelling when the *handwriting* is easy to read (Greifeneder et al., 2010) and so are spoken messages when the speaker's *accent* is easy to understand (Levy-Ari & Keysar, 2010). Similarly, the same conference talk is less impressive when its video recording has low *audio quality*, and a

Print font	% answering without noticing error
How many animals of each kind did Moses take on the Ark?	88%
How many animals of each kind did Moses take on the Ark?	53%

FIGURE 5.1 Print font and the detection of misleading information

Source: Adapted from Song and Schwarz (2008), Experiment 1.

poor phone connection during a researcher's radio interview can impair listeners' impression of the quality of her research program (Newman & Schwarz, 2018). People also find a statement to be more true when presented with a version of it that *rhymes* rather than one that doesn't, even when the two versions are substantively equivalent (McGlone & Tofighbakhsh, 2000). Even a *photo* without any probative value can increase acceptance of a statement, provided the photo makes it easier to imagine what the statement is about (for a review, see Newman & Zhang, this volume).

Merely having a name that is easy to *pronounce* is sufficient to endow the person with higher credibility and trustworthiness. For example, consumers trust an online seller more when the seller's eBay username is easy to pronounce – they are more likely to believe that the product will live up to the seller's promises and that the seller will honor the advertised return policy (Silva, Chrobot, Newman, Schwarz, & Topolinski, 2017). Similarly, the same claim is more likely to be accepted as true when the name of its source is easy to pronounce (Newman et al., 2014).

As this selective review indicates, any variable that can influence ease of processing can also influence judgments of truth. This is the case because people are very sensitive to their processing experience but insensitive to where this experience comes from. When their attention is directed to the incidental source of their experience, the informational value of the experienced ease or difficulty is undermined and its influence attenuated or eliminated, as predicted by feelings-as-information theory (for reviews, see Schwarz, 2012, 2018).

Analytic versus intuitive processing

As in other domains of judgment, people are more likely to invest the time and effort needed for careful information processing when they are sufficiently motivated and have the time and opportunity to do so (for reviews, see Greifeneder, Bless, & Pham, 2011; Greifeneder & Schwarz, 2014). One may hope that this favors careful processing whenever the issue is important. However, this optimism may not be warranted. In the course of everyday life, messages about issues we consider personally important may reach us when we have other things on our minds and lack the opportunity to engage with them. Over repeated encounters, such messages may become familiar and fluent enough to escape closer scrutiny even when the situation would allow us to engage with them. As reviewed previously, telling recipients that some of the information shown to them is false is only protective when the warning precedes the first exposure; later warnings show little effect (Jalbert et al., 2019). Similarly, the motivation and opportunity to examine a message critically may exert only a limited influence once the message has been encoded (for a review, see Lewandowsky et al., 2012).

Implications for social media

The dynamics of truth judgment have important implications for the acceptance and correction of false information in the real world. Beginning with the proliferation of cable TV and talk radio, citizens in democracies enjoyed ever more opportunities to selectively expose themselves to media that fit their worldview. The advent of social media is the latest step in this development and, in many ways, one might think that social media were designed to make questionable messages seem true. To begin with, most social media messages are short, written in simple language, and presented in optics that are easy to read, which satisfies many of the technical prerequisites for easy processing. These fluent messages are posted by one's friends, a credible source. The content they post is usually compatible with one's own beliefs, given the similarity of opinions and values in friendship networks (for a review of network homophily, see McPherson, Smith-Lovin, & Cook, 2001). Posted messages are liked by other friends, thus confirming social consensus, and reposted, thus ensuring multiple repeated exposures. With each exposure, processing becomes easier and perceptions of social consensus, coherence, and compatibility increase. Comments and related posts provide additional supporting evidence and further enhance familiarity. At the same time, the accumulating likes and reposts ensure that the filtering mechanism of the feed makes exposure to opposing information less and less likely. The *Wall Street Journal*'s "Blue Feed/Red Feed" site illustrates how Facebook's filtering mechanism resulted in profoundly different news feeds for liberals and conservatives during the 2016 elections in the United States, and a growing body of research traces how opinion homophily within networks contributes to controversies between networks (Del Vicario et al., 2016; Gargiulo & Gandica, 2017). The observed narrowing of recipients' information diet on social media is enhanced through the personalization of internet offerings outside of social media, where internet providers and search engines track users' interests to tailor information delivery (Pariser, 2011).

These processes not only increase the acceptance of claims that feel increasingly familiar and compatible with what else one knows but also foster a high sense of expertise and confidence. After all, much of what one sees in one's feed is familiar, which suggests that one knows most of what there is to know about the topic. It has also been seen without much opposing evidence, suggesting that the arguments are undisputed. This enhances what Ross and Ward (1996) described as "naïve realism" – the belief that the world is the way I see it and whoever disagrees is either ill-informed (which motivates persuasion efforts) or ill-intentioned (if persuasion fails). These beliefs further contribute to polarization and the mutual attribution of malevolence.

Implications for the correction of misinformation

That people can arrive at judgments of truth by relying more on analytic or more on intuitive strategies poses a major challenge for public information campaigns aimed at correcting false beliefs. Extensive research in education shows that students' misconceptions can be corrected by confronting them with correct information, showing students step by step why one idea is wrong and another one right, preferably repeating this process multiple times (for reviews, see Vosniadou, 2008). This works best when the recipient wants to acquire the correct information and is sufficiently motivated to pay attention, think through the issues, and remember the new insights (for a review, see Sinatra & Pintrich, 2003). Public information campaigns often follow these procedures by confronting the "myths" with "facts", consistent with content-focused theories of message learning (McQuail, 2000; Rice & Atkin, 2001). While this works in the classroom, with motivated recipients, sufficient time, and the benefit of incentives, the reality of public information campaigns is starkly different. For any given topic, only a small segment of the population will care enough to engage with the details; most are likely to notice the message only in passing, if at all, and will process it superficially while doing something else. Even if they remember the corrective message as intended when tested immediately, it may fade quickly from memory.

Under such conditions, repeating false information in order to correct it may mostly succeed in spreading the false information to disinterested recipients who may otherwise never have encountered it. Not having processed the message in detail, they may now find the false claims a bit more familiar and easier to process when they hear or see them again. This way, the attempt to correct the erroneous beliefs of a few may prepare numerous others to accept those beliefs through repeated exposure (for a review, see Schwarz, Sanna, Skurnik, & Yoon, 2007). For example, Skurnik, Yoon, Park, and Schwarz (2005) exposed older and younger adults once or thrice to product statements like "Shark cartilage is good for your arthritis", and these statements were explicitly marked as "true" or "false". When tested immediately, the corrections seemed successful – all participants were less likely to accept a statement as true the more often they were told that it is false. This is the hoped-for success and most studies stop at this point. But after a three-day delay, repeated warnings backfired and older adults were now more likely to consider a statement "true", the more often they had been explicitly told that it is false. Presumably, the recipients could no longer recall whether the statement had been originally marked as true or false, but still experienced repeated statements as easier to process and more familiar, which made the statements "feel" true.

Even exposing people to only true information can make it more likely that they accept a false version of that information as time passes. Garcia-Marques, Silva, Reber, and Unkelbach (2015) presented participants with ambiguous statements (e.g., "crocodiles sleep with their eyes closed") and later asked them to rate the truth of statements that were either identical to those previously seen or that directly contradicted them (e.g., "crocodiles sleep with their eyes open"). When participants made these judgments immediately, they rated repeated identical statements as more true, and contradicting statements as less true, than novel statements, which they had not seen before. One week later, however, identical as well as contradicting statements seemed more true than novel statements. Put simply, as long as the delay is short enough, people can recall the exact information they just saw and reject the opposite. As time passes, however, the details get lost and contradicting information feels more familiar than information one has never heard of – yes, there was something about crocodiles and their eyes, so that's probably what it was.

As time passes, people may even infer the credibility of the initial source from the confidence with which they hold the belief. For example, Fragale and Heath (2004) exposed participants two or five times to statements like "The wax used to line Cup-o-Noodles cups has been shown to cause cancer in rats". Next, participants learned that some statements were taken from the *National Enquirer* (a low credibility source) and some from *Consumer Reports* (a high credibility source) and had to assign the statements to their likely sources. The more often participants had heard a statement, the more likely they were to attribute it to *Consumer Reports* rather than the *National Enquirer*. In short, frequent exposure not only increases the apparent truth of a statement, it also increases the belief that the statement came from a trustworthy source. Similarly, well-intentioned efforts by the Centers for Disease Control and the *Los Angeles Times* to debunk a rumor about "flesh-eating bananas" morphed into the belief that the *Los Angeles Times* had warned people not to eat those dangerous bananas, thus reinforcing the rumor (Emery, 2000). Such errors in source attribution increase the likelihood that people convey the information to others, who themselves are more likely to accept (and spread) it, given its alleged credible source (Rosnow & Fine, 1976).

Such findings illustrate that attempts to correct misinformation can backfire when they focus solely on message content at the expense of the message's impact on recipients' later processing experience. Even when a corrective message succeeds in changing the beliefs of recipients who deeply care about the topic and process the message with sufficient attention, it may spread the false information to many others who don't care about the topic. Unfortunately, the latter are likely to outnumber the former. In those cases, the successful correction of a few false believers may come at the cost of misleading many bystanders. To avoid such backfire effects, it will usually be safer to refrain from any reiteration of false information and to focus solely on the facts. The more the facts become familiar and fluent, the more likely it is that they will be accepted as true and serve as the basis of judgments and decisions (Lewandowsky et al., 2012; Schwarz et al., 2007, 2016).

Unfortunately, the truth is usually more complicated than false stories, which often involve considerable simplification. This puts the truth at a disadvantage because it is harder to process, understand, and remember. It is therefore important to present true information in ways that facilitate its fluent processing. This requires clear step-by-step exposition and the avoidance of jargon. It also helps to pay close attention to incidental influences on ease of processing. Making the font easy to read and the speaker's pronunciation easy to understand, adding photos and repeating key points are all techniques that should not be left to those who want to mislead – they can also give truth a helping hand and should be used.

Finally, at the individual level, the best protection against the influence of misinformation is skepticism at the time the information is first encountered (for a review, see Lewandowsky et al., 2012). Once people have processed the false information, warnings exert little influence. In addition to explicit warnings, general feelings of suspicion and distrust increase message scrutiny and decrease message acceptance (for reviews, see Mayo, 2017; Schwarz & Lee, 2019). Explicit warnings as well as suspicion and distrust entail that the communicator may not adhere to the norms of cooperative conversational conduct (Grice, 1975), thus flagging the message for closer scrutiny. Unfortunately, in a polarized public opinion climate, merely realizing that a message supports the "other" side is itself likely to elicit suspicion and distrust, further impairing correction attempts in polarized contexts.

Acknowledgments

Preparation of this chapter was supported by the Linnie and Michael Katz Endowed Research Fellowship Fund through a fellowship to the second author and funds of the USC Dornsife Mind and Society Center to the first author.

References

Allport, F. H., & Lepkin, M. (1945). Wartime rumors of waste and special privilege: Why some people believe them. *Journal of Abnormal and Social Psychology, 40*, 3–36.
Arkes, H. R., Hackett, C., & Boehm, L. (1989). The generality of the relation between familiarity and judged validity. *Journal of Behavioral Decision Making, 2*, 81–94.
Bacon, F. T. (1979). Credibility of repeated statements: Memory for trivia. *Journal of Experimental Psychology: Human Learning and Memory, 5*, 241–252.
Begg, I., & Armour, V. (1991). Repetition and the ring of truth: Biasing comments. *Canadian Journal of Behavioural Science, 23*, 195–213.
Brown, A. S., Brown, L. A., & Zoccoli, S. L. (2002). Repetition-based credibility enhancement of unfamiliar faces. *The American Journal of Psychology, 115*, 199–2009.

Brown, A. S., & Nix, L. A. (1996). Turning lies into truths: Referential validation of falsehoods. *Journal of Experimental Psychology: Learning, Memory, and Cognition, 22,* 1088–1100.

Cialdini, R. B. (2009). *Influence: Science and practice.* Boston: Pearson Education.

Dechêne, A., Stahl, C., Hansen, J., & Wänke, M. (2010). The truth about the truth: A meta-analytic review of the truth effect. *Personality and Social Psychology Review, 14,* 238–257.

Del Vicario, M., Bessi, A., Zollo, F., Petroni, F., Scala, A., Caldarelli, G., . . . Quattro-ciocchi, W. (2016). The spreading of misinformation online. *Proceedings of the National Academy of Sciences, 113*(3), 554–559.

Eagly, A. H., & Chaiken, S. (1993). *The psychology of attitudes.* Fort Worth, TX: Harcourt Brace.

Emery, D. (2000, February 23). The great banana scare of 2000. Retrieved May 24, 2002, from http://urbanlegends.about.com/library/weekly/aa022302a.htm

Erickson, T. D., & Mattson, M. E. (1981). From words to meaning: A semantic illusion. *Journal of Verbal Learning & Verbal Behavior, 20,* 540–551.

Fazio, L. K., Brashier, N. M., Payne, B. K., & Marsh, E. J. (2015). Knowledge does not protect against illusory truth. *Journal of Experimental Psychology: General, 144*(5), 993–1002.

Fazio, L. K., Rand, D. G., & Pennycook, G. (2019). Repetition increases perceived truth equally for plausible and implausible statements. *Psychonomic Bulletin & Review, 26*(5), 1705–1710.

Festinger, L. (1954). A theory of social comparison processes. *Human Relations, 7,* 123–146.

Festinger, L. (1957). *A theory of cognitive dissonance.* Evanston, IL: Row, Peterson.

Foster, J. L., Huthwaite, T., Yesberg, J. A., Garry, M., & Loftus, E. (2012). Repetition, not number of sources, increases both susceptibility to misinformation and confidence in the accuracy of eyewitnesses. *Acta Psychologica, 139,* 320–326.

Fragale, A. R., & Heath, C. (2004). Evolving information credentials: The (mis)attribution of believable facts to credible sources. *Personality and Social Psychology Bulletin, 30,* 225–236.

Gabielkov, M., Ramachandran, A., Chaintreau, A., & Legout, A. (2016). Social clicks: What and who gets read on Twitter? *ACM SIGMETRICS Performance Evaluation Review, 44,* 179–192. http://dx.doi.org/10.1145/2896377.2901462

Garcia-Marques, T., Silva, R. R., Reber, R., & Unkelbach, C. (2015). Hearing a statement now and believing the opposite later. *Journal of Experimental Social Psychology, 56,* 126–129.

Gargiulo, F., & Gandica, Y. (2017). The role of homophily in the emergence of opinion controversies. *Journal of Artificial Societies and Social Simulation, 20*(3), 8. doi: 10.18564/jasss.3448. Retrieved from http://jasss.soc.surrey.ac.uk/20/3/8.htm

Gawronski, B., & Strack, F. (Eds.). (2012). *Cognitive consistency: A fundamental principle in social cognition.* New York: Guilford Press.

Gefen, D. (2000). E-commerce: The role of familiarity and trust. *Omega, 28,* 725–737.

Gilbert, D. T. (1991). How mental systems believe. *American Psychologist, 46,* 107–119.

Greifeneder, R., Alt, A., Bottenberg, K., Seele, T., Zelt, S., & Wagener, D. (2010). On writing legibly: Processing fluency systematically biases evaluations of handwritten material. *Social Psychological and Personality Science, 1,* 230–237.

Greifeneder, R., Bless, H., & Pham, M. T. (2011). When do people rely on cognitive and affective feelings in judgment? A review. *Personality and Social Psychology Review, 15,* 107–141.

Greifeneder, R., & Schwarz, N. (2014). Metacognitive processes and subjective experience. In J. W. Sherman, B. Gawronski, & Y. Trope (Eds.), *Dual-process theories of the social mind* (pp. 314–327). New York, NY: Guilford Press.

Grice, H. P. (1975). Logic and conversation. In P. Cole & J. L. Morgan (Eds.), *Syntax and semantics, vol. 3: Speech acts* (pp. 41–58). New York: Academic Press.

Haddock, G., Rothman, A. J., Reber, R., & Schwarz, N. (1999). Forming judgments of attitude certainty, importance, and intensity: The role of subjective experiences. *Personality and Social Psychology Bulletin, 25,* 771–782.

Harris, A. J. L., & Hahn, U. (2009). Bayesian rationality in evaluating multiple testimonies: Incorporating the role of coherence. *Journal of Experimental Psychology: Learning, Memory, and Cognition, 35,* 1366–1372.

Hasher, L., Goldstein, D., & Toppino, T. (1977). Frequency and the conference of referential validity. *Journal of Verbal Learning & Verbal Behavior, 16,* 107–112.

Hasson, U., Simmons, J. P., & Todorov, A. (2005). Believe it or not: On the possibility of suspending belief. *Psychological Science, 16,* 566–571.

Hawkins, S. A., & Hoch, S. J. (1992). Low-involvement learning: Memory without evaluation. *Journal of Consumer Research, 19,* 212–225.

Jacoby, L. L., Woloshyn, V., & Kelley, C. M. (1989). Becoming famous without being recognized: Unconscious influences of memory produced by dividing attention. *Journal of Experimental Psychology: General, 118,* 115–125.

Jalbert, M., Newman, E. J., & Schwarz, N. (2019). *Only half of what I tell you is true: How experimental procedures lead to an underestimation of the truth effect.* Manuscript under review.

Johnson-Laird, P. N. (2012). Mental models and consistency. In B. Gawronski & F. Strack (Eds.), *Cognitive consistency: A fundamental principle in social cognition* (pp. 225–243). New York: Guilford Press.

Kahneman, D. (2011). *Thinking, fast and slow.* New York: Macmillan.

Levy-Ari, S., & Keysar, B. (2010). Why don't we believe non-native speakers? The influence of accent on credibility. *Journal of Experimental Social Psychology, 46,* 1093–1096.

Lewandowsky, S., Ecker, U. K. H., Seifert, C., Schwarz, N., & Cook, J. (2012). Misinformation and its correction: Continued influence and successful debiasing. *Psychological Science in the Public Interest, 13,* 106–131.

Lewandowsky, S., Gignac, G. E., & Vaughan, S. (2013). The pivotal role of perceived scientific consensus in acceptance of science. *Nature Climate Change, 3,* 399–404.

Luhmann, N. (1979). *Trust and power.* Chichester, UK: Wiley.

Mayo, R. (2017). Cognition is a matter of trust: Distrust tunes cognitive processes. *European Review of Social Psychology, 26,* 283–327.

McGlone, M. S., & Tofighbakhsh, J. (2000). Birds of a feather flock conjointly (?): Rhyme as reason in aphorisms. *Psychological Science, 11,* 424–428.

McPherson, M., Smith-Lovin, L., & Cook. J. M. (2001). Birds of a feather: Homophily in social networks. *Annual Review of Sociology, 27,* 415–444.

McQuail, D. (2000). *McQuail's mass communication theory.* Newbury Park, CA: Sage Publications.

Morsanyi, K., & Handley, S. J. (2012). Logic feels so good: I like it! Evidence for intuitive detection of logicality in syllogistic reasoning. *Journal of Experimental Psychology: Learning, Memory, and Cognition, 38,* 596–616.

Newcomb, T. M. (1943). *Personality and social change.* New York: Holt, Rinehart, & Winston.

Newman, E. J., Sanson, M., Miller, E. K., Quigley-McBride, A., Foster, J. L., Bernstein, D. M., & Garry, M. (2014). People with easier to pronounce names promote truthiness of claims. *PLoS One, 9*(2). doi: 10.1371/journal.pone.0088671

Newman, E. J., & Schwarz, N. (2018). Good sound, good research: How audio quality influences perceptions of the researcher and research. *Science Communication, 40*(2), 246–257.

Newman, E. J., & Zhang, L. (2020). Truthiness: How nonprobative photos shape beliefs. In R. Greifeneder, M. Jaffé, E. J. Newman, & N. Schwarz (Eds.), *The psychology of fake news: Accepting, sharing, and correcting misinformation* (pp. 90–114). London, UK: Routledge.

Oyserman, D., & Dawson, A. (2020). Your fake news, our fakes: Identity-based motivation shapes what we believe, share, and accept. In R. Greifeneder, M. Jaffé, E. J. Newman, & N. Schwarz (Eds.), *The psychology of fake news: Accepting, sharing, and correcting misinformation* (pp. 173–195). London, UK: Routledge.

Pariser, E. (2011). *The filter bubble: How the new personalized web is changing what we read and how the think.* New York: Penguin Books.

Pennington, N., & Hastie, R. (1993). The story model for juror decision making. In R. Hastie (Ed.), *Inside the juror* (pp. 192–223). New York: Cambridge University Press.

Petty, R. E., & Cacioppo, J. T. (1986). The elaboration likelihood model of persuasion. *Advances in Experimental Social Psychology, 19,* 123–205.

Reber, R., & Schwarz, N. (1999). Effects of perceptual fluency on judgments of truth. *Consciousness and Cognition, 8,* 338–342.

Rice, R., & Atkin, C. (Eds.). (2001). *Public communication campaigns* (3rd ed.). Newbury Park, CA: Sage Publications.

Rosnow, R. L., & Fine, G. A. (1976). *Rumor and gossip: The social psychology of hearsay.* New York: Elsevier.

Ross, L., & Ward, A. (1996). Naive realism in everyday life: Implications for social conflict and misunderstanding. In E. S. Reed, E. Turiel, & T. Brown (Eds.), *Values and knowledge* (pp. 103–135). Hillsdale, NJ: Lawrence Erlbaum.

Ross, M., Buehler, R., & Karr, J. W. (1998). Assessing the accuracy of conflicting autobiographical memories. *Memory and Cognition, 26,* 1233–1244.

Schul, Y., Mayo, R., & Burnstein, E. (2008). The value of distrust. *Journal of Experimental Social Psychology, 44,* 1293–1302.

Schwarz, N. (1994). Judgment in a social context: Biases, shortcomings, and the logic of conversation. *Advances in Experimental Social Psychology, 26,* 123–162.

Schwarz, N. (1996). *Cognition and communication: Judgmental biases, research methods, and the logic of conversation.* Hillsdale, NJ: Erlbaum.

Schwarz, N. (1998). Accessible content and accessibility experiences: The interplay of declarative and experiential information in judgment. *Personality and Social Psychology Review, 2,* 87–99.

Schwarz, N. (2012). Feelings-as-information theory. In P. A. Van Lange, A. W. Kruglanski, & E. Higgins (Eds.), *Handbook of theories of social psychology* (pp. 289–308). Thousand Oaks, CA: Sage Publications.

Schwarz, N. (2015). Metacognition. In M. Mikulincer, P. R. Shaver, E. Borgida, & J. A. Bargh (Eds.), *APA handbook of personality and social psychology: Attitudes and social cognition* (pp. 203–229). Washington, DC: APA.

Schwarz, N. (2018). Of fluency, beauty, and truth: Inferences from metacognitive experiences. In J. Proust & M. Fortier (Eds.), *Metacognitive diversity: An interdisciplinary approach* (pp. 25–46). New York: Oxford University Press.

Schwarz, N., & Lee, S. W. S. (2019). The smell of suspicion: How the nose curbs gullibility. In J. P. Forgas & R. F. Baumeister (Eds.), *The social psychology of gullibility: Fake news, conspiracy theories, and irrational beliefs* (pp. 234–252). New York: Routledge and Psychology Press.

Schwarz, N., Newman, E., & Leach, W. (2016). Making the truth stick and the myths fade: Lessons from cognitive psychology. *Behavioral Science & Policy, 2*(1), 85–95.

Schwarz, N., Sanna, L. J., Skurnik, I., & Yoon, C. (2007). Metacognitive experiences and the intricacies of setting people straight: Implications for debiasing and public information campaigns. *Advances in Experimental Social Psychology, 39,* 127–161.

Schwarz, N., & Vaughn, L. A. (2002). The availability heuristic revisited: Ease of recall and content of recall as distinct sources of information. In T. Gilovich, D. Griffin, & D. Kahneman (Eds.), *Heuristics and biases: The psychology of intuitive judgment* (pp. 103–119). Cambridge: Cambridge University Press.

Silva, R. R., Chrobot, N., Newman, E., Schwarz, N., & Topolinski, S. (2017). Make it short and easy: Username complexity determines trustworthiness above and beyond objective reputation. *Frontiers in Psychology, 8,* 2200.

Sinatra, G. M., & Pintrich, P. (2003). The role of intentions in conceptual change learning. In G. M. Sinatra & P. R. Pintrich (Eds.), *Intentional conceptual change.* Mahwah, NJ: Lawrence Erlbaum Associates.

Skurnik, I., Yoon, C., Park, D. C., & Schwarz, N. (2005). How warnings about false claims become recommendations. *Journal of Consumer Research, 31,* 713–724.

Song, H., & Schwarz, N. (2008). Fluency and the detection of misleading questions: Low processing fluency attenuates the Moses illusion. *Social Cognition, 26,* 791–799.

Sperber, D., & Wilson, D. (1986). *Relevance: Communication and cognition.* Cambridge, MA: Harvard University Press.

Stanovich, K. E. (1999). *Who is rational? Studies of individual differences in reasoning.* Mahwah: Erlbaum.

Taber, C. S., & Lodge, M. (2006). Motivated skepticism in the evaluation of political beliefs. *American Journal of Political Science, 50*(3), 755–769.

Toland, J. (1976). *Adolf Hitler.* Garden City, NY: Doubleday.

Topolinski, S. (2012). Nonpropositional consistency. In B. Gawronski & F. Strack (Eds.), *Cognitive consistency: A fundamental principle in social cognition* (pp. 112–131). New York: Guilford Press.

Topolinski, S., & Strack, F. (2008). Where there's a will: There's no intuition: The unintentional basis of semantic coherence judgments. *Journal of Memory and Language, 58,* 1032–1048.

Topolinski, S., & Strack, F. (2009). The architecture of intuition: Fluency and affect determine intuitive judgments of semantic and visual coherence and judgments of grammaticality in artificial grammar learning. *Journal of Experimental Psychology: General, 138,* 39–63.

Tversky, A., & Kahneman, D. (1973). Availability: A heuristic for judging frequency and probability. *Cognitive Psychology, 5,* 207–232.

Unkelbach, C., & Greifeneder, R. (2018). Experiential fluency and declarative advice jointly inform judgments of truth. *Journal of Experimental Social Psychology, 79,* 78–86.

Visser, P. S., & Mirabile, R. R. (2004). Attitudes in the social context: The impact of social network composition on individual-level attitude strength. *Journal of Personality and Social Psychology, 87,* 779–795.

Vosniadou, S. (Ed.). (2008). *International handbook of research on conceptual change.* New York, NY: Routledge.

Weaver, K., Garcia, S. M., Schwarz, N., & Miller, D. T. (2007). Inferring the popularity of an opinion from its familiarity: A repetitive voice can sound like a chorus. *Journal of Personality and Social Psychology, 92,* 821–833.

Weisbuch, M., & Mackie, D. (2009). False fame, perceptual clarity, or persuasion? Flexible fluency attribution in spokesperson familiarity effects. *Journal of Consumer Psychology, 19*(1), 62–72.

Winkielman, P., Huber, D. E., Kavanagh, L., & Schwarz, N. (2012). Fluency of consistency: When thoughts fit nicely and flow smoothly. In B. Gawronski & F. Strack (Eds.), *Cognitive consistency: A fundamental principle in social cognition* (pp. 89–111). New York: Guilford Press.

Yousif, S. R., Aboody, R., & Keil, F. C. (2019). The illusion of consensus: A failure to distinguish between true and false consensus. *Psychological Science, 30*(8), 1195–1204.

6

TRUTHINESS

How non-probative photos shape belief

Eryn J. Newman and Lynn Zhang

"Breaking: Tens of thousands of fraudulent Clinton votes found in Ohio warehouse". In late 2016, an estimated six million people on social media and other news websites were exposed to this claim, which appeared with a photo of a man standing in front of stacks of ballot boxes.[1] This claim was fake news invented by a college student. And the photo? A stock photo that the same college student found using a "ballot boxes" search on google. The Clinton example is not unique. Fake news and misinformation are often accompanied by decorative photos that relate to the general topic but do not provide any probative evidence regarding whether the headline is actually correct (see examples here: Politico Staff, 2017). From a communications perspective, the use of related stock photos makes sense: photos capture attention, and can at times, aid comprehension and increase the chances that people remember the associated content (Carney & Levin, 2002; Knobloch, Hastall, Zillmann, & Callison, 2003; Waddill & McDaniel, 1992). But decorating headlines or claims with these non-probative photos can have more insidious effects on people's beliefs.

A growing body of work shows that even a brief exposure to a related but non-probative photo can bias people to believe that an associated claim is true, despite the fact that the photo offers no diagnostic evidence for the claim's veracity, a *truthiness effect*[2] (Fenn, Newman, Pezdek, & Garry, 2013; Newman, Garry, Bernstein, Kantner, & Lindsay, 2012; Newman et al., 2015). This truthiness effect holds over several days and influences a range of judgments, including judgments about general knowledge facts, predictions about future events, and judgments about our own episodic memories. We review the literature on truthiness, documenting the ways in which photos and other kinds of non-probative information can rapidly change people's beliefs, memories, and judgments about their own general knowledge. We also examine the mechanisms contributing to truthiness and explore the implications for fake news and misinformation.

Non-probative photos and truthiness

It is well-established that misleading photos can trick us. When they are doctored to represent an event that never happened, or are paired with repeated suggestion from a trusted source, they can lead people to believe and remember completely false information (Lindsay, Hagen, Read, Wade, & Garry, 2004). But photos like the ballot boxes, that simply decorate, viewed only briefly, have been treated as relatively innocuous (e.g., Carney & Levin, 2002). What is the evidence that such decorative, non-probative photos have any impact on people's beliefs?

Experimental research on truthiness

In one of the first experiments to examine the influence of non-probative photos, people were asked to participate in a trivia test where they saw a series of general knowledge claims appear on a computer screen (Newman et al., 2012). The key manipulation in this experiment was that half of the claims appeared with a related non-probative photo, much like the format one might encounter in the news or on social media, and half of the claims appeared without a photo. For example, participants in this trivia study saw claims like "Giraffes are the only mammals that cannot jump" presented either with a photo, like the headshot of a giraffe in Figure 6.1, or without a photo. Despite the fact that the photos provided no evidence of whether the claims were accurate or not – the headshot of the giraffe tells you nothing about whether giraffes can jump – the presence of a photo biased people toward saying the associated claims were true. Photos produced *truthiness*, a bias to believe claims with the addition of non-probative information. In another set of experiments, published in the same article, Newman and colleagues conceptually replicated the finding. In these experiments, participants were asked to play a different trivia game: "Dead or Alive" (a game that a co-author remembered from old radio programing). The key task was to judge whether the claim "This person is alive" was true or false for each celebrity name that appeared on the screen. Half the time, those celebrity names appeared with a non-probative photo – a photo that depicted the celebrity engaged in their profession but did not provide any evidence about the truth of the claim "This person is alive". For instance, subjects may have seen the name "Nick Cave" with a photo of Nick Cave on stage with a microphone in his hand and singing to a crowd (see Figure 6.1). Nothing about the photo provided any clues about whether Nick Cave was in fact alive or not. In many ways, the photos were simply stock photos of the celebrities. The findings from this experiment were clear: people were more likely to accept the claim "This person is alive" as true when the celebrity name appeared with a photo, compared to when there was no photo present. Perhaps more surprisingly, the same pattern of results was found when another group of subjects were shown the *same* celebrity names, with the *same* celebrity photos, but evaluated the opposite claim: "This person is dead". In other words, the very same photos nudged people toward believing

FIGURE 6.1 On the top, an example of a non-probative photo of Nick Cave in the "Dead or Alive" experiments (Newman et al., 2012); on the bottom, an example of a non-probative photo for the trivia claims experiment reported in Newman et al. (2012, 2015)

Source: Photo of Nick Cave: Creative Commons License attribution: Marco Annunziata. Giraffe: Photograph by Fir0002/Flagstaffotos, under the GFDL v1.2 www.gnu.org/licenses/old-licenses/fdl-1.2.en.html

not only claims that the celebrities were "alive" but also claims that the same people were "dead".

This truthiness effect – that non-probative photos bias people to believe claims – also holds in other domains of judgment. In a commodity market prediction task, Newman, Azad, Lindsay, and Garry (2018) asked people to guess whether claims about various commodities were true or false. Participants saw a commodity name like "Benzene" appear on a computer screen and decided whether the claim that "this commodity will increase in price" was true or false. As in the initial trivia claim studies, the commodities were paired either with or without a photo of the commodity (e.g., a photo of benzene). Although the photos simply depicted the commodities, people were biased to believe the claims when they saw a photo. This pattern was pronounced for positive claims about the future performance of a commodity (e.g., that the commodity will make a profit), which squares with general rose-colored cognitive biases about future events (e.g., Szpunar, Addis, & Schacter, 2012). In a product evaluation task, people were more likely to believe positive claims about wines (e.g., "This wine was rated high quality") when those wine labels (e.g., Two Quills Pinot Noir) were accompanied by a non-probative photograph depicting the unfamiliar noun in the wine name (e.g., a photo of quills in a pot of ink). This pattern held even when people were given the opportunity to taste the wines bearing a label that did or did not contain a related photo. In other words, even with additional sensory information – the taste of the wine – photos still biased people's judgments (Cardwell, Newman, Garry, Mantonakis, & Beckett, 2017).

In a memory for actions task, Cardwell, Henkel, Garry, Newman, and Foster (2016) found that people were biased to believe they performed certain actions (saying true more often to claims like "I gave food to this animal" in a simulated zoo game) when they saw a non-probative photo at test. Notably, photos biased people to believe they had performed a given action, regardless of whether they actually had or had not. This result is particularly surprising – while there is some evidence that photos can distort memory for recent actions, the photos in those studies are often combined with variables such as suggestion, elaboration, and repetition, all of which make it more difficult to discern whether a memory is real or not (Lindsay et al., 2004; for a review see Garry & Gerrie, 2005). The results from Cardwell et al. (2016) demonstrate that even a short exposure to non-probative photos in the absence of other suggestive techniques can lead to immediate mistakes in memory. Taken together, the addition of a non-probative photo does not simply shape belief for general knowledge claims. Rather, these photos have systematic effects on belief across a variety of domains and can influence people's estimates about the performance of commodities, the quality of products, and judgments about their own recent actions. How do photos exert these effects on assessments of truth?

Underlying mechanisms of the truthiness effect

Although these photos offer no evidence about the truth of a claim, there are several reasons why the addition of a related photo might sway people's judgments.

We consider those possibilities here and review the related empirical evidence. First, we consider the possibility that photos bias belief because photos are inherently trustworthy. Second, we consider the possibility that photos may bias people's belief via a cognitive fluency mechanism, facilitating the semantic processing of a claim. Third, we consider the possibility that photos bias belief because the addition of photos, although non-probative, creates an illusion of evidence. We present the empirical evidence for each of these theoretical accounts.

Do non-probative photos produce truthiness because photos are inherently trustworthy?

Photos are unique in many ways – they capture a moment in time, usually represent real events, and at times are the best evidence that something actually happened (Kelly & Nace, 1994; Strange, Garry, Bernstein, & Lindsay, 2011; see also Nightingale, Wade, & Watson, 2017). Moreover, people tend to trust photos and often cannot detect when a photo is altered or doctored to mislead (e.g., Nightingale et al., 2017). Thus, in the truthiness paradigm, although photos do not provide probative information for a target claim, they might nonetheless boost belief in the claim because photos are inherently credible themselves.

In order to examine the hypothesis that photos bias people to believe via their inherent credibility, Newman and colleagues (2012) examined whether the truthiness effect was tied specifically to photos, or whether people would be biased by other forms of related – non-probative – information. In an experiment testing this hypothesis, people saw celebrity names and were asked to evaluate the truth of the claim that "This person is alive [dead]". Half the time, those celebrity names were paired with some non-probative semantic information. For one group of subjects, the non-probative information was a photo depicting the celebrity engaged in their profession, as described earlier. For the other group of subjects, the non-probative information was a verbal description of the celebrity engaged in their profession. For instance, instead of seeing a photo of Nick Cave, those in the verbal condition saw a list of semantic information that could easily be extracted from the photo (e.g., male, black hair, microphone, tambourine; see Figure 6.2).

The key finding in this study was that regardless of whether people saw a photo of Nick Cave or a verbal description of Nick Cave, they were more likely to believe the claim that Nick Cave was alive [or dead], compared to when the claims appeared without the addition of non-probative information (Newman et al., 2012). That is, the addition of semantic information, not photos per se, led to a truthiness effect. These findings fit more broadly with research on truth judgments and cognitive fluency (see Schwarz, 2015). In fact, a growing body of work suggests that the addition of conceptually related information (e.g., non-probative photo or words) enhances the semantic processing of claims, biasing people to believe that associated claims are true. We consider this possibility next.

White Man
Long Black Straight Hair
Musician
Microphone

FIGURE 6.2 Examples of photo and verbal conditions, Newman et al. (2012)

Do non-probative photos produce truthiness via an increase in cognitive fluency?

From one moment to the next, people tend to notice shifts in their ongoing cognitive processing. Whether we are trying to recall general knowledge or imagine a scenario, there is variation in how much effort we must exert in information processing. We are generally aware whether perceiving, understanding, or imagining a claim feels easy and effortless, or difficult and effortful (for reviews see Alter & Oppenheimer, 2009; Jacoby, Kelley, & Dywan, 1989; Schwarz, 2015). When information processing feels easy and smooth, we tend to nod along (see Marsh & Stanley, Chapter 8; Schwarz & Jalbert, Chapter 5). That is, when we can easily retrieve related information from memory, rapidly make sense of, and quickly generate mental imagery about a claim or idea, we tend to believe that it is true. As Schwarz and Jalbert describe in this volume, ease of processing is an important cue to assessments of truth, in part, because easy processing is interpreted as evidence for many important criteria that are related to assessments of truth: information that is easy to process is rated as more coherent, credible, compatible with our own general knowledge, likely to have high social consensus, as well as being well supported by significant evidence (Schwarz, 2015; Schwarz & Newman, 2017).

Non-probative photos should (theoretically) facilitate the conceptual processing of a claim

There are several reasons why a non-probative photo (or related words) might influence the ease of processing a claim and bias people to conclude that a claim is true (see Alter & Oppenheimer, 2009 for a review of factors that lead to cognitive fluency). First, a related non-probative photo should provide a semantically rich context for evaluating a claim, facilitating rapid retrieval of information relating to a target of the claim (see Whittlesea, 1993; Wilson & Westerman, 2018). That is, in evaluating the claim "Giraffes are the only mammals that cannot jump", a photo of a giraffe should help people to more rapidly retrieve related (but likely non-probative) details about a giraffe (see Carr, McCauley, Sperber, & Parmelee, 1982). When people can rapidly retrieve information (whether that information is diagnostic or not) from memory, they tend to conclude that easy retrieval signals frequency, familiarity, and truth (see related concepts of semantic priming and cognitive availability; Begg, Anas, & Farinacci, 1992; Kelley & Lindsay, 1993; Tversky & Kahneman, 1973; Whittlesea, 1993). Second, a related photo should help people to more vividly imagine the claim at hand. Research shows that when people can easily imagine a hypothetical event, they tend to conclude that it is more likely (Sherman, Cialdini, Schwartzman, & Reynolds, 1985; see Alter & Oppenheimer, 2009 for a review). Third, pairing a related photo with a claim should make that claim more concrete, increasing the ease of understanding elements in the claim. When information is written in concrete language and is easy to understand, people are more likely to believe it (Hansen & Wanke, 2010; Oppenheimer, 2006). That is, while related non-probative information should not provide evidence for a claim, it should facilitate cognitive processing in three key ways: (1) helping people to rapidly retrieve related semantic details, (2) helping people to easily imagine claims, and (3) helping people to understand the associated claim. It is well-documented in the broader cognitive literature that any one of these variables can increase cognitive fluency and the chances that people agree with a claim, suggesting that non-probative photos may be an especially influential variable in assessments of truth.

Experimental evidence for a cognitive fluency account of truthiness

What is the evidence that photos influence people's assessments of truth via a change in the ease of processing of the claim? There are several predictions that arise from the cognitive fluency literature. The first is that a non-probative photo should bias people to think a claim is true, to the extent that the photo facilitates conceptual processing of the claim. Thus, non-probative photos should produce truthiness when they are semantically related to a claim, but not when they are semantically unrelated (see Alter & Oppenheimer, 2009). The addition of semantically related photos should facilitate conceptual processing of the claim, while the addition of semantically unrelated photos should interfere with the processing of the claim, compared to when there is no photo present at all (Figure 6.3). In order to test this idea, Newman and colleagues (2015) used the general knowledge paradigm described earlier and added one additional tweak to the method: they manipulated the semantic relationship between the photos and the claims.

As in the studies described earlier, people saw trivia claims either paired with a photo or not and had to decide whether those claims were true or false. The key manipulation in these new studies was that half of the subjects saw photos that were semantically related to the claims (e.g., the claim "Magnesium is the liquid metal inside a thermometer" was paired with a photo of a thermometer), and half the subjects saw photos that were semantically unrelated to the claims (e.g., the claim "Magnesium is the liquid metal inside a thermometer" was paired with a photo of a lizard). The results of these studies are consistent with a cognitive fluency interpretation of truthiness – relative to when there was no photo, semantically related photos that should have facilitated conceptual processing of the claim biased people to think an associated claim was true, whereas semantically unrelated photos that should have interfered with conceptual processing of the claim biased people to think an associated claim was false, i.e., a *falsiness effect*.

Another prediction from the fluency literature is that the truthiness effect should be larger when the claims that appear with photos are presented among other claims that appear with no photo. A growing body of work shows that well-established fluency effects are more robust in within-subject, rather than between-subject designs (e.g., Mere Exposure Effect, Truth Effect, Recognition

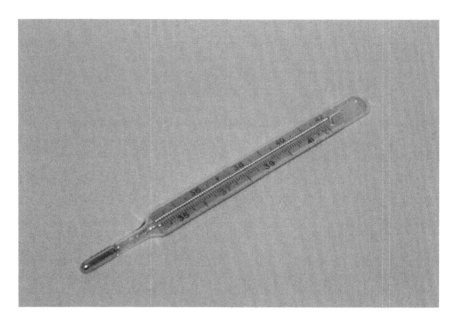

FIGURE 6.3 Representative examples of semantically related and unrelated photos from Newman et al. (2015)

Source: Photo of Thermometer: Creative Commons License attribution, Da Sal. www.flickr. com/photos/112931986@N07/11646098174. Lizard: Free Usage, https://routespartnership.org/ industry-resources/images-video-library/free-use-wildlife-images/reptiles

Memory Effects: Hansen, Dechêne, & Wänke, 2008; Westerman, 2008; for a review, see Wänke & Hansen, 2015). Put simply, an important component of fluency-based effects is the relative ease of processing information. This is not unique to fluency. Indeed, changes in experience are generally more informative than steady states (Berelson & Steiner, 1964). This is exactly what is found in truthiness paradigms: the truthiness effect is more robust in experimental designs that manipulate the presence of a photo within, but not between-subjects (Newman et al., 2015).

A fluency account also predicts that the extent to which photos facilitate processing of a claim should depend on the familiarity of key elements in the claim (see Parks & Toth, 2006; Whittlesea & Williams, 1998). That is, claims with elements that are easy to understand should be closer to a "fluency ceiling" than claims that contain unfamiliar elements (see Cardwell, Newman, Garry, Mantonakis, & Beckett, 2017; Zhang, Newman, & Schwarz, 2018). Therefore, claims with familiar elements like "Two Roses Pinot Noir was rated high quality" should benefit less from the presence of a photo than claims like "Two Quills Pinot Noir was rated high quality". Several findings within the truthiness literature fit with these predictions. The initial truthiness experiments showed that truthiness was most pronounced for unfamiliar celebrity names like Nick Cave compared to more familiar celebrity names like Brad Pitt (Newman et al., 2012). More recently, Abed, Fenn, and Pezdek (2017) found that photos biased people to believe claims about unfamiliar others, but not claims about oneself, perhaps due to differences in available, relevant knowledge. Moreover, Cardwell et al. (2017) found that the extent to which photos led to a truthiness bias was dependent on how much the presence of a photo had increased comprehension of unfamiliar elements in a claim.

Taken together, these effects are consistent with a fluency account – photos (or words) likely bias people to believe by facilitating the conceptual processing of associated claims. Although these studies provide converging evidence for a fluency account of truthiness, there is at least one other possibility: perhaps photos bias people's judgments, in part, because people assume that the experimenters, across these different studies, are offering relevant evidence that participants should use to answer the claim.

Do non-probative photos produce truthiness via an illusion of evidence?

When communicating, people expect speakers to provide only information that is relevant to the ongoing conversation and refrain from providing more information than necessary (Grice, 1975). Therefore, when a related, although non-probative, photo is presented with a claim, people may reasonably assume that the photo is relevant to the judgment at hand and that the placement of the photo is the communicator's attempt to provide supportive evidence for the claim (for reviews on Gricean effects see Schwarz, 1994, 1996). From this perspective, truthiness may be driven, in part, by an illusion of evidence created by the photo, rather than changes in the ease of processing produced by the photo.

In order to disentangle the illusion-of-evidence account from a fluency account, Zhang et al. (2020) examined truthiness effects in the context of comparative claims. Zhang et al. altered materials from the commodity market prediction task described earlier (Newman, Azad, Lindsay, & Garry, 2018), so that (1) each claim was presented in a comparative format and (2) half of the participants saw comparative claims about easy-to-visualize commodities (e.g., "Shrimp will have increased more in price than rose in three months") and the other half saw claims about difficult-to-visualize commodities (e.g., "Betal will have increased more in price than leghorn in three months"). A third of the time, those claims appeared with a photo of the linguistic subject of the claim (e.g., *Shrimp* for the high and *Betal* for the low imageability group), a third of the time those claims appeared with a photo of the linguistic referent in the claim (e.g., *Rose* for the high and *Leghorn* for the low imageability group), and a third of the time, those claims appeared with no photo. Using comparative claims and varying the imageability of the items allowed Zhang and colleagues to disentangle a fluency account from an illusion-of-evidence account for the following reasons. From an illusion-of-evidence perspective, photos of both the subject (*Betal/Shrimp*) and the referent (*Leghorn/Rose*) are conversationally and conceptually relevant to the claim and can be treated as supportive evidence for both high and low imageability claims. If the truthiness effect is indeed produced by an illusion of evidence, either photo should bias people to accept the claim as true in both high and low imageability conditions.

From a fluency perspective, however, photos of the subject should produce truthiness, whereas photos of the referent should produce falsiness. Moreover, the truthiness and falsiness effects should depend on the changes in the ease of processing produced by the photos. Research on comparative judgments shows that a comparison begins with an assessment of features of the subject, which are then checked against features of the referent (e.g., Tversky, 1977; Tversky & Gati, 1978). Put simply, the subject is the focus of the claim and people tend to process the subject before the referent. Accordingly, facilitation and impairment in the processing of the subject should have consequences for the processing and consequently the acceptance of the claim. Thus, a fluency account would predict that relative to the no photo condition, a photo of the subject in a comparative claim should increase acceptance of the claim by facilitating the processing of the subject (e.g., presenting a photo of *Betal* for the claim "Betal will have increased more in price than leghorn in three months"), especially when the subject is otherwise difficult to visualize without a photo. In contrast, a photo of the referent should decrease acceptance of the claim by making processing of the subject (and consequently processing of the claim) more difficult than when no photo is presented (e.g., presenting a photo of *Rose* for the claim "Shrimp will have increased more in price than leghorn in three months"), especially when the subject is otherwise easy to visualize without a photo.

Indeed, Zhang et al.'s findings were consistent with these fluency predictions. Photos of the subject increased, whereas photos of the referent decreased, acceptance of the comparative claim depending on the changes in the ease of processing produced by the photos. In other words, instead of being treated as supportive evidence, photos of the referent acted more like the semantically unrelated photos used in previous research (see Newman et al., 2015), producing a *falsiness* effect. These findings are at odds with an illusion-of-evidence account, which predicts that any related photo would produce truthiness.

Considered together, converging evidence across a range of manipulations supports a cognitive fluency account of truthiness. The addition of related, but non-probative photographs can facilitate the processing of a claim, biasing people to conclude that a claim is true.

Truthiness and illusions of familiarity and knowledge

Although the key focus of this chapter is truthiness, there is a growing body of evidence showing that non-probative photos also shift people's assessments of familiarity, having implications for how people remember and how they estimate their own general knowledge when they encounter a claim. These findings are critically relevant to how people evaluate fake news and misinformation. We therefore describe those findings here.

Assessments of familiarity are often influenced by how rapidly an idea or associated information is retrieved from memory (see Jacoby et al., 1989). This makes sense – compared to something that is new, when something has been seen before, it is easier to retrieve and easier to identify (e.g., Feustel, Shiffrin, & Salasoo, 1983; Tulving & Schacter, 1990). However, a feeling of familiarity can be manufactured by variables in the current context that happen to facilitate the processing of information, and yet have nothing to do with prior exposure (Whittlesea, 1993). For instance, it is well-established that features of a recognition memory test that make test items feel fluent, can bias people to claim that they have seen the items before, regardless of whether they actually have or not (Westerman, 2008; Jacoby et al., 1989). For example, in a recognition test, people are more likely to claim they have studied a target word ("boat") when that word appears in a semantically predictive sentence at test (e.g., "The stormy seas tossed the *boat*".) rather than in a more neutral sentence (e.g., "He saved up his money and bought a *boat*"; Whittlesea, 1993). Recently, Wilson and Westerman (2018) demonstrated that adding non-probative photos to a recognition memory test influences people's memory judgments in a similar way. Photos not only facilitated the speed by which people identified test items, but also produced illusions of familiarity – leading people to claim they had previously seen words that they had never studied (see Brown & Marsh, 2008; repeated photos can also rapidly lead to illusions of familiarity).

Given that photos can produce illusions of familiarity, it is perhaps not surprising that they can also lead people to overestimate how familiar they are with complex concepts in a knowledge estimation task. Across a series of experiments, Cardwell, Lindsay, Förster, and Garry (2017) asked people to rate how much they knew about various complex processes (e.g., how rainbows form). Half the time, people also saw a non-probative photo with the process statement (e.g., seeing a photo of a watch face with the cue "How watches work"). Although the watch face provides no relevant information about the mechanics of a watch, when people saw a photo with a process cue, they claimed to know more about the process in question. When Cardwell et al. examined actual knowledge for these processes, those who saw photos had explanations that were similar in quality to those who did not see a photo. In the context of fake news and misinformation, such findings are particularly worrisome and suggest that stock photos in the media may not only bias people's assessments of truth but also lead to an inflated feeling of knowledge or memory about a claim they encounter.

Reducing truthiness

Given the powerful effects of non-probative information, one critical question is: how can one reduce truthiness? We address this question from three different perspectives, considering (1) the conditions under which people are susceptible to truthiness, (2) individual differences in susceptibility to truthiness, and (3) whether instructions or alerts about the photos influence susceptibility.

Under what conditions are people susceptible to truthiness?

Prior knowledge

Across the cognitive fluency literature, people are typically less influenced by experiences of easy processing when they have high prior knowledge about the claims they are judging (e.g., Dechêne, Stahl, Hansen, & Wänke, 2010; Parks & Toth, 2006; Unkelbach, 2007). This pattern also holds for truthiness. As described earlier, truthiness effects are typically smaller and less robust when people are evaluating claims that can be easily answered with one's own general knowledge (Newman et al., 2012). That is, trivia claims like "Mount Everest is the tallest mountain", tend to produce smaller truthiness effects (Newman et al., 2012; see also Cardwell et al., 2016, 2017; Zhang et al., 2018 for effects of noun familiarity discussed earlier). Notably, while the truthiness effect is reduced under these conditions, it is not fully eliminated (Cardwell et al., 2016, 2017; Newman et al., 2012). This effect of attenuation, is consistent with research on the repetition-based truth effect. The key finding from the truth effect literature is that repeated claims are more likely to be judged as true than new claims (Bacon, 1979; Begg et al., 1992; Hasher, Goldstein, & Toppino, 1977; for a review see Dechêne et al., 2010). Like truthiness, this effect is most robust when people are judging ambiguous claims, via an increase in processing fluency from repeated exposures (see Dechêne et al., 2010). But Fazio and colleagues (2015) showed that the tendency to believe repeated claims holds even when, under other testing conditions, participants demonstrate that they know the correct answer to the claims (Fazio et al., 2015; see also Henkel & Mattson, 2011). Relatedly, Unkelbach and Greifeneder (2018) found robust effects of fluency when clues about the accuracy of the claims were presented to participants while they made judgments of truth. Considered together, the findings from the truthiness literature and the truth effect literature suggest that an experience of easy processing is a robust input in assessments of truth, despite the presence of general knowledge and other more probative inputs (see Unkelbach & Greifeneder, 2018 for an analysis of the combined effects of fluency and declarative inputs).

Negative valence

Another consistent pattern within the truthiness literature is that the bias to believe claims with photos is often completely eliminated or reversed when people are asked to judge negatively valenced claims. For example, in one line of research when people were asked to judge the claim that "This wine was rated *low* quality", the presence of a photo either had no effect or produced a tendency to disbelieve the claim (Cardwell et al., 2017). Similarly, in the experiments on claims about one's own actions, when people were asked to judge the claim "I gave this animal *unhealthy* food" a photo of the animal led people to disbelieve the claim (Cardwell et al., 2016). Notably, the typical truthiness effect was found for the corresponding positive claims in these studies; that is, people were more likely to believe that the same wine was rated *high* quality and that they gave the same animal *healthy* food when a photo accompanied the claims. Why would the typical truthiness effect attenuate or reverse for a negatively valenced claim? A large literature shows that a feeling of cognitive ease is an inherently positive experience (Reber, Schwarz, & Winkielman, 2004; Winkielman, Schwarz, Fazendeiro, & Reber, 2003). Indeed, ease of processing generally increases positive, but not negative judgments. For instance, an experience of cognitive fluency leads to higher ratings of beauty and liking, but not disliking, or ugliness (Reber, Winkielman, & Schwarz, 1998; Seamon, McKenna, & Binder, 1998). Moreover, an experience of easy processing is reflected in facial expressions – fluently processed stimuli lead to activation of the zygomaticus, a psychophysiological marker of positive affect (Topolinski, Likowski, Weyers, & Strack, 2009; Winkielman & Cacioppo, 2001). These findings may explain why, in the context of a negative evaluative judgments, the presence of a non-probative photo has little effect on people's assessments of truth and can in fact bias people to say false to negative claims.

Of course, the findings of the dead or alive study seem at odds with this account. One might expect that a judgment about whether a celebrity is dead or not is also negatively valenced. But in the dead or alive study, people made judgments about a series of famous names, thus it is possible that the dead or alive status may have been evaluated with fame on the mind, rather than the negative valence of death and loss (see also Cardwell et al., 2017 for a discussion of whether the dead or alive statements were more likely to be interpreted as facts about the world, rather than valenced claims). Better understanding the limitations for the valence effect is a topic worthy of future research. For instance, would priming people to consider infamy versus losing a star influence the extent to which a truthiness effect was detected?

Another related and compelling question to consider – especially in the context of fake news – is whether identity consistent or inconsistent claims can act in the same way as positive or negatively valenced claims. Consider for instance, the opening paragraph. If I am a Hillary or Democratic supporter, the addition of a photo may do less to sway my beliefs than if I am a Republican supporter. That is, the truthiness effect may vary by the extent to which claims align with my own beliefs and political ideology. This is another question that could be addressed in future work.

Who is susceptible to truthiness?

Cognitive styles

The literature on persuasion and attitude change shows that some people are more likely to draw on heuristic cues in evaluating a message than others. This individual difference is usually assessed with the Need for Cognition scale (NFC; Cacioppo & Petty, 1982), which measures how much people enjoy and engage in deep thinking. Those who score high on NFC are more likely to consider the quality of an argument or message as well as the consistency of the evidence presented. As a result, they are more persuaded by strong than by weak arguments. In contrast, those who score low on NFC attend less to the substance of the arguments and are more likely to rely on heuristic cues (such as the status of the communicator) and tangential, non-diagnostic information (for reviews, see Petty & Cacioppo, 1986; Priester & Petty, 1995; see also Reinhard & Sporer, 2008). This may suggest that those who are high in NFC should be less likely to fall victim to truthiness, because they tend to rely less on tangential cues and should be more likely to notice that the photos are non-probative. But we find no reliable evidence for this idea (see Newman, Jalbert, Schwarz, & Ly, 2020). One might expect that perhaps other measures that capture people's tendency to engage in more analytical processing may reduce truthiness. For instance, the Cognitive Reflection Test (CRT) measures one's ability to override an initial intuitive response in favor of a more analytical answer (see Pennycook, Fugelsang, & Koehler, 2015). Those who do well on the CRT may thus be less swayed by the intuitive ease with which the claim is processed, and more likely to notice that the photos are non-probative.

Age

It is well-documented that as people age, their ability to recollect episodic details decreases, while feelings of familiarity are relatively unaffected (for a review see Jacoby & Rhodes, 2006). In the context of memory, this means that older adults are often more susceptible to illusions of memory because they tend to draw on familiarity rather than recollection (Jacoby & Rhodes, 2006; see also illusions of truth Skurnik, Yoon, Park, & Schwarz, 2005). In the context of general knowledge, however, recent evidence suggests that aging may not impair performance, but instead provide protection against biases in assessments of truth. Research on the repetition-based truth effect shows that while older adults and younger adults are similarly susceptible to the truth effect when judging ambiguous claims, older adults show a smaller truth effect than younger adults when judging easier or better-known claims (Brashier, Umanath, Cabeza, & Marsh, 2017, see also Parks & Toth, 2006). One explanation for these findings is that older adults simply know more and could more easily answer the better-known claims. But Brashier and colleagues controlled for knowledge between the two age groups by conducting a knowledge check. Why then, would older adults be less susceptible to the truth effect than younger adults for better-known claims? One possibility that Brashier et al. offer is that older adults have more developed knowledge networks, which increases the likelihood that they can apply relevant knowledge in the moment (see Umanath & Marsh, 2014).

It is possible that similar patterns are observed for truthiness and other fluency-based effects on general knowledge. To date, there has only been one initial study investigating the effects of age on susceptibility to the truthiness effect. In a recent study at a local science center, Derksen, Giroux, Newman, and Bernstein (2019) recruited participants from age 3 to age 60 and asked them to participate in an age-adjusted version of the truthiness paradigm (using claims that both three-year-olds and older adults might find difficult to answer, such as "Woodpeckers are the only bird that can fly backwards"). These data showed no reliable differences in the size of the truthiness effect across different age groups (see also Thapar & Westerman, 2009). This initial research shows that pictures might persuade despite one's age, although more research is called for here. But this research also raises an interesting possibility – just as older adults are less susceptible to the effect of repeated exposure for better-known claims (Brashier et al., 2017), age may also guard against the effect of non-probative photos for claims that are easy to answer or are better known. This is also an interesting empirical question for future research.

Can instructions or warnings reduce truthiness?

In a world where social media giants like Facebook and Google are scrambling to develop algorithms to detect misleading photos and questionable news stories, are there person-level interventions that can help people protect themselves from falling victim to the biasing effects of photos? The truth effect literature suggests that the answer is yes. Indeed, giving people a warning about the truth status of claims reduces (although does not eliminate) people's susceptibility to repetition-based truth effect (Jalbert, Newman, & Schwarz, 2020; see also Nadarevic & Aßfalg, 2017). One possible mechanism for this reduction in the truth effect is that people examined claims with a more skeptical lens, overriding feelings of familiarity. Would such a mechanism also reduce the impact of non-probative photos? In recent work, Ly and Newman (2019) found that while a general warning about truth – "take your time and think critically before responding to each claim" – can increase accuracy in judging claims (i.e., ability to discriminate between true and false claims), it did not reduce the truthiness effect (bias to judge claims presented with photos as true). This pattern is compatible with research on misinformation, showing that general warnings typically do not fully eliminate the effects of misinformation (e.g., Butler, Zaromb, Lyle, & Roediger, 2009; Ecker, Lewandowsky, & Tang, 2010).

Explicitly alerting people to the fact that the photos only illustrate elements in the claim, and do not provide evidence for the associated claims, also does not eliminate truthiness, suggesting that photos have an insidious effect on people's assessments of truth (Newman, Garry, Feigenson, & Marsh, 2014). Indeed, in one study, after completing the commodity market prediction task, Newman et al. (2018) asked people how they thought the photos of commodities had influenced their judgments. A total of 62% of participants said that the photos helped them understand or imagine the claim, while another 28% said the photo did nothing or slowed them down. Only 10% said they thought the photo added credibility to the claim. Put simply, people had little insight into how photos shape their judgments (see Pronin, 2007 for a general review of failure to identify bias in judgment). The only instructional manipulation that has successfully eliminated truthiness was to tell people to ignore the photos (Newman et al., 2014). This "ignore" approach may work in an experimental setting but have limited application in natural settings where photos and images tend to capture attention and affect time spent on engaging with online material (e.g., Knobloch et al., 2003).

Truthiness and fake news

The photo-headline formula is a standard template for news – real or fake. At first glance these decorative photos seem to be innocuous, but the research reviewed here suggests they signal truth and can bias people to believe within just a few seconds. The size of the truthiness effect varies across studies and materials, but in a typical trivia claim experiment we recently estimated effect size to be Cohen's $d = .23$, 95% CI [.15, .30]. While participants in these studies were directed to assess truth, those who are scrolling through the news are not necessarily testing truth or on alert for false information. In fact, those who read news online spend on average only 2.5 minutes per visit to newspapers sites (Pew Research Center, 2019), and this time on news stories is further reduced when browsing news on mobile devices (Dunaway, Searles, Sui, & Paul, 2018). Relatively relaxed processing of news items, combined with disinformation campaigns where stories and headlines are designed to mislead, may mean that photos produce larger biases than we typically detect in laboratory settings. Indeed, recent research shows that when people are not alerted to the possibility of false claims, the illusory truth effect nearly doubles (Jalbert et al., 2020).

The ease of sharing information online may also make the influence of photos more widespread. Although it is difficult to estimate "truthiness in the wild" from lab experiments, recent evidence suggests the effects of non-probative photos hold when participants are tested in a simulated social media environment (Fenn, Ramsay, Kantner, Pezdek, & Abed, 2019). Compared to claims that appeared without photos, participants not only found both true and false information accompanied by photos more likely to be true, but also liked the information more and were more likely to share it on a simulated social media platform. Yet people have little insight into the influence of photos on their judgment (Newman et al., 2018; see Pronin, 2007 for a general review of failure to identify bias in judgment). In fact, individuals tend to believe that others are more vulnerable to fake news and media effects than themselves (Jang & Kim, 2018; Sun, Pan, & Shen, 2008). These findings are worrying, given that an estimated 68% of Americans report getting news from social media platforms (Matsa & Shearer, 2018), while many more are incidentally exposed to news when using such platforms.

Although the focus of this book is on fake news, a headline may not need to be intentionally deceptive in order for photos to promote false beliefs. For example, photos may promote false beliefs when paired with headlines that are designed to entertain. Indeed, sites like *The Onion* or *The Borowitz Report*, which publish satirical articles about fictional events, are often mistaken for real news (Garrett, Bond, & Poulsen, 2019). Although these articles are written in exaggerated language to highlight their satirical nature, they are almost always accompanied by decorative, and sometimes doctored photos, that relate to the fictional events. If people miss the satire, the decorative photos likely encourage false beliefs for stories that are entertainment, not facts. Moreover, some news headlines are exaggerated, although not entirely false, to catch readers' attention. Paired with a related photo, such headlines may seem real at first, but many readers do not click beyond the headline itself, missing nuances in the longer text (Gabielkov, Ramachandran, Chaintreau, & Legout, 2016). Given that photos can have lasting effects on belief (Fenn et al., 2013) as well as producing false memories (Cardwell et al., 2016; Strange, Garry, Brenstein, & Lindsay, 2011), mere exposure to such photo–headline combinations might create and make false beliefs stick.

Technological advancements and the future of fake news

With the advancement of technology making digital access and spread of information more convenient, detecting instances of fake news on different media platforms will be critical in addressing the potential for false beliefs. An estimated 64% of adult Americans report that fake news stories are causing them a great deal of confusion about current affairs, and nearly a quarter of Americans report having shared political misinformation online knowingly and unknowingly (Barthel, 2016). Since warnings tend to be more effective when given before than after exposure (Jalbert, Newman & Schwarz, 2020), developing algorithms to detect clickbaits and misinformation online prior to exposure is particularly important.

Reducing the media attention that often follows false headlines may also help to ward off false beliefs. Text analysis on social media reveals that misinformation tends to resurface multiple times after its initial publication, while facts do not (Shin, Jian, Driscoll, & Bar, 2018). This is particularly concerning given that repeated exposure to false information increases the familiarity of the fake news, making false details stick in memory over time (Bacon, 1979; Begg et al., 1992; Hasher et al., 1977; for a review see Dechêne et al., 2010). This holds true even when the intention of the repetition is to correct false details, such as the "myth versus fact" approach commonly used in campaigns that are intended to combat misinformation (e.g., Skurnik et al., 2005; Schwarz, Sanna, Skurnik, & Yoon, 2007; see also Schwarz & Jalbert, Chapter 5). To avoid ironically increasing the chance that false information is misremembered as being true once exposed, perhaps the misinformation is best left ignored. In the meantime, repeating correct information and its corresponding facts while decorating them with photos may help people remember the facts without promoting the myths. It is important to note that while photos can promote acceptance and sharing of misinformation, they can also promote facts (Fenn et al., 2019). Thus, in addition to current investigations of how photos may bias judgment, future work on truthiness should explore how non-probative photos can be used to correct bias and combat misinformation.

Summary

Deciding whether information is accurate or not pervades our everyday lives, whether that is considering a claim from social media, a claim in the news, or a claim in more high stakes contexts such as in the courtroom. Photos appear in each of these contexts, either as decorations or communication tools aimed to capture attention or illustrate a message. But these photos do more than decorate or illustrate – with only a short exposure, a seemingly innocuous, related photo can wield significant and consistent effects on judgment, biasing people toward believing and liking claims within just a few seconds. The truthiness effect adds to a larger literature on cognitive fluency and is yet another example of how the availability of conceptually relevant information can enhance processing, but bias judgment. While people may be confident in their ability to discern fact from fiction, truth from lies, and real from fake, the truthiness effect squares with broader research on eyewitness memory, lie detection and truth, showing that assessments of truth are fallible and vulnerable to biases we are often unaware of. But the future is not completely bleak. Just as photos bias people to believe false claims, they also make facts stick. The science of truthiness should therefore not stop at the understanding of how judgment can be biased by photos, but be used as a weapon to combat misinformation and promote facts in the post-truth era.

Notes

1 See full story: www.nytimes.com/2017/01/18/us/fake-news-hillary-clinton-cameron-harris.html
2 Newman and colleagues called this biasing effect of non-probative photos a *truthiness effect,* borrowing a word that US satirist Stephen Colbert coined for "truth that comes from the gut and not books". See www.colbertnation.com/the-colbert-report-videos/24039/october-17-2005/the-word-truthiness

References

Abed, E., Fenn, E., & Pezdek, K. (2017). Photographs elevate truth judgments about less well-known people (but not yourself). *Journal of Applied Research in Memory and Cognition, 6,* 203–209.

Alter, A. L., & Oppenheimer, D. M. (2009). Uniting the tribes of fluency to form a metacognitive nation. *Personality and Social Psychology Review, 13,* 219–235. doi: 10.1177/1088868309341564

Bacon, F. T. (1979). Credibility of repeated statements: Memory for trivia. *Journal of Experimental Psychology: Human Learning and Memory, 5,* 241–252. doi: 10.1037/0278-7393.5.3.241

Barthel, M. (2016, December 15). Many Americans believe fake news is sowing confusion. *Pew Research Center, Journalism and Media.* Retrieved from www.journalism.org/2016/12/15/many-americans-believe-fake-news-is-sowing-confusion/#fn-59275-1

Begg, I. M., Anas, A., & Farinacci, S. (1992). Dissociation of processes in belief: Source recollection, statement familiarity, and the illusion of truth. *Journal of Experimental Psychology: General, 121*(4), 446.

Berelson, B., & Steiner, G. A. (1964). *Human behavior: An inventory of scientific findings.* Oxford, UK: Harcourt, Brace & World.

Brashier, N. M., Umanath, S., Cabeza, R., & Marsh, E. J. (2017). Competing cues: Older adults rely on knowledge in the face of fluency. *Psychology and Aging, 32*(4), 331.

Brown, A. S., & Marsh, E. J. (2008). Evoking false beliefs about autobiographical experience. *Psychonomic Bulletin & Review, 15*(1), 186–190.

Butler, A. C., Zaromb, F. M., Lyle, K. B., & Roediger III, H. L. (2009). Using popular films to enhance classroom learning: The good, the bad, and the interesting. *Psychological Science, 20*(9), 1161–1168.

Cacioppo, J. T., & Petty, R. E. (1982). The need for cognition. *Journal of Personality and Social Psychology, 42*(1), 116.

Cardwell, B. A., Henkel, L. A., Garry, M., Newman, E. J., & Foster, J. L. (2016). Non-probative photos rapidly lead people to believe claims about their own (and other people's) pasts. *Memory & Cognition, 44,* 883–896.

Cardwell, B. A., Lindsay, D. S., Förster, K., & Garry, M. (2017). Uninformative photos can increase people's perceived knowledge of complicated processes. *Journal of Applied Research in Memory and Cognition, 6,* 244–252.

Cardwell, B. A., Newman, E. J., Garry, M., Mantonakis, A., & Beckett, R. (2017). Photos that increase feelings of learning promote positive evaluations. *Journal of Experimental Psychology: Learning, Memory, and Cognition, 43*(6), 944.

Carney, R. N., & Levin, J. R. (2002). Pictorial illustrations still improve students' learning from text. *Educational Psychology Review, 14,* 5–26.

Carr, T. H., McCauley, C., Sperber, R. D., & Parmelee, C. M. (1982). Words, pictures, and priming: On semantic activation, conscious identification, and the automaticity of information processing. *Journal of Experimental Psychology: Human Perception and Performance, 8*(6), 757–777.

Dechêne, A., Stahl, C., Hansen, J., & Wänke, M. (2010). The truth about the truth: A meta-analytic review of the truth effect. *Personality and Social Psychology Review, 14,* 238–257.

Derksen, D. G., Giroux, M. E., Newman, E. J., & Bernstein, D. (2019, June). *Truthiness bias from 3–60 years.* Poster presented at the bi-annual conference of the Society for Applied Research on Memory and Cognition. Cape Cod, MA.

Dunaway, J., Searles, K., Sui, M., & Paul, N. (2018). News attention in a mobile era. *Journal of Computer-Mediated Communication, 23*(2), 107–124.

Ecker, U. K., Lewandowsky, S., & Tang, D. T. (2010). Explicit warnings reduce but do not eliminate the continued influence of misinformation. *Memory & Cognition, 38*(8), 1087–1100.

Fazio, L. K., Brashier, N. M., Payne, B. K., & Marsh, E. J. (2015). Knowledge does not protect against illusory truth. *Journal of Experimental Psychology: General, 144,* 993–1002.

Fenn, E., Newman, E. J., Pezdek, K., & Garry, M. (2013). The effect of non-probative photographs on truthiness persists over time. *Acta Psychologica, 144*(1), 207–211.

Fenn, E., Ramsay, N., Kantner, J., Pezdek, K., & Abed, E. (2019). Nonprobative photos increase truth, like, and share judgments in a simulated social media environment. *Journal of Applied Research in Memory and Cognition, 8*(2), 131–138.

Feustel, T., Shiffrin, R., & Salasoo, A. (1983). Episodic and lexical contributions to the repetition effect in word recognition. *Journal of Experimental Psychology: General, 112,* 309–346.

Gabielkov, M., Ramachandran, A., Chaintreau, A., & Legout, A. (2016, June). Social clicks: What and who gets read on Twitter? In *Proceedings of the 2016 ACM SIGMETRICS international conference on measurement and modeling of computer science* (pp. 179–192).

Garrett, R. K., Bond, R., & Poulsen, S. (2019, August 16). Too many people think satirical news is real. *The Conversation.* Retrieved from https://theconversation.com/too-many-people-think-satirical-news-is-real-121666

Garry, M., & Gerrie, M. P. (2005). When photographs create false memories. *Current Directions in Psychological Science, 14*(6), 321–325.

Grice, H. P. (1975). Logic and conversation. In P. Cole & J. L. Morgan (Eds.), *Syntax and semantics, vol. 3: Speech acts* (pp. 41–58). New York: Academic Press.

Hansen, J., Dechêne, A., & Wänke, M. (2008). Discrepant fluency increases subjective truth. *Journal of Experimental Social Psychology, 44*(3), 687–691.

Hansen, J., & Wanke, M. (2010). Truth from language and truth from fit: The impact of linguistic concreteness and level of construal on subjective truth. *Personality and Social Psychology Bulletin, 36,* 1576–1588. doi: 10.1177/0146167210386238

Hasher, L., Goldstein, D., & Toppino, T. (1977). Frequency and the conference of referential validity. *Journal of Verbal Learning and Verbal Behavior, 16,* 107–112.

Henkel, L. A., & Mattson, M. E. (2011). Reading is believing: The truth effect and source credibility. *Consciousness and Cognition, 20*(4), 1705–1721.

Jacoby, L. L., Kelley, C. M., & Dywan, J. (1989). Memory attributions. In H. L. Roediger III & F. I. M. Craik (Eds.), *Varieties of memory and consciousness: Essays in honour of Endel Tulving* (pp. 391–422). Hillsdale, NJ: Erlbaum.

Jacoby, L. L., & Rhodes, M. G. (2006). False remembering in the aged. *Current Directions in Psychological Science, 15*(2), 49–53.

Jalbert, M., Newman, E. J., & Schwarz, N. (2019). *Only half of what I tell you is true: Expecting to encounter falsehoods reduces illusory truth.* Manuscript under review.

Jang, S. M., & Kim, J. K. (2018). Third person effects of fake news: Fake news regulation and media literacy interventions. *Computers in Human Behavior, 80,* 295–302.

Kelley, C. M., & Lindsay, D. S. (1993). Remembering mistaken for knowing: Ease of retrieval as a basis for confidence in answers to general knowledge questions. *Journal of Memory and Language, 32,* 1–24. doi: 10.1006/jmla.1993.1001

Kelly, J. D., & Nace, D. (1994). Knowing about digital imaging and believing news photographs. *Visual Communication Quarterly, 18*(1), 4–5.

Knobloch, S., Hastall, M., Zillmann, D., & Callison, C. (2003). Imagery effects on the selective reading of Internet newsmagazines. *Communication Research, 30* (1), 3–29.

Lindsay, D. S., Hagen, L., Read, J. D., Wade, K. A., & Garry, M. (2004). True photographs and false memories. *Psychological Science, 15,* 149–154.

Ly, D. P., & Newman, E. J. (2019, April). *Thinking more does not protect people from truthiness.* Poster presented at the Experimental Psychology Conference, Victoria University of Wellington, New Zealand.

Matsa, K. E., & Shearer, E. (2018). News use across social media platforms 2018. *Pew Research Center, Journalism and Media.* Retrieved from www.journalism.org/2018/09/10/news-use-across-social-media-platforms-2018/

Marsh, E., & Stanley, M. (2020). False beliefs: byproducts of an adaptive knowledge base? In R. Greifeneder, M. Jaffé, E. J. Newman, & N. Schwarz (Eds.), *The psychology of fake news: Accepting, sharing, and correcting misinformation* (pp. 202–225). London, UK: Routledge.

Nadarevic, L., & Aßfalg, A. (2017). Unveiling the truth: Warnings reduce the repetition-based truth effect. *Psychological Research, 81,* 814–826.

Newman, E. J., Azad, T., Lindsay, D. S., & Garry, M. (2018). Evidence that photos promote rosiness for claims about the future. *Memory & Cognition, 46*(8), 1223–1233.

Newman, E. J., Garry, M., Bernstein, D. M., Kantner, J., & Lindsay, D. S. (2012). Non-probative photos (or words) promote truthiness. *Psychonomic Bulletin & Review, 19,* 969–974. doi: 10.3758/s13423-012-0292-0

Newman, E. J., Garry, M., Feigenson, N., & Marsh, E. J. (2014, May). *To what extent can jury instructions protect people from truthiness?* Poster presented at the 26th Association for Psychological Science Annual Convention, San Francisco, CA.

Newman, E. J., Garry, M., Unkelbach, C., Bernstein, D. M., Lindsay, D. S., & Nash, R. A. (2015). Truthiness and falsiness of trivia claims depend on judgmental contexts. *Journal of Experimental Psychology: Learning, Memory, and Cognition, 41,* 1337–1348. doi: 10.1037/xlm0000099

Newman, E. J., Jalbert, M. C., Schwarz, N., & Ly, D. P. (2020). Truthiness, the illusory truth effect, and the role of need for cognition. *Consciousness and Cognition, 78,* 102866.

Nightingale, S. J., Wade, K. A., & Watson, D. G. (2017). Can people identify original and manipulated photos of real-world scenes? *Cognitive Research: Principles and Implications, 2*(1), 30.

Oppenheimer, D. M. (2006). Consequences of erudite vernacular utilized irrespective of necessity: Problems with using long words needlessly. *Applied Cognitive Psychology: The Official Journal of the Society for Applied Research in Memory and Cognition, 20*(2), 139–156.

Parks, C. M., & Toth, J. P. (2006). Fluency, familiarity, aging, and the illusion of truth. *Aging, Neuropsychology, and Cognition, 13*(2), 225–253.

Pennycook, G., Fugelsang, J. A., & Koehler, D. J. (2015). Everyday consequences of analytic thinking. *Current Directions in Psychological Science, 24*(6), 425–432.

Petty, R. E., & Cacioppo, J. T. (1986). The elaboration likelihood model of persuasion. In *Communication and persuasion* (pp. 1–24). New York, NY: Springer.

Pew Research Center. (2019, July 9). Newspapers fact sheet. *Pew Research Center, Journalism and Media.* Retrieved from www.journalism.org/fact-sheet/newspapers/

Politico Staff. (2017, November 1). The social media ads Russia wanted Americans to see. *Politico.* Retrieved from www.politico.com/story/2017/11/01/social-media-ads-russia-wanted-americans-to-see-244423

Priester, J. R., & Petty, R. E. (1995). Source attributions and persuasion: Perceived honesty as a determinant of message scrutiny. *Personality and Social Psychology Bulletin, 21*(6), 637–654.

Pronin, E. (2007). Perception and misperception of bias in human judgment. *Trends in Cognitive Sciences, 11*, 37–43.

Reber, R., Schwarz, N., & Winkielman, P. (2004). Processing fluency and aesthetic pleasure: Is beauty in the perceiver's processing experience? *Personality and Social Psychology Review, 8*(4), 364–382.

Reber, R., Winkielman, P., & Schwarz, N. (1998). Effects of perceptual fluency on affective judgments. *Psychological Science, 9*, 45–48.

Reinhard, M. A., & Sporer, S. L. (2008). Verbal and nonverbal behaviour as a basis for credibility attribution: The impact of task involvement and cognitive capacity. *Journal of Experimental Social Psychology, 44*(3), 477–488.

Schwarz, N. (1994). Judgment in a social context: Biases, shortcomings, and the logic of conversation. In M. Zanna (Ed.), *Advances in experimental social psychology* (Vol. 26, pp. 123–162). San Diego, CA: Academic Press.

Schwarz, N. (1996). *Cognition and communication: Judgmental biases, research methods, and the logic of conversation.* Hillsdale, NJ: Erlbaum.

Schwarz, N. (2015). Metacognition. In E. Borgida & J. A. Bargh (Eds.), *APA handbook of personality and social psychology: Attitudes and social cognition.* Washington, DC: APA.

Schwarz, N., & Jalbert, M. (2020). When (fake) news feels true: Intuitions of truth and the acceptance and correction of misinformation. In R. Greifeneder, M. Jaffé, E. J. Newman, & N. Schwarz (Eds.), *The psychology of fake news: Accepting, sharing, and correcting misinformation* (pp. 113–139). London, UK: Routledge.

Schwarz, N., & Newman, E. J. (2017). Psychological science agenda, August 2017. *Psychological Science.*

Schwarz, N., Sanna, L. J., Skurnik, I., & Yoon, C. (2007). Metacognitive experiences and the intricacies of setting people straight: Implications for debiasing and public information campaigns. *Advances in Experimental Social Psychology, 39*, 127–161.

Seamon, J. G., McKenna, P. A., & Binder, N. (1998). The mere exposure effect is differentially sensitive to different judgment tasks. *Consciousness and Cognition, 7*(1), 85–102.

Sherman, S. J., Cialdini, R. B., Schwartzman, D. F., & Reynolds, K. D. (1985). Imagining can heighten or lower the perceived likelihood of contracting a disease: The mediating effect of ease of imagery. *Personality and Social Psychology Bulletin, 11,* 118–127. doi: 10.1177/0146167285111011

Shin, J., Jian, L., Driscoll, K., & Bar, F. (2018). The diffusion of misinformation on social media: Temporal pattern, message, and source. *Computers in Human Behavior, 83,* 278–287.

Skurnik, I., Yoon, C., Park, D. C., & Schwarz, N. (2005). How warnings about false claims become recommendations. *Journal of Consumer Research, 31*(4), 713–724.

Strange, D., Garry, M., Bernstein, D. M., & Lindsay, D. S. (2011). Photographs cause false memories for the news. *Acta Psychologica, 136*(1), 90–94.

Sun, Y., Pan, Z., & Shen, L. (2008). Understanding the third-person perception: Evidence from a meta-analysis. *Journal of Communication, 58*(2), 280–300.

Szpunar, K. K., Addis, D. R., & Schacter, D. L. (2012). Memory for emotional simulations: Remembering a rosy future. *Psychological Science, 23*(1), 24–29.

Thapar, A., & Westerman, D. L. (2009). Aging and fluency based illusions of recognition memory. *Psychology and Aging, 24,* 595–603.

Topolinski, S., Likowski, K. U., Weyers, P., & Strack, F. (2009). The face of fluency: Semantic coherence automatically elicits a specific pattern of facial muscle reactions. *Cognition and Emotion, 23*(2), 260–271.

Tulving, E., & Schacter, D. L. (1990). Priming and human memory systems. *Science, 247,* 301–306.

Tversky, A. (1977). Features of similarity. *Psychological Review, 84,* 327–352.

Tversky, A., & Gati, I. (1978). Studies of similarity. In E. Rosch & B. Lloyd (Eds.), *Cognition and categorization* (pp. 79–98). Hillsdale, NJ: Erlbaum.

Tversky, A., & Kahneman, D. (1973). Availability: A heuristic for judging frequency and probability. *Cognitive Psychology, 5*(2), 207–232.

Umanath, S., & Marsh, E. J. (2014). Understanding how prior knowledge influences memory in older adults. *Perspectives on Psychological Science, 9*(4), 408–426.

Unkelbach, C. (2007). Reversing the truth effect: Learning the interpretation of processing fluency in judgments of truth. *Psychological Science, 20,* 135–138. doi: 10.1037/0278-7393.33.1.219

Unkelbach, C., & Greifeneder, R. (2018). Experiential fluency and declarative advice jointly inform judgments of truth. *Journal of Experimental Social Psychology, 79,* 78–86.

Waddill, P. J., & McDaniel, M. A. (1992). Pictorial enhancement of text memory: Limitations imposed by picture type and comprehension skill. *Memory & Cognition, 20*(5), 472–482.

Wänke, M., & Hansen, J. (2015). Relative processing fluency. *Current Directions in Psychological Science, 24*(3), 195–199.

Westerman, D. L. (2008). Relative fluency and illusions of recognition memory. *Psychonomic Bulletin & Review, 15*(6), 1196–1200.

Whittlesea, B. W. A. (1993). Illusions of familiarity. *Journal of Experimental Psychology: Learning, Memory, and Cognition, 19,* 1235–1253. doi: 10.1037/0278-7393.19.6.1235

Whittlesea, B. W., & Williams, L. D. (1998). Why do strangers feel familiar, but friends don't? A discrepancy-attribution account of feelings of familiarity. *Acta psychologica, 98*(2–3), 141–165.

Wilson, J. C., & Westerman, D. L. (2018). Picture (im) perfect: Illusions of recognition memory produced by photographs at test. *Memory & Cognition, 46*(7), 1210–1221.

Winkielman, P., & Cacioppo, J. T. (2001). Mind at ease puts a smile on the face: Psychophysiological evidence that processing facilitation elicits positive affect. *Journal of Personality and Social Psychology, 81*(6), 989.

Winkielman, P., Schwarz, N., Fazendeiro, T., & Reber, R. (2003). The hedonic marking of processing fluency: Implications for evaluative judgment. *The Psychology of Evaluation: Affective Processes in Cognition and Emotion, 189*, 217.

Zhang, L., Newman, E.J., & Schwarz, N. (2020). When photos backfire: Truthiness and falsiness effects in comparative judgements. *Manuscript under review.*

7

CAN THAT BE TRUE OR IS IT JUST FAKE NEWS?

New perspectives on the negativity bias in judgments of truth

Mariela E. Jaffé and Rainer Greifeneder

Introduction

Which of the two statements do you believe is true: (1) 80% of marriages last ten years or longer or (2) 20% of marriages are divorced within the first ten years? Which one of them is more likely to be fake news? As a reader, you may come to the conclusion that the authors must have made a mistake – both statements are content-wise identical and therefore can only both be true or false. Indeed, logically speaking, the statements are identical. Nevertheless, when individuals are asked to judge the statements' truthfulness, the estimates differ depending on whether they read the positively (1) or negatively (2) framed version of the same fact. In particular, research has shown that the negatively framed statement (2) that focuses on the divorce rate is more likely to be judged as true compared to the positively framed version (1) that focuses on marriage duration (Hilbig, 2009). This bias has been coined *negativity bias in truth judgments* (Hilbig, 2009, 2012a, 2012b) and describes the tendency that negatively framed compared to positively framed but content-wise identical statements are more likely to be judged as true. In this chapter, we deep dive into the bias's psychological mechanics and suggest that there is more to understand about this bias than previously assumed. We summarize current research on the bias and further analyze how and when the negativity bias does (not) influence and eventually bias individuals' judgments of truth. This summary sheds light on the malleability of truth judgments and provides information on how the communication format can make information sound very compelling while its content still is false or fake.

Truth or post-truth? A currently ongoing discussion

Telling the truth is crucial to our daily interactions. If we ask somebody a question, we generally assume that the person will reply with information that he or she believes is true. This belief is a pragmatic necessity for the successful functioning of human communication: when engaging in interpersonal interactions individuals are expected and expect from their counterparts that they follow the so-called cooperative principle (Grice, 1975). This cooperative principle asks individuals to "make your conversational contribution such as it is required, at the stage at which it occurs, by the accepted purpose or direction of the talk exchange in which you are engaged" (Grice, 1975, p. 45). This cooperative principle is the summary of sub-principles, of which one is the maxim of quality. The maxim of quality states that one should not say what one believes to be false and one should also not say something for which one lacks adequate evidence. In sum, one should speak the truth and therefore the counterpart can expect to be told the truth.

Although truthfulness appears to be fundamental for human interactions, *post-truth* has been elected as word of the year 2016, "relating or denoting circumstances in which objective facts are less influential in shaping public opinion than appeals to emotion and personal beliefs" (Oxford Dictionary, 2016). The Oxford Dictionary argued that the frequency of usage spiked in the context of the 2016 EU referendum in the United Kingdom and the 2016 presidential election in the United States and has therefore been associated with the particular noun of post-truth politics. It reflects the general assumption that we are entering a time "in which the specified concept [of truth] has become unimportant or irrelevant", especially in the context of politics (Oxford Dictionary, 2016). *The Independent* author Matthew Norman agrees and notes "the truth has become so devalued that what was once the gold standard of political debate is now a worthless currency" (Norman, 2016) – and instead so called *alternative facts* are presented by candidates and politicians alike.

In a world of post-truth politics, alternative facts, and uncertainty, telling what is true or false has arguably become more difficult than before. *The Guardian* suggested that countering fake news with "fact checkers" as weapons of choice is crucial, and that journalism has to get better at spreading facts to show people what is actually happening (Jackson, 2017). However, to be able to convince individuals of the truthfulness of these facts and successfully warn them about fake news, one first needs to better understand how individuals decide whether they believe something is true or false. In this chapter, we focus on one particular aspect of this question, the *negativity bias in judgments of truth*.

How do individuals judge truth?

Grice (1975) assumed that individuals start from the premise that others are telling the truth (see also Marsh & Stanley, this volume). Consistent with this basic tenet, individuals overestimate others' truthfulness, which is known as the truth bias (Burgoon, Blair, & Strom, 2008; Reinhard, Greifeneder, & Scharmach, 2013) and has been amply documented in a variety of contexts (e.g., Anolli, Balconi, & Ciceri, 2003; Buller, Burgoon, White, & Ebescu, 1994; Vrij & Mann, 2001).

If individuals, however, are not willing to start from the basic premise of truthfulness, they may resort to strategies to decide whether some piece of information is true or false. Dunwoody (2009), for example, summarized that the principles of *coherence* and *correspondence* (C&C; Hammond, 1996, 2007) can be used as criteria to assess the truth-value of a statement, belief, or judgment. The *correspondence theory of truth* argues that a belief can be said to be true if it corresponds with the facts (Dunwoody, 2009, p. 117). As an example, to test correspondence, the accuracy of a weather forecast may be checked by comparing it to reality (Hammond, 1996, p. 95). For instance, if rain was predicted and it rained, the prediction was true, if not, it was false. However, this rather philosophical approach to truth was criticized by pragmatists and idealists in the nineteenth century (Dunwoody, 2009), as the notion of a *fact* was objected. This critic strengthened an alternative approach, the *coherence theory of truth*, in which truth is assessed via consistency of beliefs (Hammond, 1996). To test coherence or also rationality, one could check whether the arguments that lead to a certain conclusion meet the test of logical or mathematical consistency (Hammond, 1996, p. 95). Although coherence alone does not guarantees truth (Dunwoody, 2009), both C&C theories of truth are informative about how individuals might come to a judgment regarding the truthfulness of a statement – they test whether the statement corresponds with facts that they know and/or if it is coherent to their beliefs.

The C&C approach can be translated to distinct processes with which individuals judge a statement's truth. Reder (1982), for example, argues that individuals can verify a statement by either directly finding a close match to the query in memory (which may be perceived as being parallel to the correspondence principle), or by judging the plausibility of the statement (which may be perceived as being in parallel to the coherence principle). Reder (1982) furthermore argues that in everyday life it is unlikely that all facts or even the majority of facts on which people are queried are directly stored in memory, which render plausibility judgments the more frequent case.

But how do individuals derive and judge the plausibility of a message or piece of information? Especially when statements are ambiguous and when individuals do not have a lot of knowledge or strong beliefs (Dechêne, Stahl, Hansen, & Wanke, 2010)? At least three sources of information may be relied upon to gauge plausibility: *cues about the statement's source* (e.g., the source's level of expertise on the subject matter), *attributes of the context* in which it is presented (e.g., at a scientific conference), and *attributes of the statement itself* to judge its veracity (see Dechêne et al., 2010).

Especially the attributes of the statements itself could impact the statements' plausibility directly and, by making them seem logically sound, also increase the associated coherence of the information. Attributes of the statement itself could include repetition (see, e.g., Stanley, Yang, & Marsh, 2019) but also recognition, familiarity, processing experiences or fluency (e.g., Reber & Schwarz, 1999; for a review, see Reber & Greifeneder, 2017), and mental references (Unkelbach & Koch, 2019; Unkelbach & Rom, 2017).

In this chapter, we focus on one attribute of the statement itself, namely the statement's conceptual frame, as detailed next. Consistent with Hilbig (2009) we here define conceptual frame as denoting something positive or negative. In research on the negativity bias, a statement's positive or negative frame is manipulated by describing something positive or negative (Hilbig, 2009). To illustrate, when talking about the status of marriages, one can focus on (1) the percentage of marriages that last ten years or longer or (2) the percentage of marriages that are divorced within the first ten years. Research on the negativity bias in truth judgments generally observed that individuals use the framing of the statement itself as a cue to gauge truthfulness (Hilbig, 2009, 2012b, 2012a). Ceteris paribus, individuals perceive the negatively framed information (2) more likely true than the positively framed information (1).

The negativity bias in truth judgments

The negativity bias in truth judgments (Hilbig, 2009) is consistent with the broadly observable principle that negative instances tend to be more influential than comparably positive ones (Baumeister, Bratslavsky, Finkenauer, & Vohs, 2001). This general bad-is-stronger-than-good principle applies to everyday events, major life events (e.g., trauma), close relationship outcomes, social network patterns, interpersonal interactions, and learning processes. Presumably this general principle arises due to the potentially detrimental impact of negative (compared to positive) information and events on the organisms' survival. Moreover, the self seems to be more motivated to avoid bad self-definitions than to pursue good ones, and therefore bad information is considered to be more salient and diagnostic, and is processed more thoroughly compared to good information (Baumeister et al., 2001).

The general negativity bias also pertains more specifically to judgments of truth: messages that are formally equivalent are deemed more true when framed negatively compared to positively (Hilbig, 2009). Different accounts can be recruited to explain this bias. For instance, negative instances attract more attention (Pratto & John, 1991) and are perceived as more informative (Peeters & Czapinski, 1990), as negative instances are more rare and more threatening (Dijksterhuis & Aarts, 2003; Lewicka, Czapinski, & Peeters, 1992; Peeters & Czapinski, 1990). Due to higher diagnosticity and salience, negative (bad) information is processed more thoroughly than positive (good) information (Baumeister et al., 2001). More thorough, deeper, or repeated processing can then increase the messages' persuasiveness (Petty & Brinol, 2008; Shiv, Britton, & Payne, 2004).

In regards to judgments of truth, Hilbig (2012a) argues that a negative frame might not only lead to more thorough processing, but instead to a stimulation of more attention or activation, which, in turn, allows for easier retrieval of relevant knowledge or generation of evidence. More specifically, the negative frame results in a more fluent retrieval or generation of relevant information, which suggests more fluent processing, and an associated higher subjective veracity

(Hilbig, 2012a, p. 39). As described by Schwarz and Jalbert (this volume), the processing experience of fluency can be used as an alternative basis to evaluate the truthfulness of information. More specifically, when evaluating plausibility or coherence, individuals may rely on fluency to answer questions such as "Is it compatible with other things I believe?" or "Is it internally consistent?" (see Schwarz & Jalbert, this volume).

Refining the perspective on the negativity bias

Previous research (Hilbig, 2012b) described the negativity bias as a general response bias. Using a multinomial processing tree model, Hilbig (2012b) found support that a bias in responses, and not differences in knowledge, accounts for the framing effect. Given insufficient knowledge, individuals are more likely to guess "true" when faced with a negatively framed compared to positively framed (identical) statistical statement.

This chapter offers an extended perspective on the negativity bias in judgments of truth. In our own work, we have investigated potential moderating circumstances of the occurrence of a negativity bias in judgments of truth. In a first study, we developed eight correct statements about women in German-speaking countries. The statements related to topics of health, well-being, and social security. Participants read either a negatively framed or positively framed version of the statements and subsequently judged each statements' truthfulness. To our surprise, and inconsistent with prior evidence reported by Hilbig (2009), a first analysis yielded a positivity bias; that is, statements framed positively were more likely to be judged as true compared to negatively framed statements (Jaffé & Greifeneder, 2019). Against the background of this evidence, it appears that there is more to understand about the negativity bias than previously thought. This chapter summarizes findings on three groups of potential moderating variables: individuals' expectations, the source of negativity, and psychological distance toward the statements' content. Furthermore, this chapter discusses other potentially influencing variables on individuals' biases in judgments of truth.

Potential moderators of the negativity bias in judgments of truth

Expectations

The preceding review has highlighted that individuals use different strategies to evaluate a statements' truthfulness, for example, its plausibility (Dunwoody, 2009; Reder, 1982). Previous negativity bias research indicates that negative information might appear more plausible (see, e.g., Hilbig, 2009). However, although valence of the frame is the key variable in negativity bias research, it is not the only possible cue that individuals may rely on when gauging plausibility and truthfulness. Furthermore, interactions between framing and other cues are conceivable. For instance, Koch and Peter (2017) investigate the occurrence of a negativity bias in the context of political communication and argue that negativity is associated with news, and positivity with persuasion attempts. In particular, individuals might have learned that politicians sharing negative information are sharing news, which increases perceptions of truthfulness. In contrast, a politician sharing positive information may raise suspicion that he or she just wants to persuade the recipient, therefore triggering reactance and doubt, resulting in decreased perceptions of the message's truthfulness. These findings suggest that other communication cues – here communication context – may interact with frame, and thus may moderate negativity bias findings. In the case made by Koch and Peter (2017), the context should strengthen the generally observed negativity bias, as the negative compared to positive framing is even more likely to be perceived as true.

Koch and Peter (2017) suggest that context channels expectations about what is more plausible. In extending this general notion of expectations, we argue that it matters whether the message itself meets or clashes with an individual's expectations. To illustrate, learning that 80% versus 40% of marriages last at least ten years is a very different piece of information, although the framing of the sentence is identical. The percentage numbers that are presented in the statements may directly influence the plausibility and credibility of a statement. Individuals might ask themselves if the number is coherent with their experiences or knowledge, that is, if the number is in a range in which they would expect it to be. Implausible information may seem fishy and therefore lead to assumptions of deception (Bond et al., 1992). On a more fine-grained level, research on the Expectancy Violation Theory (Burgoon & Jones, 1976) further suggests that the direction of expectancy violation may be crucial: a positive violation (information is better than expected) leads to a less negative judgment compared to a negative violation (information is worse than expected).

Jaffé and Greifeneder (2019) systematically tested the effect of individuals' expectations in regard to the percentage numbers and found throughout four studies that individuals' expectations moderate the negativity bias. Using a new set of items, the initial studies in this line failed to replicate the negativity bias. As an example, an original and negatively framed statement read "61% of German-speaking women are dissatisfied with their looks" whereas the positively framed version read "39% of German-speaking women are satisfied with their looks". Participants were more likely to judge the positively framed version as true compared to the negatively framed version. The authors then exploratorily investigated individuals' expectations in regards to the stated content. Participants' mean expectations differed markedly from the true values presented in the initial study. In regards to the exemplary statement, participants believed that only 54% of women would be dissatisfied with their looks (negative frame) and 45% were satisfied with their looks (positive frame). More importantly, when looking at all eight statements, a systematic pattern emerged as a function of over-/underestimation and truth judgments when comparing data across studies: a negativity bias in judgments of truth was more likely to occur when the likelihood of an aspect was overestimated in the negatively framed version and underestimated in the positively framed version. Building on this insight, we systematically adjusted the numbers in negatively framed statements to be lower than expected in a subsequent study. The new statements then read, for example, "41% of German-speaking women are dissatisfied with their looks" (negatively framed) or "59% of German-speaking women are satisfied with their looks" (positively framed). With this change in place, a negativity bias could be created for the same set of items where a positivity bias was observed in the initial study. In a next step, we systematically decreased and increased numbers in both framing conditions, showing statements framed negatively and positively with numbers higher or lower than expected. This setup allowed to investigate the impact of under- versus overestimating in the context of framing. While expectations had no consistent effects for positive frames, overestimation (compared to underestimation) led to a higher likelihood of perceived truth in the negative framing condition.

These results indicate that expectations with regard to the stated content play a crucial role in the occurrence of the negativity bias. Using the same set of statements, a negativity and a positivity bias could be found, depending on how the numbers presented deviated from individuals' expectations. Presumably this is because learning that actual numbers are lower than expected for something negative is good news, and therefore individuals have a tendency to believe it to be true. In turn, learning that the actual numbers are higher than expected for something negative is bad news, which may trigger a preference for this statement to be false. This tendency matches the general definition of a self-serving bias as a "cognitive or perceptual process that is distorted by the need to maintain and enhance self-esteem" (Forsyth, 2008, p. 429). Although such optimistic perspectives on the outside world reflect a bias, believing in good news and discarding bad news might be a helpful tendency, as optimistic tendencies might promote better health and well-being (Taylor & Brown, 1988).

Implications of the impact of expectations

If expectations impact the outcome of judgments of truth, those interested in disseminating fake news and post-truth politics may take advantage. In the worst case, a false statement is communicated in a way that mocks credibility by systematically underbidding individuals' expectations in regards to negative concerns. As a result, individuals may be well advised to pay special attention to the statement's details and how they relate to their own expectations. Am I surprised that the numbers are so high or low? Have the numbers eventually been chosen to exceed or fall below expectations? How does reading such a statement make me feel? Questions like these might be asked to activate a mindful handling of ambivalent information: somebody might try to make the statement feel good and therefore true.

Sources of negativity

It is noteworthy that the negativity bias has been investigated with framing statements either negatively or positively. What does framing negatively or framing positively exactly mean? The working definition is to describe something in positive versus negative ways, without changing content. To illustrate, one of Hilbig's original statements (2012b) reads: "In Africa, 40% of people make less than 1 Dollar per day" (negatively framed) and "In Africa, 60% of people make more than 1 Dollar per day" (p. 46). However, another exemplary statement reads: "20% of German under-17-year-olds are smokers" (negatively framed) and "80% of German under-17-year-olds are *non*-smokers" (positively framed, emphasis added). This illustrates that there are different ways to build a negative versus positive frame: on the one hand, one can focus on *concept valence* and present a negative (earning only very little money) versus positive concept (earning a little more money). On the other hand, one can focus on semantic negation. By negating a positive concept a negative frame can be derived, and by negating a negative concept, a positive frame can be built (see Jaffé & Greifeneder, 2019).

Previous research that is cited in the context of the negativity bias in judgments of truth is often related to the concept valence of information (e.g., Baumeister et al., 2001). Negation, however, is not discussed as often, but, as we described earlier, also allows to build a negative or positive frame. Furthermore, the arguments why negative information could have a stronger impact might also pertain to negation, as research indicates that actively encoding negated statements demands controlled processing (Deutsch, Kordts-Freudinger, Gawronski, & Strack, 2009). Just as when focusing on the negative frame, negation could also lead to more thorough processing that could, in turn, increase perceptions of plausibility.

To allow for a better understanding of framing effects, it is critical to disentangle the potential drivers of the framing: concept valence of a statement (negative versus positive) and whether the statement is semantically negated or not. That is, both forms of negativity need to be separately manipulated in order to understand what drives the effect of the negativity bias. To this end, Jaffé and Greifeneder (2020a) conducted a set of studies in which they systematically varied valence and negation (see Table 7.1 for an exemplary item).

TABLE 7.1 Exemplary item with an orthogonal variation of concept valence and negation

| | | Concept valence | |
		Positive	Negative
Negation	Present	30% of adults in Germany are not free from allergies.	70% of adults in Germany do not suffer from allergies.
	Absent	70% of adults in Germany are free from allergies.	30% of adults in Germany suffer from allergies.

The authors find that negation contributes to the negativity bias, meaning that negated statements are generally more likely to be judged as true. Why does negation play such an important role? One might speculate that the integration of a negation into a sentence could also signal expertise and preciseness of the communicator. If a negation is used, the communicator must possess a certain level of knowledge about the topic – how else could they be so specific in their phrasing?

In addition to the increase in specificity, a negation could also increase the realm of possible states. Looking back at the example provided in Table 7.1, there might be many ways in which something is not the case ("not suffering from allergies", e.g., by not having an allergy at all, by not noticing one's allergy, or by not actually suffering from it), but usually only one way in which something *is* the case ("suffering from allergies", i.e., having and suffering from an allergy). If there are indeed more ways how something is not the case than how something is the case, relying on these base rate differences when judging truth might be a very reasonable thing to do, especially when not having any specific knowledge. Furthermore, if participants have no previous knowledge and simply judge the plausibility by trying to imagine potential scenarios, it might be easier to imagine scenarios that pertain to the negated version but more difficult to imagine scenarios for the not-negated version, as it allows for less variety.

Other work in this volume also refers to the impact of negation (see chapter by Marsh & Stanley, this volume). The authors describe recent findings that individuals are better at correcting false beliefs when they initially believed in a negated claim, and then received a not-negated claim (compared to first learning a not-negated piece of information, which should then be corrected by learning a negated claim). One could speculate that individuals are cognitively more likely to replace a negated claim with a simpler and more specific positive claim than the other way around.

Implications of the impact of negation

So far, the data from Jaffé and Greifeneder (2020a) indicate that negation is another important piece of the puzzle on how individuals proceed when forming judgments of truth. Again, negation could be used in a manipulative manner when communicating fake news and post-truth information. A false statement could contain a negation to appear more credible and to systematically lead individuals to judge the information as true. In a protective fashion, again, individuals could carefully investigate whether the negation to them appears plausible. Why is a certain piece of information presented in a negated way? What if individuals simply reframe the item without the negation? Does it sound different?

Psychological distance

A third likely candidate for moderating the occurrence of a negativity bias in judgments of truth is the mindset of individuals, as it influences how individuals integrate and weigh veracity cues. Here we focus on individuals' construal level (Liberman & Trope, 2008; Trope & Liberman, 2003, 2010), as one theory on mindsets that has been related to how individuals encode, process, and integrate information. Construal Level Theory (CLT; Liberman & Trope, 2008) assumes that individuals can think about objects or events on a continuum from concreteness to abstractness. When thinking about a forest in detail, individuals might picture the colors of stems, of branches, of different leaves and therefore have a very concrete representation of the concept forest. The other extreme would be thinking of a forest in absolute abstract patterns, such as a green recreational location in the countryside. One can easily see that depending on where on this continuum individuals construe, very different pieces of information about a forest are considered. On a concrete mindset level (or also low construal level), individuals include a high number of specific details, but also subordinate information. On a more abstract mindset level (or high construal level) instead, individuals include less details but more abstract and central components of the object or event, considered as superordinate information. Construal Level Theory assumes that individuals construe on a lower level if objects and events are psychologically close (in time, space, socially, or in probability of occurrence), whereas individuals construe on a higher level if objects and events are psychologically distant.

Construal Level Theory makes specific assumptions about the weighing of positive and negative information (Trope & Liberman, 2010). The authors assume that arguments in favor are superordinate to arguments against something, as the subjective importance of cons depends on whether or not pros are present more than the reverse (Eyal, Liberman, Trope, & Walther, 2004; Herzog, Hansen, & Wänke, 2007). Common examples are medical treatments. To illustrate: if a medical treatment seems beneficial (has pros), only then would one consider and discuss the potential negative side effects (cons). If, however, no benefits are apparent (no pros), potential side effects seem irrelevant and will not be discussed. Equating pros with positive information and cons with negative information, Construal Level Theory allows for the prediction that when individuals construe on a higher level, positive compared to negative information is processed more thoroughly and therefore is deemed more true. This notion receives support from several angles. For instance, it has been shown that the mental salience of positive and societal outcomes of an action increases as social distance increases, and the framing of persuasive messages in terms of gains compared to losses becomes more powerful when participants make judgments for socially distant versus proximal entities (Nan, 2007). Individuals also seem to judge both negative and positive emotional experiences as more pleasant when construing abstractly, as abstractness increases the positivity of these experiences (Williams, Stein, & Galguera, 2014). Presumably, while individuals are concerned with negative and preventional outcomes in the here-and-now (such as disappointing oneself when failing an exam), with increasing psychological distance (two weeks before the exam) individuals also focus on positive and promotional outcomes (such as getting a high score; Pennington & Roese, 2003). Summing up, positive aspects are more strongly weighed in conditions of abstractness or psychological distance, whereas more negative concerns come into play when construing more concretely and decreasing distance.

Against this background, we (Jaffé & Greifeneder, 2020b) hypothesized that the negativity bias in judgments of truth is particularly pronounced in conditions of psychological proximity and when individuals construe concretely, but not as strong in conditions of psychological distance and when individuals construe abstractly. We investigated this hypothesis in a first set of studies, using negatively and positively framed statements pertaining to places spatially close to the participants versus far away, therefore manipulating psychological distance via spatial distance. The results of these first studies provide preliminary support for the attenuation or reversal of the negativity bias with increased psychological distance. However, this first set of studies awaits further testing and replication, as for example other distance dimensions may be investigated. Furthermore, it appears interesting to investigate idiosyncratic differences in psychological distance. Depending on the content of the statement, perceptions of relevance and importance might be changed, and a highly relevant topic might per se feel psychologically closer than another one that individuals do not care about.

Implications of the impact of psychological distance

Individuals might benefit from learning that psychological distance impacts the weighing of information. To free themselves from this impact, individuals could attempt to vary the distance toward the statement by themselves. How would they feel about the statement if it was related to a faraway place instead of their hometown? Or if it concerned sometime in the past and not now? Applying this procedure could aid individuals to overcome their own negativity bias in judgments of truth, as by increasing psychological distance, negative instances may be weighted less strongly and might be less likely to increase perceived plausibility and credibility.

The mechanisms underlying negativity bias in judgments of truth

The current overview indicates that there is more to tell about the negativity bias in judgments of truth. The original research (Hilbig, 2009, 2012b) has shown that negatively framed versus positively framed statements are more likely to be judged as true. This chapter argues that a negative frame alone might not always be a sufficient condition for an increase in plausibility and expected truthfulness. Other aspects such as individuals' expectations, the semantics of the statements, and individuals' mindset at least moderate the impact of the valence of the frame on judgments of truth.

Investigating potential moderators of the negativity bias appears commendable, as it allows a deeper understanding of the underlying processes. Several explanations for the general negative-is-stronger-than-good have been discussed in the literature, such as that negative instances are perceived as more informative (Peeters & Czapinski, 1990), that negative instances stand a higher chance of being cognitively elaborated (Lewicka, 1997; Peeters & Czapinski, 1990), and that negative instances are detected more reliably, because they are more rare and more threatening (Dijksterhuis & Aarts, 2003). Other research also taps into this notion, showing that positive information is more alike than negative information (Alves, Koch, & Unkelbach, 2017; Koch, Alves, Krueger, & Unkelbach, 2016). Positive information is therefore more redundant, whereas negative information is more distinct, and individuals therefore benefit from taking it into account (Alves et al., 2017). Last but not least, negative framing and truth might be perceived to be associated, because other individuals are less likely to lie to us when bringing bad news (Hilbig, 2009; see also Koch & Peter, 2017 for a perspective on politicians' communication). All of these suggested underlying processes are defined by a strong cognitive perspective. This is consistent with previous research that individuals with good numeracy skills are less susceptible to framing effects (Peters, 2012), which might indicate that cognitive capacity is especially relevant when investigating biases in truth judgments. However, the research by Jaffé and Greifeneder (2019) about expectations suggests that motivational mechanisms may be important, too, and have been neglected so far in the array of possible of underlying processes. To recapitulate, the authors observed that negative facts that are less frequent (and therefore eventually also less negative) than expected are more likely judged true. Perhaps this is because individuals misattribute the relief of a better-than-expected world to truth or that they simply wish that good things are true.

Future directions

Given that the mere phrasing of information, be it valence, negation, or distance, impacts individuals' judgments of truth, implications of research on the negativity bias are likely far reaching and important for all types of communication, be it spoken or written. Implications pertain, for instance, to detecting deception in interpersonal interactions (Bond et al., 1992), judging the truthfulness of messages sent by politicians (Koch & Peter, 2017), or survey responding in day-to-day polls or longitudinal representative surveys. Further research may fruitfully investigate how framing information impacts individuals' judgments across a multitude of different contexts. In our work, we often focus on domains in which we believe there is a shared consensus about what is positive (e.g., health) and what is negative (e.g., illness). However, looking at a variety of contexts could allow for investigations on how idiosyncratic beliefs and opinions might interact with framing effects in judgments of truth. Furthermore, research could also investigate how effects might not only change depending on the context, but also how effects might change when statements increase or decrease in relevance. As an example, when comparing a statement that informs individuals about a personal risk (versus a risk that impacts their opponents), attributes of the statement might be processed differently.

Furthermore, future research may also investigate potential differences between information shared offline versus through online channels. Looking at the incredible speed of information sharing that is characteristic for communication over the internet in general, or social media platforms more specifically, it is important to understand differential processing of information (see Baumeister et al., 2001) and its impact on subsequent judgments of truth. One could speculate that individuals are more inclined to deeply process a newspaper article that they read after breakfast on a Sunday morning, compared to a news snippet in their Facebook online feed. This difference could then moderate potential framing biases. If, for example, negation is indeed an indicator for the expertise of the communicator, as we speculated, it may have a more powerful impact in conditions of low processing intensity, such as the Facebook online feed (cf. the Elaboration Likelihood Model of Persuasion, Petty & Cacioppo, 1986).

Technological progress has made it easier to spread information, but it has also become easier to fact check information. However, given the sheer amount of shared information, the likelihood of engaging in fact checking might be lower. This opens the door widely for effects of framing, negation, or expectations as documented here.

We have argued throughout this chapter that further knowledge about the negativity bias may help those who wish to disseminate fake news, and those who wish to protect themselves or others against unwanted manipulation. In a battle for truth (or falsehood), knowledge about the power of phrasing is likely important for all players.

Conclusion: new perspectives on the negativity bias in judgments of truth

In this chapter, we discussed the negativity bias in judgments of truth. We highlighted why, in post-truth times, it is important to better understand how individuals come to make their judgments of truth. Deep-diving into the concept of the negativity bias, we offered insights into potential moderators of the negativity bias that impact individuals' tendency to believe a certain statement to be true. We conclude that, especially for those who intend to debias, it is important to gain insight ino the malleability of truth judgments and to understand how slight adjustments in the framing or content of information impact evaluations.

References

Alves, H., Koch, A., & Unkelbach, C. (2017). Why good is more alike than bad: Processing implications. *Trends in Cognitive Sciences*, *21*, 69–79. https://doi.org/10.1016/j.tics.2016.12.006

Anolli, L., Balconi, M., & Ciceri, R. (2003). Linguistic styles in deceptive communication: Dubitative ambiguity and elliptic eluding in packaged lies. *Social Behavior and Personality: An International Journal, 31*, 687–710. https://doi.org/10.2224/sbp. 2003.31.7.687

Baumeister, R. F., Bratslavsky, E., Finkenauer, C., & Vohs, K. D. (2001). Bad is stronger than good. *Review of General Psychology, 5*, 323–370. https://doi.org/10.1037// 1089-2680.5.4.323

Bond, C. F., Jr., Omar, A., Pitre, U., Lashley, B. R., Skaggs, L. M., & Kirk, C. T. (1992). Fishy-looking liars: Deception judgment from expectancy violation. *Journal of Personality and Social Psychology, 63*, 969–977. http://dx.doi.org/10.1037//0022-3514. 63.6.969

Buller, D. B., Burgoon, J. K., White, C. H., & Ebescu, A. S. (1994). Interpersonal deception VII behavioral profiles of falsification, equivocation, and concealment. *Journal of Language and Social Psychology, 13*, 366–395. https://doi.org/10.1177/0261927X94134002

Burgoon, J. K., Blair, J. P., & Strom, R. E. (2008). Cognitive biases and nonverbal cue availability in detecting deception. *Human Communication Research, 34*, 572–599. https://doi.org/10.1111/j.1468-2958.2008.00333.x

Burgoon, J. K., & Jones, S. B. (1976). Toward a theory of personal space expectations and their violations. *Human Communication Research, 2*, 131–146. https://doi. org/10.1111/j.1468-2958.1976.tb00706.x

Dechêne, A., Stahl, C., Hansen, J., & Wanke, M. (2010). The truth about the truth: A meta-analytic review of the truth effect. *Personality and Social Psychology Review, 14*, 238–257. https://doi.org/10.1177/1088868309352251

Deutsch, R., Kordts-Freudinger, R., Gawronski, B., & Strack, F. (2009). Fast and fragile: A new look at the automaticity of negation processing. *Experimental Psychology, 56*, 434–446. https://doi.org/10.1027/1618-3169.56.6.434

Dijksterhuis, A., & Aarts, H. (2003). On wildebeests and humans: The preferential detection of negative stimuli. *Psychological Science, 14*, 14–18. https://doi.org/10.1111/1467-9280.t01-1-01412

Dunwoody, P. T. (2009). Theories of truth as assessment criteria in judgment and decision making. *Judgement and Decision Making, 4*, 116–125.

Eyal, T., Liberman, N., Trope, Y., & Walther, E. (2004). The pros and cons of temporally near and distant action. *Journal of Personality and Social Psychology, 86*, 781–795. https://doi.org/10.1037/0022-3514.86.6.781

Forsyth, D. R. (2008). Self-serving bias. In W. A. Darity (Ed.), *International encyclopedia of the social sciences* (2nd ed., Vol. 7, p. 429). Retrieved from http://scholarship.richmond. edu/jepson-faculty-publications

Grice, H.-P. (1975). Logic and conversation. In P. Cole & J. L. Morgan (Eds.), *Syntax and semantics 3: Speech arts* (pp. 41–58). New York: Academic Press.

Hammond, K. R. (1996). *Human judgment and social policy*. New York: Oxford University Press.

Hammond, K. R. (2007). *Beyond rationality*. Oxford: Oxford University Press.

Herzog, S. M., Hansen, J., & Wänke, M. (2007). Temporal distance and ease of retrieval. *Journal of Experimental Social Psychology, 43*, 483–488. https://doi.org/10.1016/j.jesp. 2006.05.008

Hilbig, B. E. (2009). Sad, thus true: Negativity bias in judgments of truth. *Journal of Experimental Social Psychology, 45*, 983–986. https://doi.org/10.1016/j.jesp.2009.04.012

Hilbig, B. E. (2012a). Good things don't come easy (to mind): Explaining framing effects in judgments of truth. *Experimental Psychology, 59*, 38–46. https://doi.org/ 10.1027/1618-3169/a000124

Hilbig, B. E. (2012b). How framing statistical statements affects subjective veracity: Validation and application of a multinomial model for judgments of truth. *Cognition, 125*, 37–48. https://doi.org/10.1016/j.cognition.2012.06.009

Jackson, J. (2017). Fact-checkers are weapons in the post-truth wars, but they're not all on one side. *The Guardian.* Retrieved from www.theguardian.com/media/2017/feb/15/fact-checkers-are-weapons-in-the-post-truth-wars-but-theyre-not-all-on-one-side

Jaffé, M. E., & Greifeneder, R. (2019). Less than I expected and oh so true? On the interplay between expectations and framing effects in judgments of truth. *Journal of Language and Social Psychology*, 1–21. https://doi.org/10.1177/0261927X19869392

Jaffé, M. E., & Greifeneder, R. (2020a). Negative or negated, thus true? An investigation of concept valence and semantic negation as drivers of framing effects in judgments of truth. *Manuscript in Preparation.*

Jaffé, M. E., & Greifeneder, R. (2020b). Negative is true here and now, but not so much there and then: On the impact of psychological distance on the negativity bias. *Manuscript in Preparation.*

Koch, A., Alves, H., Krueger, T., & Unkelbach, C. (2016). A general valence asymmetry in similarity: Good is more alike than bad. *Journal of Experimental Psychology: Learning, Memory, and Cognition, 42*, 1171–1192. https://doi.org/10.1037/xlm0000243

Koch, T., & Peter, C. (2017). Effects of equivalence framing on the perceived truth of political messages and the trustworthiness of politicians. *Public Opinion Quarterly, 81*, 847–865. https://doi.org/10.1093/poq/nfx019

Lewicka, M. (1997). Is hate wiser than love? Cognitive and emotional utilities in decision making. In R. Ranyard, W. R. Crozier, & O. Svenson (Eds.), *Decision making: Cognitive models and explanations.* London, UK: Routledge.

Lewicka, M., Czapinski, J., & Peeters, G. (1992). Positive-negative asymmetry or "when the heart needs a reason". *European Journal of Social Psychology, 22*, 425–434. https://doi.org/10.1002/ejsp.2420220502

Liberman, N., & Trope, Y. (2008). The psychology of transcending the here and now. *Science, 322*, 1201–1205. https://doi.org/10.1126/science.1161958

Marsh, E. J., & Stanley, M. L. (n.d.). False beliefs: Byproducts of an adaptive knowledge base? In R. Greifeneder, M. E. Jaffé, E. J. Newman, & N. Schwarz (Eds.), *The psychology of fake news: Accepting, sharing, and correcting misinformation* (pp. 131–146). Abingdon, UK: Routledge.

Nan, X. (2007). Social distance, framing, and judgment: A construal level perspective. *Human Communication Research, 33*, 489–514. https://doi.org/10.1111/j.1468-2958.2007.00309.x

Norman, M. (2016, November 8). Whoever wins the US presidential election, we've entered a post-truth world: There's no going back now. *The Independent.* Retrieved from www.independent.co.uk/voices/us-election-2016-donald-trump-hillary-clinton-who-wins-post-truth-world-no-going-back-a7404826.html

Oxford Dictionary. (2016). Oxford Dictionary Word of the Year 2016.

Peeters, G., & Czapinski, J. (1990). Positive-negative asymmetry in evaluations: The distinction between affective and informational negativity effects. *European Review of Social Psychology, 1*, 33–60. https://doi.org/10.1080/14792779108401856

Pennington, G. L., & Roese, N. J. (2003). Regulatory focus and temporal distance. *Journal of Experimental Social Psychology, 39*, 563–576. https://doi.org/10.1016/S0022-1031(03)00058-1

Peters, E. (2012). Beyond comprehension: The role of numeracy in judgments and decisions. *Current Directions in Psychological Science, 21*, 31–35. https://doi.org/10.1177/0963721411429960

Petty, R. E., & Brinol, P. (2008). Persuasion: From single to multiple to metacognitive processes. *Perspectives on Psychological Science, 3,* 137–147.

Petty, R. E., & Cacioppo, J. T. (1986). The elaboration likelihood model of persuasion. In L. Berkowitz (Ed.), *Advances in exprimental social psychology* (Vol. 19, pp. 123–205). https://doi.org/10.1016/S0065-2601(08)60214-2

Pratto, F., & John, O. P. (1991). Automatic vigilance: The attention-grabbing power of negative social information. *Journal of Personality and Social Psychology, 61,* 380–391. https://doi.org/10.1037/0022-3514.61.3.380

Reber, R., & Greifeneder, R. (2017). Processing fluency in education: How metacognitive feelings shape learning, belief formation, and affect. *Educational Psychologist, 52,* 84–103. https://doi.org/10.1080/00461520.2016.1258173

Reber, R., & Schwarz, N. (1999). Effects of perceptual fluency on judgments of truth. *Consciousness and Cognition, 8,* 338–342. https://doi.org/ccog.1999.0386

Reder, L. M. (1982). Plausibility judgments versus fact retrieval: Alternative strategies for sentence verification. *Psychological Review, 89,* 250–280. https://doi.org/10.1037//0033-295X.89.3.250

Reinhard, M.-A., Greifeneder, R., & Scharmach, M. (2013). Unconscious processes improve lie detection. *Journal of Personality and Social Psychology, 105,* 721–739. https://doi.org/10.1037/a0034352

Schwarz, N., & Jalbert, M. (n.d.). When news feels true: Intuitions of truth and the acceptance and correction of misinformation. In R. Greifeneder, M. E. Jaffé, E. J. Newman, & N. Schwarz (Eds.), *The psychology of fake news: Accepting, sharing, and correcting misinformation* (pp. 73–89). Abingdon, UK: Routledge.

Shiv, B., Britton, J. A. E., & Payne, J. W. (2004). Does elaboration increase or decrease the effectiveness of negatively versus positively framed messages? *Journal of Consumer Research, 31,* 199–208. https://doi.org/10.1086/383435

Stanley, M. L., Yang, B. W., & Marsh, E. J. (2019). When the unlikely becomes likely: Qualifying language does not influence later truth judgments. *Journal of Applied Research in Memory and Cognition, 8,* 118–129. https://doi.org/10.1016/j.jarmac.2018.08.004

Taylor, S. E., & Brown, J. D. (1988). Illusion and well-being: A social psychological perspective on mental health. *Psychological Bulletin, 103,* 193–210. https://doi.org/10.1037/0033-2909.103.2.193

Trope, Y., & Liberman, N. (2003). Temporal construal. *Psychological Review, 110,* 403–421. https://doi.org/10.1037/0033-295X.110.3.403

Trope, Y., & Liberman, N. (2010). Construal-level theory of psychological distance. *Psychological Review, 117,* 440–463. https://doi.org/10.1037/a0018963

Unkelbach, C., & Koch, A. (2019). Gullible but functional? Information repetitions and the formation of beliefs. In J. P. Forgas & R. F. Baumeister (Eds.), *The social psychology of gullibility: Conspiracy theories, fake news and irrational beliefs* (pp. 42–60). Abingdon-on-Thames: Routledge.

Unkelbach, C., & Rom, S. C. (2017). A referential theory of the repetition-induced truth effect. *Cognition, 160,* 110–126. https://doi.org/10.1016/j.cognition.2016.12.016

Vrij, A., & Mann, S. (2001). Who killed my relative? Police officers' ability to detect real-life high-stake lies. *Psychology, Crime & Law, 7,* 119–132. https://doi.org/10.1080/10683160108401791

Williams, L. E., Stein, R., & Galguera, L. (2014). The distinct affective consequences of psychological distance and construal level. *Journal of Consumer Research, 40,* 1123–1138. https://doi.org/10.1086/674212

8

FALSE BELIEFS

Byproducts of an adaptive knowledge base?

Elizabeth J. Marsh and Matthew L. Stanley

Pizzagate. The Bowling Green Massacre. Pope Francis endorsing Donald Trump for president. Such "fake news" stories often go viral, hijacking typical cues for credibility while spinning fictions about familiar people and places. It is almost impossible to completely eliminate exposure to factually incorrect information (misinformation), especially as such stories rarely (if ever) really disappear, living on through the internet (Shin, Jian, Driscoll, & Bar, 2018). Although some stories were never meant to be believed at face value (e.g., satires from *The Onion*), others are concerning because they serve as highly effective propaganda tools (e.g., the stories attributed to Russian Bots on Twitter and Facebook). Oftentimes, they play on emotions and motivations by scaring viewers with, for example, images of immigrants crossing the southern border or false information about the future implementation of bureaucratic "death panels" with the power to terminate an individual's medical care.

But this "hot cognition" occurs within a system tuned to learn, maintain, and update knowledge and beliefs about the world. The likelihood that we come to believe fake news stories (and our ability to correct false beliefs) is dependent upon everyday cognitive processes underlying knowledge and belief, and not upon unique, special processes or strategies (Isberner & Richter, 2014; Marsh, Cantor, & Brashier, 2016; Rapp & Donovan, 2017; Rapp & Salovich, 2018). In this chapter, we begin by briefly describing the knowledge base, defining its contents and comparing it to other forms of memory. We then describe five properties of the knowledge base that often make it efficient and powerful – but which sometimes yield false beliefs, with implications for why people sometimes believe fake news stories. In the last section of the chapter, we summarize potentially valuable strategies for combatting the problem of fake news.

The knowledge base

Humans know a lot, and this knowledge can take many forms, from discrete facts (e.g., knowing the capital of Peru) to scripts (abstractions of past experience, such as a script for navigating airport security) to understanding complex systems (e.g., how the economy works, and how changing interest rates will have downstream implications for other parts of the system). It is accumulated over a lifetime, sometimes formally (in school, through deliberate instruction) and other times informally (through trial-and-error, exposure to media, interpersonal interactions, etc.).

In psychological science, knowledge is often defined by what it is not: It is *not* thinking back to a specific event that occurred at a particular time and place in the past. The distinction between knowledge and retrieving specific events (episodic memory) is perhaps best captured with examples. An individual might know what a prom is, for example, but might recollect a specific episode that involves receiving a pink corsage for her own senior prom. An individual might know the steps involved in taking a typical airplane flight, or that individual might think back to a particularly bumpy flight from Columbus to St. Louis. An individual might know who Abraham Lincoln is, without remembering having learned about him in a specific lesson in a particular classroom.

We suggest that combatting errors in the knowledge system (false beliefs, illusions of knowledge, misconceptions) may require different strategies than the ones that are sometimes recommended to combat false memories of specific events. Correcting someone's false beliefs about the purported link between vaccines and autism, for example, differs from helping a person remember a specific event accurately and completely. Some of the current suggestions for combatting fake news are based on the large literature on how people misremember specific events from their pasts (e.g., strategies for thinking about the particular person, or source, who presented the information at a particular time and place, and whether that person is trustworthy or has adequate expertise; Lewandowsky, Ecker, & Cook, 2017; Rapp & Salovich, 2018). These strategies might work in some contexts, but we suggest that a different set of strategies might be better suited for correcting false beliefs instilled by fake news.[1]

Consider the so-called "birtherism" movement in which many people came to falsely believe that Barack Obama was born *outside* of the United States. Of course, it is possible that people have false memories about a specific event in which they heard the claim that Barack Obama was (or was not) born outside of the United States. However, we suggest that whether people can accurately and completely recollect the event in which they were exposed to this claim matters less than whether they currently hold the belief that the statement "Barack Obama was born outside of the United States" is true. It is the false belief that needs to be corrected, not one's memory of when one heard it. This suggests that we should look to the literature on belief correction rather than to the literature aimed at helping people to accurately remember specific past events.

In short, in this chapter we briefly describe several properties of the knowledge base that have implications for processing fake news, before turning to implications for combatting the problem.

Principle #1

We are biased to believe information is true. All else being equal, upon initially encountering information, people are biased to assume that it is true rather than false. Gilbert (1991) argues that this bias is cognitively efficient, and it means we only need to tag information when it is false (and otherwise we can assume it is true). This bias allegedly reflects a disposition to believe in a generally truthful world, where any given piece of information is more likely to be true than false. But in this model, tagging a piece of information as false is effortful and requires a second step of unbelieving, setting up a problem if the process of unbelieving is disrupted.

Multiple studies support this prediction, namely that interrupted falsehoods are later remembered as true (e.g., Gilbert, Tafarodi, & Malone, 1993). In one study (Gilbert, Krull, & Malone, 1990), participants simulated learning a foreign language in an immersion setting that required them to routinely guess the meanings of words before receiving feedback. Participants read a series of Hopi-English translations, each of which was immediately followed by a true or false label; critically, a subset of trials were interrupted with a tone that required participants to press a key. Later, participants took a true/false test. As predicted, interrupted false trials were often later misremembered as true, consistent with the idea that the tone interfered with the additional, effortful process of "unbelieving" the false translations.

A second example from Gilbert and colleagues (1990) involved participants viewing videos and judging whether smiles were real or fake. After seeing each face, participants were explicitly told whether the smile was real or fake. On some of the trials, cognitive load was induced by requiring participants to respond as quickly as possible to a tone or to identify which of two tones was higher or lower in pitch. During the subsequent test phase, participants were more likely to make errors and claim that individuals in the videos had expressed real smiles if the real/fake label had been paired with the secondary task. As with the Hopi-English translations, the explanation was that increased cognitive load resulted in the effortful unbelieving stage being bypassed. Consequently, judgments on the test reflected only the initial belief-assenting stage (see also, Mandelbaum, 2014).

If Gilbert and colleagues are correct, then people might generally be biased to believe in headlines like "Clint Eastwood Refuses to Accept Presidential Medal of Freedom from Obama, Says He Is Not My President" with unbelieving only occurring after a second, effortful step.[2] The implication is that that people who are distracted or otherwise busy will be less likely to "unbelieve" false information. Lending credence to Gilbert and colleagues' view, people who are being "cognitively lazy" (i.e., fail to engage more reflective, effortful reasoning processes when encountering new information) are more likely to believe in the veracity of relatively implausible fake news headlines, whereas those who tend to engage more reflective, effortful reasoning processes are less likely to believe in those same implausible fake news headlines (Bronstein, Pennycook, Bear, Rand, & Cannon, 2019; Pennycook & Rand, 2019). That is, people who gave the obvious but incorrect answer to questions such as "How many cubic feet of dirt are there in a hole that is three feet deep by three feet wide by three feet long?" were also more likely to accept the fake news headlines (note: there is no dirt in a hole). Relatedly, those individuals who are more likely to engage reflective, effortful reasoning processes when encountering new information are more likely to reject conspiracy theories than those who fail to engage those same processes (Swami, Voracek, Stieger, Tran, & Furnham, 2014).

One caveat to Principle #1 must be made: This effect occurs when people are forced to choose between truth and falseness. When remaining uncertain is an option, the effect disappears (Street & Richardson, 2015; see also, Street & Kingstone, 2017). In other words, Principle #1 describes a heuristic that is used in a specific situation. When a true/false judgment must be made, the heuristic holds because people assume that most people tell the truth most of the time (DePaulo, Kashy, Kirkendol, Wyer, & Epstein, 1996).

Principle #2: we use shortcuts to judge truth

More generally, people use heuristics to judge the truth of incoming information, judging easy-to-process information as more likely to be true than harder-to-process information. That is, statements that are easy to process (to read, to hear, to understand) are more likely to be judged as true relative to claims that are harder to process. Consequently, statements written in an easy-to-read font are more likely to be judged as true than those written in more difficult-to-read fonts (Reber & Schwarz, 1999). Relatedly, rhyming aphorisms (*woes unite foes*) are judged as more likely to be true than ones that do not rhyme ("fools live poor to die rich"; McGlone, & Tofighbakhsh, 2000).

Repetition is perhaps the easiest way to make some statements feel easier to process that others, as a statement will be read more easily (more quickly) the second time it is seen. Experimentally, this is typically demonstrated by having participants read a series of trivia statements in the first phase and then make truth ratings about a larger set of statements in the second phase (commonly one-half old and one-half new). Repeated statements are judged as more likely to be true than new statements, a finding called the *illusory truth effect*. Originally demonstrated in the 1970s (Hasher, Goldstein, & Toppino, 1977), this effect has been replicated many times, is robust across procedural variations and materials, and can last for many weeks (see Dechêne, Stahl, Hansen, & Wänke, 2010, for a meta-analysis).

The illusory truth effect is not merely a laboratory phenomenon nor is it restricted to obscure trivia statements: The effect has been obtained for fake news headlines that were actually seen on Facebook (Pennycook, Cannon, & Rand, 2018). Pennycook and colleagues (2018) showed that just a single, brief exposure to a fake news headline (e.g., 'Donald Trump Sent His Own Plane to Transport 200 Stranded Marines') increased the likelihood that people believed the headline was true. This boost in the perceived accuracy of the fake news headlines persisted after a week-long delay, and additional exposures further increased belief in the veracity of the headlines. Surprisingly, these same effects were obtained even when the participants were told that the articles were disputed by an independent group of fact checkers. This finding suggests that labelling information as false or disputed (as is done by third-party fact-checking organizations like PolitiFact and Snopes) may not be using the most effective means for combatting fake news and misinformation, a point we return to later in this chapter.

Principle #3: we interpret incoming information

Fake news stories are interesting because they are typically about real people and places, like Hillary Rodham Clinton and Russia; they are rarely about people or places we have never heard of before. The familiar actors and places mean we draw on our prior knowledge when processing fake news stories, making them easy to understand and to elaborate upon. Furthermore, we have a script for news stories – a set of expectations about what kinds of information they will typically contain: who, what, when, where, why, and a little human interest. We have some idea about what to expect when reading this type of story.

Because our default goal is normally to extract meaning and to fit new information into our existing schemas and belief structures, we do not store information verbatim, and we seldom remember the exact wording of conversations or form of other communications. For example, the sentence "the karate expert *hit* the block" is misremembered as "the karate expert *broke* the block" (Brewer, 1977). A similar effect occurs in the visual domain; people falsely remember having seen causal actions (e.g., a foot hitting a ball) that were only implied by the surrounding video footage (Strickland & Keil, 2011).

Furthermore, we are wired to go beyond what is given, to make inferences, and to fill in the gaps. In other words, the system is cognitively efficient, leveraging the past to prepare for the future. We learn things that are not explicitly stated. For example, young children do not need to be explicitly told that "dolphins communicate by squeaking" after learning that "dolphins travel in pods" and that "pods communicate by squeaking" (Bauer & San Souci, 2010). We transfer our knowledge to new situations and to new instances. For example, identifying the artist of a painting we are seeing for the first time, based on our past experiences with that artist's work (Kornell & Bjork, 2008).

Our ability to interpret allows us to handle imperfect inputs, so long as they are "close enough". Speech is notoriously disfluent – we stutter, speak ungrammatically, and use ambiguous referents. Accordingly, the system is designed to handle imperfect inputs, allowing a certain amount of "deviation" in messaging (Ferreira, Bailey, & Ferraro, 2002). A word is recognized in many different fonts, accents, contexts – such flexibility is advantageous as we encounter new variations of stored information. On the other hand, a flexible system has the side effect of missing inaccuracies that are "close enough". For example, people often fail to detect incorrect presuppositions in questions, even when warned to do so. Many people will attempt to provide a numerical answer to the question "How many animals of each kind did Moses take on the ark?" even when warned about this type of trick, and later demonstrate knowledge that the reference should be to Noah, not to Moses (the 'Moses Illusion'; Bottoms, Eslick, & Marsh, 2010; Erickson & Mattson, 1981).

Many different strategies have been implemented in efforts to reduce or eliminate the "Moses Illusion" and related phenomena. Ironically, however, many of these implemented strategies backfire, making people even more likely to remember or rely upon the misinformation. For example, Eslick, Fazio, and Marsh (2011) attempted to draw participants' attention to false information in claims by highlighting it in red font. But this only made participants more likely to repeat those errors on a later test. One strategy that does seem to reduce the influence of misinformation, however, is to encourage individuals to play the role of a professional fact checker when reading new information (Rapp, Hinze, Kohlhepp, & Ryskin, 2014; Brashier, Eliseev, & Marsh, 2020). Doing so makes people more likely to identify misinformation and less likely to rely on that misinformation later on.

Principle #4: knowledge feels different

The phenomenology of retrieving knowledge is very different from what one experiences when retrieving a personal memory (which will involve mentally traveling back in time and place to a specific event). Knowledge "pops to mind", and is labeled as "known" rather than "remembered" (Tulving, 1972). When retrieving the fact that George Washington was the first president of the United States, for example, most people do not think back to a specific instance of learning that information; instead, they simply know it. Of course, there can be exceptions, where one remembers the circumstances of learning information (e.g., Conway, Gardiner, Perfect, Anderson, & Cohen, 1997), but in most cases the things we know are relatively decontextualized from original learning. While people are less likely to be persuaded by sources perceived as untrustworthy (Guillory & Geraci, 2013; Mills & Jellison, 1967; Priester & Petty, 1995), the source of information is typically forgotten over even relatively brief periods of time (e.g., Underwood & Pezdek, 1998) and as one encounters information in multiple different contexts (Watkins & Kerkar, 1985).

At the moment, a popular suggestion for dealing with fake news involves training people to better evaluate and remember sources of information (Rapp &

Salovich, 2018; Swire & Ecker, 2018). This advice is based on the large literature on how people misremember the past, which can often be traced to problems in *source monitoring* (Johnson, Hashtroudi, & Lindsay, 1993): a presupposition embedded in a question is misattributed to experience; a statement in a narrative is misattributed to a video; or a photo provides details that are incorporated into one's memory. The natural solution is to focus people's attention on the origin of their memories, either at the time of learning (e.g., discounting information from a low credibility source) or specifically discriminating sources at test (Lindsay & Johnson, 1989). This approach is endorsed by professional organizations such as IFLA (the International Federation of Library Associations and Institutions), which has issued a number of recommendations for spotting fake news, including researching the quality of the hosting website and the credibility of the author.

But source monitoring is unlikely to solve the problem that fake news poses (Marsh & Yang, 2017). Aside from the fact that people do not always agree about whether a source is credible (e.g., Fox News is more credible to some than others), source credibility is often inferred from cues that can potentially mislead, such as the number of citations included (Putnam & Phelps, 2017) or the ease with which a message is read (Fragale & Heath, 2004). In fact, ease of processing information is typically more likely to influence truth judgments than is the source of the information: Statements that are initially labeled as false or obtained from an unreliable source are nevertheless more likely to be judged as true relative to novel statements (Begg & Armour, 1991; Begg, Anas, & Farinacci, 1992; Stanley, Yang, & Marsh, 2019).

Even if sources are correctly evaluated and that information is stored in memory, it is likely to have no impact on later judgments, as our bias toward cognitive efficiency means that our default is to use information without spontaneously thinking about where it came from (reflecting the fact that much of what we know is decontextualized, Tulving, 1972). The result is that people may be able to identify statements as having come from a reliable or unreliable source (two weeks after exposure, if explicitly prompted), and yet fail to apply that knowledge when asked to judge the truth of the statements (Henkel & Mattson, 2011).

Furthermore, because information often is associated with multiple sources, remembering that something came from a low credibility source does not necessarily mean it should be ignored (Marsh, Meade, & Roediger, 2003). That is, it is possible that Donald Trump made the same claim as Nancy Pelosi, and thus, the low credibility source is ignored given the memory of (or misattribution to) the higher credibility source. Third, a major problem is that source information simply isn't well remembered over time. This is the problem captured in the classic "sleeper effect" – a low credibility source is not persuasive initially, but over time the message has more impact as the source information is forgotten (e.g., Underwood & Pezdek, 1998).

Principle #5: we do not always retrieve and/or apply what we know

People often think of knowledge as something that is always used if stored in memory, but knowing something does not guarantee that it will come to mind, or be applied, when needed. The most common example of this phenomena is the tip-of-the-tongue state (TOT state; see Brown, 1991). Most commonly encountered when trying to remember specific terms or names, a TOT state involves the frustrating feeling that what we know is "just out of reach". When in a TOT state, one is hyper-aware of the problem; however, at other times the remember may not be aware that they are having a retrieval failure. More generally, information that has not been used recently is less likely to be spontaneously retrieved (Cantor, Eslick, Marsh, Bjork, & Bjork, 2015).

We already gave one example of the general principle that knowledge isn't always utilized, noting how our system accepts inputs that are "close enough" even when we know better (e.g., failing to notice the error in the question "How many animals of each kind did Moses take on the ark?"). This problem occurs even with well-learned information. Cantor and Marsh (2017) created biology (e.g., "Water contains two atoms of Helium and how many atoms of oxygen?") and history questions with incorrect presuppositions ("The British congress imposed fees on the colonies' sugar, tea, and stamps that were called what?") and posed them to PhD students in biology and history. All participants were warned not to answer questions with incorrect presuppositions, as illustrated in an example. These disciplinary experts performed slightly better in their thesis domain, but they still missed about 30% of the incorrect presuppositions in questions that targeted their field of graduate study (Cantor & Marsh, 2017).

A second example involves the illusory truth effect; the assumption in the literature has been that this fluency heuristic comes into play in the face of ignorance, when someone does not know better. But recent evidence suggests that this is not always the case. For example, exposure to blatantly false facts (e.g., "The short-pleated skirt worn by Scotsmen is the sari") increases the likelihood they are later judged true, as compared to new statements. This effect occurs regardless of whether knowledge is estimated based on norms of general knowledge or measured in a given individual (Fazio, Brashier, Payne, & Marsh, 2015). It is not clear how far one can push these effects; initial results suggested a boundary condition, with no illusory truth effect for implausible statements like "The earth is a perfect square" (Pennycook et al., 2018) – but more recent work suggests this finding is due to a floor effect in belief, rather than the nature of the items themselves (Fazio, Rand, & Pennycook, under review).

A third example involves reliance on information clearly labeled as false. In our own studies (Stanley et al., 2019), participants studied qualified statements (e.g., "It is *unlikely* that that the body of a rotten tree is called a daddock" or "It is *impossible* that the study of snakes is called ophiology"). In the critical experiment, all qualifiers were negative, meaning that every single statement

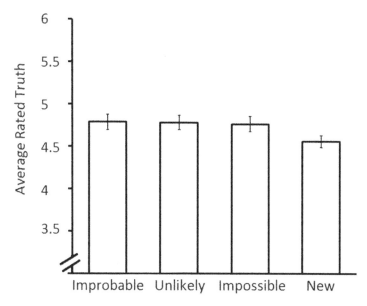

FIGURE 8.1 Average truth rating for statements previously qualified as improbable, unlikely, or impossible, as compared to new statements

was qualified as being impossible, improbable, or unlikely. Two days later, participants rated the truth of those statements without the qualifiers, as well as new statements. Previously qualified statements were rated as more likely to be true than new statements (see Figure 8.1), even though every single one of the original qualifiers cast doubt on the veracity of the statements. When prompted, the majority of subjects correctly identified the qualifiers presented in the first part of the experiment; they knew that the statements were part of a set that was very unlikely to be true, and yet exposure in that set increased the likelihood of calling a negatively qualified statement "true".

Implications for the fake news problem

Thus far, we have focused on the processing of fake news stories, emphasizing that we are not optimistic about interventions that focus solely on source credibility. While it is appealing to offload the problem to third parties (e.g., to fact checkers like PolitiFact or Snopes) or to algorithms that diagnose content and warn if sources are low credibility, such solutions will likely be incomplete ones. To the extent that such labels prevent people from reading any of the content, they may help; however, once information is processed, a source-based strategy is not likely to help, especially as time passes.

Instead, we focus on the aftermath of fake news, and the problem of correcting the misinformation conveyed by fake news stories. One issue is the distribution of corrections – it cannot be assumed that people see them and process them. On twitter, at least, the distribution of corrections is quite discouraging. Shin and colleagues analyzed over 400,000 tweets about 57 different political rumors, and reached the following conclusion: "Overall, there were few tweets rejecting any rumor in our dataset, be it true or false" (Shin, Jian, Driscoll, & Bar, 2017, p. 1222). They found that less than 4% of tweets rejected rumors, as opposed to endorsing them. And to the extent that fact checks are shared, they are likely to be ones that confirm one's own opinion. An examination of Twitter shares in 2012 showed that people were more likely to share fact-checks (e.g., from the Washington Post's Fact Checker) that matched their political affiliations. That is, Democrats were responsible for sharing fact-checks that favored Obama, whereas fact-checks favoring Romney were more likely to be shared by Republicans (Shin & Thorson, 2017). Finally, we note that even if people encounter the corrections, they may not be successful. Newspaper retractions, for example, do not always stick; some Americans continued to hold false beliefs about the existence of weapons of mass destruction in Iraq, even though they also remembered reading retractions of those claims (Lewandowsky, Stritzke, Oberauer, & Morales, 2005).

One question is whether debunking fake news is as difficult as debunking serious misconceptions (e.g., about the vaccine-autism link). Misconceptions such as the vaccine-autism link are notoriously difficult to correct (Lewandowsky, Ecker, Seifert, Schwarz, & Cook, 2012), with corrections often losing their effectiveness over time and sometimes even backfiring and increasing belief (Nyhan & Reifler, 2010; cf. Wood & Porter, 2019). It is an open question whether fake news stories are in this category. In one experimental study, for example, the researchers examined belief in statements such as "Anthony Scaramucci subject of Senate Russian Investigation" and "President Obama fakes birth certificate" and then corrected them (Porter, Wood, & Kirby, 2018). Corrections were quite successful – although it is not clear how much participants believed the stories in the first place (participants who never received the corrections were described as 'credulous' of the original headlines). Furthermore, long-term effects were not examined, and it is quite possible that corrections would lose their efficacy as time passed (Butler, Fazio, & Marsh, 2011).

We believe the prudent path is to follow the insights generated from the larger literature and assume that debunking is not as easy as it might seem initially. Lewandowsky and colleagues (2012) have outlined a number of principles to follow when debunking; we briefly review those before turning to some additional recommendations based on our own work. The clearest advice is to avoid repeating the fake news claim when debunking it (Lewandowsky et al., 2012). That is, every message that says "Pizzagate is false" is increasing the fluency of the word "Pizzagate", which is problematic since increasing the fluency of a concept can increase the likelihood of entire statements being labeled as true.

Other recommendations include using simple language that is easy to read and also to add photographs. Photographs are interesting as people show a bias to consider statements paired with photos as truer than statements presented alone (Newman, Garry, Bernstein, Kantner, & Lindsay, 2012). That is, showing a picture of a turtle paired with the claim "turtles are deaf" increases belief in the veracity of that statement, as opposed to simply reading the statement "turtles are deaf" (perhaps because the photos help readers to generate evidence to support the claim; Newman et al., 2015). It is interesting to note that the Pennycook and colleagues' finding of an illusory truth effect for fake news paired photos with the fake headlines, because that is the way such headlines typically appear on social media.

In our own recent work, we have identified an asymmetry in the likelihood that corrections induce reliable belief revision. False beliefs are more likely to be corrected when the correction involves instilling a new positive belief, compared to rescinding an existing belief (see also, Lewandowsky et al., 2012). More specifically, people are better at correcting false beliefs when they initially believe in a negated claim like "A poem written for a bride is *not* an epithalamium" but then receive the correction that "A poem for a bride is an epithalamium". In contrast, false beliefs are more difficult to correct when the initial, false belief is an affirmation (e.g., "Michelangelo's statue of David is located in Venice") and the correction takes the form of a negation (e.g., "Michelangelo's statue of David is *not* located in Venice"). This general strategy of changing beliefs by instilling new beliefs (affirmations) instead of rescinding existing beliefs (negations) may be a particularly promising strategy for combatting fake news and misinformation. In fact, Horne and colleagues (2015) were able to successfully change some individuals' false beliefs and intentions about vaccinations by providing individuals with information about the dangers of diseases like measles and mumps (i.e., instilling a new, affirmative belief about disease risk) rather than just stating that there is no link between vaccines and autism (i.e., belief negation).

Conclusions and future directions

Humans are capable of learning an impressive amount of information and can retain much of it over very long retention intervals. In this chapter, we have described how this system has properties that facilitate the acquisition of new information and allow inferences and transfer to new situations. For example, the system is flexible, both in terms of inputs (accommodating noise) and outputs (going beyond encountered information to generate new insights). The system is cognitively efficient, with shortcuts that reflect the state of the world (e.g., bias to assume truth, using fluency as a heuristic to judge truth). Finally, the representations tend to be decontextualized (sourceless, retrieved without a sense of reliving) in a way that facilitates their usage across contexts and applications.

But as described here, the properties that make the system powerful also facilitate the learning of misinformation from fake news. Upon encountering a fake news source, people may or may not recognize the source as low credibility. Once reading commences, people are often biased to believe incoming information is true; in fact, they may have to believe it to comprehend it (and take a second step to unbelieve it). Readers of fake news will draw on a wealth of prior knowledge when processing the article, likely generating inferences that go beyond the stated text. And people may repeatedly encounter the same claims, increasing their fluency and, thus, the likelihood that they believe the claims are true.

These issues are particularly problematic today, which some have dubbed the "post-truth" era (Lewandowsky, Ecker, & Cook, 2017) due to the sheer amount of misinformation being circulated widely and quickly through social media platforms. These social media platforms can foster the creation of cliques, or "echo chambers" comprised of people who come to hold the same (often false) beliefs and who collectively seek out and share information that reinforces their shared beliefs (i.e., "echo chambers"). Such echo chambers have been identified on Twitter (Barberá, Jost, Nagler, Tucker, & Bonneau, 2015; Williams, McMurray, Kurz, & Lambert, 2015), Facebook (Del Vicario, et al., 2016), and various blogs (Suhay, Blackwell, Roche, & Bruggeman, 2015). Members may not realize they are receiving information from low-credibility sources; they are biased to believe that information from other community members is true. And when the same claims and information are repeated without correction, belief in those claims is likely to increase, and potentially spawn new misinformation as people make inferences that go beyond what has already been provided, thereby generating even more misinformation.

It is likely impossible to stop the spread of and belief in fake news; instead, we are forced to develop viable strategies for correcting this misinformation. Such efforts should not focus on the source of the original misinformation. Instead, our recommendations focus on the content of the messaging: The content should be simple and accompanied by pictures (to increase fluency), should avoid qualifying claims, and should affirm correct information rather than negating the myth (and more generally the myth should not be stated). Furthermore, the propagation of retractions/debunking messages must be considered, given that people seem much more interested in the initial claims than the corrections.

In this chapter, we argued that combatting errors in the knowledge system (false beliefs, illusions of knowledge, misconceptions) may require different strategies than those recommended to prevent the misremembering of specific events. There may, however, be viable approaches to correction that go beyond the focus on source that also make use of episodic memory. For example, a particularly memorable event (e.g., an emotional, charged press conference that is witnessed in person) in which some false claim is corrected (or retracted) might be more likely to instill lasting belief change than a less memorable event that involves the correction. In this way, knowledge and episodic memory might *interact* in certain contexts to increase the chances that a correction sticks over time. Whether this kind of interaction is useful for making corrections stick over time warrants further research.

Notes

1 Of course, it is possible for a false belief to be driven by a false memory, as demonstrated in Polage (2012); but we believe this is much less likely than illusions of knowledge.
2 Although controversial, more recent work argues for a different position, namely that validation may sometimes accompany comprehension (Richter, 2015; Richter, Schroeder, & Wöhrmann, 2009). On this view, validating incoming information tends to be a relatively automatic and effortless process that occurs with comprehension, instead of a separate, effortful step after comprehension.

References

Barberá, P., Jost, J. T., Nagler, J., Tucker, J. A., & Bonneau, R. (2015). Tweeting from left to right: Is online political communication more than an echo chamber? *Psychological Science*, *26*(10), 1531–1542.

Bauer, P. J., & San Souci, P. (2010). Going beyond the facts: Young children extend knowledge by integrating episodes. *Journal of Experimental Child Psychology*, *107*, 452–465.

Begg, I. M., Anas, A., & Farinacci, S. (1992). Dissociation of processes in belief: Source recollection, statement familiarity, and the illusion of truth. *Journal of Experimental Psychology: General*, *121*(4), 446.

Begg, I. M., & Armour, V. (1991). Repetition and the ring of truth: Biasing comments. *Canadian Journal of Behavioural Science*, *23*(2), 195.

Bottoms, H. C., Eslick, A. N., & Marsh, E. J. (2010). Memory and the Moses illusion: Failures to detect contradictions with stored knowledge yield negative memorial consequences. *Memory*, *18*(6), 670–678.

Brashier, N. M., Eliseev, E. D., & Marsh, E. J. (2020). An initial accuracy focus prevents illusory truth. *Cognition*, *194*, 104054.

Brewer, W. F. (1977). Memory for the pragmatic implications of sentences. *Memory & Cognition*, *5*, 673–678.

Bronstein, M. V., Pennycook, G., Bear, A., Rand, D. G., & Cannon, T. D. (2019). Belief in fake news is associated with delusionality, dogmatism, religious fundamentalism, and reduced analytic thinking. *Journal of Applied Research in Memory and Cognition*, *8*(1), 108–117.

Brown, A. S. (1991). A review of the tip-of-the-tongue experience. *Psychological Bulletin*, *109*, 204–223.

Butler, A. C., Fazio, L. K., & Marsh, E. J. (2011). The hypercorrection effect persists over a week, but high-confidence errors return. *Psychonomic Bulletin & Review*, *18*, 1238–1244.

Cantor, A. D., Eslick, A. N., Marsh, E. J., Bjork, R. A., & Bjork, E. L. (2015). Multiple-choice tests stabilize access to marginal knowledge. *Memory & Cognition*, *43*, 193–205.

Cantor, A. D., & Marsh, E. J. (2017). Expertise effects in the Moses illusion: Detecting contradictions with stored knowledge. *Memory*, *25*, 220–230.

Conway, M. A., Gardiner, J. M., Perfect, T. J., Anderson, S. J., & Cohen, G. M. (1997). Changes in memory awareness during learning: The acquisition of knowledge by psychology undergraduates. *Journal of Experimental Psychology: General*, *126*, 393–413.

Dechêne, A., Stahl, C., Hansen, J., & Wänke, M. (2010). The truth about the truth: A meta-analytic review of the truth effect. *Personality and Social Psychology Review*, *14*, 238–257.

Del Vicario, M., Vivaldo, G., Bessi, A., Zollo, F., Scala, A., Caldarelli, G., & Quattrociocchi, W. (2016). Echo chambers: Emotional contagion and group polarization on facebook. *Scientific Reports, 6,* 37825.

DePaulo, B. M., Kashy, D. A., Kirkendol, S. E., Wyer, M. M., & Epstein, J. A. (1996). Lying in everyday life. *Journal of Personality and Social Psychology, 70*(5), 979–995.

Erickson, T. D., & Mattson, M. E. (1981). From words to meaning: A semantic illusion. *Journal of Verbal Learning & Verbal Behavior, 20,* 540–551.

Eslick, A. N., Fazio, L. K., & Marsh, E. J. (2011). Ironic effects of drawing attention to story errors. *Memory, 19*(2), 184–191.

Fazio, L. K., Brashier, N. M., Payne, B. K., & Marsh, E. J. (2015). Knowledge does not protect against illusory truth. *Journal of Experimental Psychology: General, 144*(5), 993–1002.

Fazio, L. K., Rand, D. G., & Pennycook, G. (under review). Repetition increases perceived truth equally for plausible and implausible statements.

Ferreira, F., Bailey, K. G., & Ferraro, V. (2002). Good-enough representations in language comprehension. *Current Directions in Psychological Science, 11,* 11–15.

Fragale, A. R., & Heath, C. (2004). Evolving informational credentials: The (mis) attribution of believable facts to credible sources. *Personality and Social Psychology Bulletin, 30*(2), 225–236.

Gilbert, D. T. (1991). How mental systems believe. *American Psychologist, 46,* 107–119.

Gilbert, D. T., Krull, D. S., & Malone, P. S. (1990). Unbelieving the unbelievable: Some problems in the rejection of false information. *Journal of Personality and Social Psychology, 59,* 601–613.

Gilbert, D. T., Tafarodi, R. W., & Malone, P. S. (1993). You can't not believe everything you read. *Journal of Personality and Social Psychology, 65,* 221–233.

Guillory, J. J., & Geraci, L. (2013). Correcting erroneous inferences in memory: The role of source credibility. *Journal of Applied Research in Memory and Cognition, 2*(4), 201–209.

Hasher, L., Goldstein, D., & Toppino, T. (1977). Frequency and the conference of referential validity. *Journal of Verbal Learning and Verbal Behavior, 16,* 107–112.

Henkel, L. A., & Mattson, M. E. (2011). Reading is believing: The truth effect and source credibility. *Consciousness and Cognition, 20*(4), 1705–1721.

Horne, Z., Powell, D., Hummel, J. E., & Holyoak, K. J. (2015). Countering antivaccination attitudes. *Proceedings of the National Academy of Sciences, 112*(33), 10321–10324.

Isberner, M. B., & Richter, T. (2014). Does validation during language comprehension depend on an evaluative mindset? *Discourse Processes, 51*(1–2), 7–25.

Johnson, M. K., Hashtroudi, S., & Lindsay, D. S. (1993). Source monitoring. *Psychological Bulletin, 114,* 3–28.

Kornell, N., & Bjork, R. A. (2008). Learning concepts and categories: Is spacing the "enemy of induction"? *Psychological Science, 19*(6), 585–592.

Lewandowsky, S., Ecker, U. K., & Cook, J. (2017). Beyond misinformation: Understanding and coping with the "post-truth" era. *Journal of Applied Research in Memory and Cognition, 6*(4), 353–369.

Lewandowsky, S., Ecker, U. K., Seifert, C. M., Schwarz, N., & Cook, J. (2012). Misinformation and its correction: Continued influence and successful debiasing. *Psychological Science in the Public Interest, 13,* 106–131.

Lewandowsky, S., Stritzke, W. G., Oberauer, K., & Morales, M. (2005). Memory for fact, fiction, and misinformation: The Iraq War 2003. *Psychological Science, 16,* 190–195.

Lindsay, D. S., & Johnson, M. K. (1989). The eyewitness suggestibility effect and memory for source. *Memory & Cognition, 17,* 349–358.

Mandelbaum, E. (2014). Thinking is believing. *Inquiry: An Interdisciplinary Journal of Philosophy, 57*(1), 55–96.

Marsh, E. J., Cantor, A. D., & Brashier, N. M. (2016). Believing that humans swallow spiders in their sleep: False beliefs as side effects of the processes that support accurate knowledge. *Psychology of Learning and Motivation, 64*, 93–132.

Marsh, E. J., Meade, M. L., & Roediger III, H. L. (2003). Learning facts from fiction. *Journal of Memory and Language, 49*(4), 519–536.

Marsh, E. J., & Yang, B. W. (2017). A call to think broadly about information literacy. *Journal of Applied Research in Memory and Cognition, 6*, 401–404.

McGlone, M. S., & Tofighbakhsh, J. (2000). Birds of a feather flock conjointly (?): Rhyme as reason in aphorisms. *Psychological Science, 11*, 424–428.

Mills, J., & Jellison, J. M. (1967). Effect on opinion change of how desirable the communication is to the audience the communicator addressed. *Journal of Personality and Social Psychology, 6*(1), 98.

Newman, E. J., Garry, M., Bernstein, D. M., Kantner, J., & Lindsay, D. S. (2012). Nonprobative photographs (or words) inflate truthiness. *Psychonomic Bulletin & Review, 19*, 969–974.

Newman, E. J., Garry, M., Unkelbach, C., Bernstein, D. M., Lindsay, D. S., & Nash, R. A. (2015). Truthiness and falsiness of trivia claims depend on judgmental contexts. *Journal of Experimental Psychology: Learning, Memory, and Cognition, 41*, 1337–1348.

Nyhan, B., & Reifler, J. (2010). When corrections fail: The persistence of political misperceptions. *Political Behavior, 32*, 303–330.

Pennycook, G., Cannon, T. D., & Rand, D. G. (2018). Prior exposure increases perceived accuracy of fake news. *Journal of Experimental Psychology: General, 147*(12), 1865–1880.

Pennycook, G., & Rand, D. G. (2019). Lazy, not biased: Susceptibility to partisan fake news is better explained by lack of reasoning than by motivated reasoning. *Cognition, 188*, 39–50.

Polage, D. C. (2012). Making up history: False memories of fake news stories. *Europe's Journal of Psychology, 8*, 245–250.

Porter, E., Wood, T. J., & Kirby, D. (2018). Sex trafficking, Russian infiltration, birth certificates, and Pedophilia: A survey experiment correcting fake news. *Journal of Experimental Political Science, 5*, 159–164.

Priester, J. R., & Petty, R. E. (1995). Source attributions and persuasion: Perceived honesty as a determinant of message scrutiny. *Personality and Social Psychology Bulletin, 21*(6), 637–654.

Putnam, A. L., & Phelps, R. J. (2017). The citation effect: In-text citations moderately increase belief in trivia claims. *Acta Psychologica, 179*, 114–123.

Rapp, D. N., & Donovan, A. M. (2017). Routine processes of cognition result in routine influences of inaccurate content. *Journal of Applied Research in Memory and Cognition, 6*(4), 409–413.

Rapp, D. N., Hinze, S. R., Kohlhepp, K., & Ryskin, R. A. (2014). Reducing reliance on inaccurate information. *Memory & Cognition, 42*, 11–26.

Rapp, D. N., & Salovich, N. A. (2018). Can't we just disregard fake news? The consequences of exposure to inaccurate information. *Policy Insights from the Behavioral and Brain Sciences, 5*(2), 232–239.

Reber, R., & Schwarz, N. (1999). Effects of perceptual fluency on judgments of truth. *Consciousness and Cognition, 8*, 338–342.

Richter, T. (2015). Validation and comprehension of text information: Two sides of the same coin. *Discourse Processes, 52*(5–6), 337–355.

Richter, T., Schroeder, S., & Wöhrmann, B. (2009). You don't have to believe everything you read: Background knowledge permits fast and efficient validation of information. *Journal of Personality and Social Psychology, 96*(3), 538.

Shin, J., Jian, L., Driscoll, K., & Bar, F. (2017). Political rumoring on Twitter during the 2012 US presidential election: Rumor diffusion and correction. *New Media & Society, 19*, 1214–1235.

Shin, J., Jian, L., Driscoll, K., & Bar, F. (2018). The diffusion of misinformation on social media: Temporal pattern, message, and source. *Computers in Human Behavior, 83*, 278–287.

Shin, J., & Thorson, K. (2017). Partisan selective sharing: The biased diffusion of fact-checking messages on social media. *Journal of Communication, 67*, 233–255.

Stanley, M. L., Yang, B. W., & Marsh, E. J. (2019). When the unlikely becomes likely: Qualifying language does not influence later truth judgments. *Journal of Applied Research in Memory and Cognition, 8*(1), 118–129.

Street, C. N., & Kingstone, A. (2017). Aligning Spinoza with Descartes: An informed Cartesian account of the truth bias. *British Journal of Psychology, 108*(3), 453–466.

Street, C. N., & Richardson, D. C. (2015). Descartes versus Spinoza: Truth, uncertainty, and bias. *Social Cognition, 33*(3), 227–239.

Strickland, B., & Keil, F. (2011). Event completion: Event based inferences distort memory in a matter of seconds. *Cognition, 121*, 409–415.

Suhay, E., Blackwell, A., Roche, C., & Bruggeman, L. (2015). Forging bonds and burning bridges: Polarization and incivility in blog discussions about Occupy Wall Street. *American Politics Research, 43*(4), 643–679.

Swami, V., Voracek, M., Stieger, S., Tran, U. S., & Furnham, A. (2014). Analytic thinking reduces belief in conspiracy theories. *Cognition, 133*, 572–585.

Swire, B., & Ecker, U. K. H. (2018). Misinformation and its correction: Cognitive mechanisms and recommendations for mass communication. *Misinformation and Mass Audiences*, 195–211.

Tulving, E. (1972). Episodic and semantic memory. In E. Tulving & W. Donaldson (Eds.), *Organization of memory* (pp. 381–403). New York, NY: Academic Press.

Underwood, J., & Pezdek, K. (1998). Memory suggestibility as an example of the sleeper effect. *Psychonomic Bulletin & Review, 5*, 449–453.

Watkins, M. J., & Kerkar, S. P. (1985). Recall of a twice-presented item without recall of either presentation: Generic memory for events. *Journal of Memory and Language, 24*, 666–678.

Williams, H. T., McMurray, J. R., Kurz, T., & Lambert, F. H. (2015). Network analysis reveals open forums and echo chambers in social media discussions of climate change. *Global Environmental Change, 32*, 126–138.

Wood, T., & Porter, E. (2019). The elusive backfire effect: Mass attitudes' steadfast factual adherence. *Political Behavior, 41*, 135–163.

9

PSYCHOLOGICAL INOCULATION AGAINST FAKE NEWS

Sander van der Linden and Jon Roozenbeek

Acknowledgments

We would like to thank the Cambridge Social Decision-Making Lab, Ruurd Oosterwoud and DROG, Design Studio Gusmanson, the Economic and Social Research Council (ESRC), and the University of Cambridge for their support and for funding this research. We also thank the editors and reviewers for their helpful feedback on an earlier version of this chapter.

What is fake news?

Fake news appears everywhere. After gaining steam during the 2016 US presidential election, the phrase has become ubiquitous in popular media. US President Donald Trump uses it to lambast journalists and media outlets for what he sees as biased coverage; researchers build algorithms to detect false and misleading stories and document their spread; Facebook is regularly forced to explain how it intends to prevent fake news from going viral on its platform; and governments are taking steps to crack down on fake news stories circulating on the internet (Bremner, 2018; Shao et al., 2018; Wakabayashi, 2017).

Accordingly, "fake news" has rapidly become a catchall phrase that lacks an accepted working definition (Tandoc Jr, Lim, & Ling, 2018). Although some have attempted to explicate the "science of fake news" (e.g., Lazer et al., 2018), if parties with such diverse interests as the BBC and President Donald Trump are using the term and take it to mean entirely different things in different contexts, it becomes difficult to know what we talk about when we talk about fake news.

It is also quite clear that the term does not do a very good job at describing the full breadth of the problem. Perhaps a sensible definition of "fake news" could be "fabricated information that mimics news media content in form, but not in organizational process or intent" (Lazer et al., 2018, p. 1). Snopes is one of the websites that keeps track of stories like this. Examples are not hard to find: headlines like "Australia to Forcibly Vaccinate Citizens via Chemtrails", "Melania Trump Bans White House Staff from Taking Flu Shot" and "Muslim Doctor Refuses to Treat Christian Girl on Board a Flight" are just one Google search away (Adl-Tabatabai, 2016; Baxter, 2018; Patriot United, 2018).

But news stories do not have to be completely false to be misleading. It is easy to quote people out of context to make it look like they are saying something that they never said, or to add misleading context to a video or image. For example, see Figure 9.1. This was a commentary posted by the Facebook page "News World" on March 20, 2018. The video purports to show Muslim immigrants in France attacking a Catholic church during mass. It was viewed about 1.2 million times within a day after it was posted. Politicians, including Front National leader Marine le Pen, expressed their outrage on Twitter, writing that the church had been "desecrated" (Le Pen, 2018).

However, fact checkers were quick to point out a number of problems with these claims. There was no evidence of the protesters' religion or the time of their arrival to France. Furthermore, the church was not "attacked", at least not according to church members themselves. Instead, the people in the video were protesting a proposed bill that would make obtaining asylum in the country more difficult (Snopes, 2018). The demonstration remained nonviolent.

News World

Yesterday at 6:35am ·

Saint-Denis (France) Muslim immigrants attack a Catholic church during the mass. The police try to stop them

1.2M Views

FIGURE 9.1 News World Facebook post (20 March 2018)

The problem with the Facebook post in Figure 9.1 is not that the information is completely false or that the events shown in the video never happened. Rather, it is the misleading context provided in the post that does most of the actual damage. In short, from a psychological perspective, intent matters, and *misleading* and *fake* are not entirely the same thing. It is therefore worthwhile to think of the different types of "fake news" along a spectrum. On one end of the spectrum we have *misinformation*, which is simply information that is false or incorrect (and can include human error). Next, we have *disinformation*, which involves misinformation coupled with a deliberate *intent* to deceive an audience. Compared to simple human error, the involvement of intent has important psychological connotations (van der Linden, 2017; van der Linden, Roozenbeek, Oosterwoud, Compton, & Lewandowsky, 2018). Propaganda is then defined as disinformation paired with an explicit or implicit political agenda (van der Linden, 2017). To keep things simple, we will be using the term *disinformation* instead of *fake news* in the current chapter, to ensure that we are not just talking about fake stories but about media manipulation more generally.

The disinformation problem

Although clearly not a new phenomenon, disinformation has become a much more serious issue with the advent of the internet. The possibility of instant and anonymous communication makes the internet an ideal vehicle for deception. Perhaps it is no surprise then that disinformation is commonly used by a variety of actors, including some governments, to influence public opinion. Social media platforms are a particularly fertile breeding ground. To give an example, around 47 million Twitter accounts (approximately 15%) are bots (Varol, Ferrara, Davis, Menczer, & Flammini, 2017) and many of these bots are used to purposefully spread political disinformation, especially during election campaigns (Ferrara, 2017).

Recent examples of influential disinformation include conspiracy theories about COVID-19, the MacronLeaks during the French presidential elections in 2017, the Pizzagate controversy during the 2016 US elections, the various "alternative" explanations surrounding the downing of Malaysia Airlines flight MH17 in July 2014, and rumors circulating in Sweden about the country's cooperation with NATO (Kragh & Åsberg, 2017). This onslaught of online disinformation is taking its toll. For example, consider that a majority of Americans admit that fake news has left them feeling confused about basic facts (Barthel, Mitchell, & Holcomb, 2016), and 83% of Europeans think that fake news is a threat to democracy (Eurobarometer, 2018). Moreover, a recent British study by YouGov indicated that only 4% of participants were able to discern fake news from real news (Channel 4, 2017). In some ways, this is not surprising: people are bombarded with information as they scroll through their news feeds.

As any functioning democracy relies on a well-informed populace, the rise of disinformation is proving to be a real threat to the democratic process

(Lewandowsky, Ecker, & Cook, 2017; van der Linden et al., 2017). The political landscape in many countries is also getting more and more polarized. This level of polarization is reinforced by the emergence of ideologically homogeneous filter bubbles, where people are exposed to stories that are congenial to their ideological worldviews (Del Vicario et al., 2016). If vast amounts of people are in the dark about what to believe and whom to trust, this can have serious consequences for evidence-based decision making on a whole range of issues, from climate change and vaccinations to international relations (Lewandowsky et al., 2017; Poland & Spier, 2010; van der Linden, Leiserowitz, Rosenthal, & Maibach, 2017). In some cases, the viral spread of fake stories has led to injury and even death (BBC, 2018a).

We also know that effective disinformation campaigns are not easily reversed. Studies on the continued influence of misinformation consistently show that acquired beliefs are very difficult to correct, even when people acknowledge that their views are based on erroneous information (Lewandowsky, Ecker, Seifert, Schwarz, & Cook, 2012). Thus, while disinformation is probably as old as the spread of rumor itself, it has become easier than ever to create and disseminate disinformation and more and more people are exposed to false content simply by virtue of their daily news consumption. Accordingly, governments, public officials, and media companies all have proposed a range of potential solutions to combat the growing disinformation problem.

Potential solutions

The solutions that are being proposed to solve the problem of disinformation can be divided into four broad categories: (1) algorithmic, (2) corrective, (3) legislative, and (4) psychological. In terms of the first category, Google and Facebook are discovering how to tweak their algorithms to disincentivize fake or unreliable news sites and prevent disinformation from appearing on people's newsfeeds in the same way as "reliable" news sites (Calfas, 2017; Elgin & Wang, 2018). However, algorithms are clearly imperfect at detecting misleading content and past attempts, such as by Facebook, have often backfired (Wakefield, 2017). The second category refers to the post-hoc correction of false stories through fact-checking tools. Fact-checking initiatives abound, and some (such as PolitiFact and Snopes) have even become household names. However, although fact-checking initiatives are laudable, evidence for their efficacy remains mixed (Nyhan, Porter, Reifler, & Wood, 2019). Moreover, it is impossible to debunk every fake or misleading story, as producing fake news requires less resources than debunking it, and the potential audience for fact-checking reports remains limited (Kurtzleben, 2016). Recent research also indicates that false stories spread more easily on social media than any other kind of news, even when controlling for stories spread by bots (Vosoughi, Roy, & Aral, 2018).

A more radical approach involves the introduction of new regulation and legislation to combat disinformation. A prominent example is France's "Fake

News Law", which during election time would place tougher restrictions on media outlets as to what content they are allowed to put online (Bremner, 2018). Similar initiatives have been proposed in the United Kingdom (e.g., the "fake news unit" (BBC News, 2018b). Yet, granting any organization, governmental or not, the power to decide what information is "real" and what is "fake" can easily backfire. For example, a European Union-funded working group named "EUvsDisinfo" was heavily criticized for flagging a number of Dutch non-mainstream news sites and one local newspaper as "spreading Kremlin disinformation" (Pieters, 2018). Dutch parliamentarians expressed their concern that EUvsDisinfo was infringing on freedom of speech, and voted to lobby to scrap the working group altogether.

Insights from psychology: inoculation against disinformation

Accordingly, more attention is now being directed toward the role of psychology, education, and the behavioral sciences in combating fake news to help empower people at the individual level (European Commission, 2018). Of course, the basic idea that fostering critical and well-informed news consumers will make disinformation less effective in the long term is sensible. Yet, the problem with most traditional media literacy approaches lies in the fact that it is neither feasible nor possible to correct every false story. Another key problem is that developing better *debunking* techniques is unlikely to be sufficient by itself to stem the onslaught of fake news. In fact, even when corrections are issued, the damage has often already been done: once people have acquired a false belief, they are unlikely to update their views. Indeed, research on the "continued influence effect" suggests that corrections are often ineffective as people continue to rely on false (and debunked) information, especially in the face of politically motivated cognition (Lewandowsky et al., 2012). This raises the following question: is it possible to *prevent* false narratives from taking hold in the first place? To investigate this question, we turn to what Eagly and Chaiken (1993, p. 561) referred to as the "grandparent theory of resistance to persuasion": *inoculation theory*. During World War II, the United States War Department had an experimental research branch in a unit called the "Department of Information and Education". This division, led by the social psychologist, Carl Hovland, was tasked specifically with conducting research on political persuasion and propaganda campaigns (Hovland, Lumsdaine, & Sheffield, 1949). Their studies formed the basis of what later became known as one of the most foundational groups in social psychology: the Yale Attitude and Persuasion Program (Huddy, Sears, & Levy, 2013). Their mission was to uncover "the basic laws of persuasion" using controlled experimental methods. Yet, in the 1960s, a new concern arose; the potential brainwashing of captured American soldiers in the Far East. Accordingly, psychologist William McGuire shifted his focus toward a different question: how can we help people resist persuasion attempts? This ultimately led him to develop "inoculation theory", which he described as a "vaccine for brainwash" (see Figure 9.2).

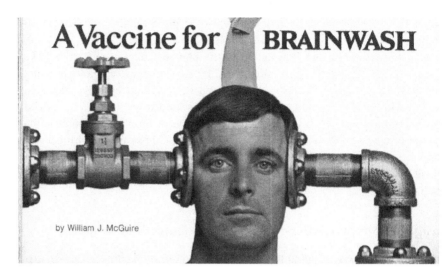

FIGURE 9.2 A vaccine for brainwash (McGuire, 1970)

Inoculation theory is based on an analogy from immunology (McGuire, 1970; McGuire & Papageorgis, 1961, 1962; Papageorgis & McGuire, 1961). Vaccines are weakened versions of pathogens (e.g., a virus) that, upon introduction to the body, trigger the production of antibodies. These antibodies become active once the real version of the pathogen enters the body thus conferring protection (immunity) against future infection. Inoculation theory postulates that the same can occur with information: by preemptively presenting someone with a weakened version of a misleading piece of information, a thought process is triggered that is analogous to the cultivation of "mental antibodies", rendering the person immune to (undesirable) persuasion attempts (Compton, 2013; McGuire & Papageorgis, 1961). Over the years, a large body of evidence has been amassed showing that public attitudes can be inoculated across domains, including health (Compton, Jackson, & Dimmock, 2016) and politics (Pfau, Park, Holbert, & Cho, 2001). Meta-analyses also confirm that inoculation messages are effective at conferring resistance to persuasion (Banas & Rains, 2010). The inoculation process consists of two main components, namely: (1) a warning to elicit and activate threat in message recipients (the affective basis) and (2) refutational preemption (the cognitive basis). Forewarning people that they are about to be exposed to counter-attitudinal content is thought to elicit *threat* to motivate the protection of existing beliefs. In turn, two-sided refutational messages both inform and teach in the sense that they model the counterarguing process for people and provide specific content that can be used to resist persuasion attempts (McGuire, 1970; Compton, 2013).

Interestingly, a number of important open questions remain about the theory, particularly with regard to its application to fake news and disinformation. For example, inoculation theory has traditionally been applied to so-called cultural truisms or widely held beliefs (e.g., the belief that brushing your teeth twice a day is good for your health, see McGuire, 1970). As such, a major open question has been how the inoculation process operates, theoretically, when people have divergent prior attitudes about an issue (as is often the case with fake news). When audiences do not already possess the desired attitude, the inoculation process is not prophylactic in the traditional sense, but rather takes on a "therapeutic" role – analogous to the emerging use of therapeutic vaccines (Compton, 2019). Second, from an intervention science perspective, it remains unclear how the inoculation process can be scaled at population level, as clearly, it is neither feasible nor possible to preemptively refute every fake news story specifically. Lastly, inoculation treatments have traditionally relied on a "passive" process where recipients read a persuasive message that forewarns and refutes potential counterarguments. However, McGuire theorized early on that a more active inoculation process could be more powerful by letting people generate their own pro- and counterarguments.[1] Accordingly, in three studies, we sought to provide initial answers to these important yet unresolved questions.

In the lab: inoculating the public against misinformation about climate change (study 1)

To answer the first question, we wanted to see whether exposing the public to a weakened version of a falsehood, and preemptively debunking that falsehood with scientific facts (a vaccine), could offer resistance against fake news about a highly polarized and contested issue: global warming. Our lab conducted two large online studies to test these hypotheses. In the first study, we used a national probability sample ($N = 1,000$) of the US population to evaluate what popular "falsehoods" about climate change people were most familiar with. The most commonly recognized source of misinformation was a real online petition (The Oregon Petition), which claims to have gathered over 31,000 signatures from scientists who disagree that human-caused global warming is real (fueling the most popular fake news story about climate change on social media in 2016, see Readfearn, 2016).

   In the second study, we relied on a large and diverse sample ($N = 2,167$) of US adults from Amazon Mechanical Turk. We used a real screenshot of the petition website as the experimental "misinformation" treatment and the simple fact that over 97% of climate scientists have concluded that human-induced global warming is happening as the "factual" statement (Cook et al., 2016). We then randomly assigned participants to one of six conditions and asked about their judgments of the scientific consensus both before and after (see Figure 9.4). The six conditions were (1) simple facts (the 97% consensus), (2) real misinformation (the petition), (3) false balance (the consensus versus the petition), (4) partial inoculation (forewarning only), (5) full inoculation (forewarning plus preemptive refutation), and (6) a "pure" control group in which participants solved a neutral word puzzle.

In Figure 9.3, from left to right (panel a), in the "facts" condition, participants only read about the evidence and shifted their views (pre-post) on climate change in line with the scientific consensus (97%) by about 20 percentage points (d = 1.23). In the "misinformation" condition, subjects were only shown the misinformation and shifted their views down by about 10% (d = 0.48). In the "false balance" condition, participants viewed both treatments side by side; here, the presence of "sticky" misinformation completely neutralized the facts (d = 0.04). In the last two "inoculation" conditions, participants were informed of the facts with either a short warning (W) that politically motivated actors may try to influence public opinion using misleading tactics or additional arguments were used to *prebunk* the misinformation in detail (e.g., that signatories of this petition include Charles Darwin and the Spice Girls). The inoculation treatments (labeled "W" for warning only and "F" for full in Figure 9.3) proved effective, preserving about one-third (d = 0.33) and two-thirds (d = 0.75) of the factual message, respectively. Crucially, the same pattern replicated across the political spectrum as well as across participants' prior attitudes about climate change (panel b).

In short, this study provided an important and compelling answer to our first question: even outside of the context of politically neutral "truisms", inoculation can be effective. In fact, rather than backfire, inoculation appears to have important retroactive or "therapeutic" benefits, even among people who reject climate science for political reasons. An independent study conceptually replicated these findings with generally stronger results (see Cook, Lewandowsky, & Ecker, 2017).

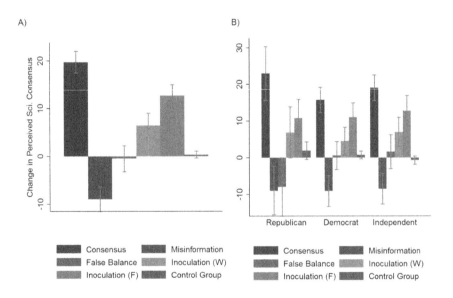

FIGURE 9.3   Inoculating against climate change misinformation (van der Linden et al., 2017)

In the field: actively inoculating against fake news (study 2)

Our initial research still left us with two important questions: (1) instead of passively reading articles is it possible to inoculate people in a more "active" and "experiential" manner to aid the learning process; and (2) can the "vaccine" be generalized and extended to other domains? For example, although it is possible to tailor inoculation messages to a particular issue by creating weakened doses of specific misinformation, what about the prospect of conferring general resistance against disinformation? To answer these questions, we established a partnership with the Dutch Media Collective "Bad News", an organization that creates novel educational materials to combat disinformation. Jointly, we extended our initial work by translating the laboratory findings into an interactive educational experience: *The Fake News Game*. We theorized that taking on the role of someone who is actively trying to deceive you will be an effective way of conferring more general resistance to misinformation. Accordingly, the game lets players walk a mile in the shoes of a fake news producer. Initially, we produced a paper-based version of the game (see Figure 9.4) where students pick a specific character, such as a conspiracy theorist or a clickbait monger, and assemble structured news articles in a way that is consistent with their role.

We pilot tested the game with 95 senior students (aged 16–18) in a Dutch high school in the context of fake news about the Syrian refugee crisis (Roozenbeek & van der Linden, 2018). Classes were randomized into a treatment and a control group. After playing the game for about 30 minutes, students in the treatment

FIGURE 9.4   The Fake News card game (Roozenbeek & van der Linden, 2018)

group significantly downgraded the reliability of previously unseen fabricated news articles about the refugee crises compared to a control group who simply watched a video as part of the standard lesson plan. To evaluate whether threat was elicited in the process, a sentiment analysis on the open-ended responses revealed significantly higher negative affect levels in the treatment group. Although these results were encouraging, the power of the study was relatively low and students did not necessarily change their attitudes about immigration. This is consistent with other recent work which finds that although media interventions can reduce misperceptions, this doesn't necessarily reflect changes in political beliefs (Nyhan et al., 2019). To be fair, however, the intervention is not aimed at changing political beliefs, but simply to help people spot disinformation techniques. Crucially, in our field study, the "weakened" fake news article the students were "trained on" was different from the article they were tested on – providing preliminary evidence that the boundary conditions of the inoculation metaphor can be extended.

Into the wild: the bad news game (study 3)

Based on these results, we designed a multiple award-winning online version of the Fake News game (FastCompany, 2018). We called it "*Bad News*" (Roozenbeek & van der Linden, 2019). The online game simulates a social media engine (Twitter) so that players have to attract followers by spreading fake news online. The interface of the game is user-friendly (see Figure 9.5a); players are shown a short text or image (such as a meme or headline) and can react to them in a variety of ways. In the game, scores are measured via a "followers" and "credibility" meter (panel b). The aim of the game is to gather as many followers as possible without losing credibility. Choosing an option that is in line with what a "real" producer of disinformation would choose gets players more followers and credibility. If, however, they lie too blatantly to their followers or act too much in line with journalistic best practices, the game either takes followers away or lowers their credibility score.

Disinformation strategies

Following the inoculation metaphor, the game exposes players to severely weakened doses of disinformation by *actively* letting them generate their own content. However, in contrast to issue-based inoculations, we hypothesized that it may be possible to "vaccinate" people against the very tactics that underlie the production of most fake news (analogous to a *broad-spectrum* vaccine). As it is impossible to cover all aspects of disinformation in detail in a 15-minute game, we chose to cover only the most common strategies. Over the course of six theory-driven "badges", players learn about impersonating people online, using emotional language, group polarization, floating conspiracy theories, building echo chambers, discrediting opponents, trolling, and false amplification. These strategies are partially derived from the report "Digital Hydra" by NATO's East Strategic

(a)

(b)

FIGURE 9.5   Screen captions of the Bad News game (www.getbadnews.com)

Command (East StratCom), which details the various forms that disinformation can take as well as academic work on deception strategies (Bertolin, Agarwal, Bandeli, Biteniece, & Sedova, 2017). The following sections offer a quick summary of the scenarios and theoretical background of each badge specifically.

Impersonation

It is no longer difficult to start a website and publish content that looks entirely legitimate. Since there is almost no entry barrier in terms of costs, pretty much anyone can become a content producer (Goga, Venkatadri, & Gummadi, 2015; Orita & Hada, 2009; Reznik, 2013). The purpose of this badge is to show how easy this process is and how a professional look or name does not necessarily imply legitimacy. "Impersonation" has two main components: (1) impersonating a real person or organization by mimicking their appearance, for example, by using a slightly different username, for example when a hoaxer impersonated billionaire investor Warren Buffett on Twitter in late 2018 (BBC News, 2018c), and (2) posing as a legitimate news website or blog without the usual journalistic norms and credentials.

In the game, players first post a tweet about something that frustrates them, which can be anything from a failing government to the Flat Earth Society. This gets them their first followers, and the game explains how the follower counter and credibility meter functions. Players then impersonate the official account of either Donald Trump (who declares war on North Korea), NASA (which announces that a massive meteor is about to hit the earth), or Nickelodeon (declaring the impending cancellation of *SpongeBob SquarePants*). Players are subsequently shown tweets by Twitter users who fell for the impersonation hoax. The game then prompts them to go professional and start their own news site. They pick a website name, title, and slogan.

Emotional content

Emotional content is content that is not necessarily "fake" or "real" but deliberately plays into people's basic emotions, such as fear, anger, or empathy (Aday, 2010; Bakir & McStay, 2017; Gross & D'Ambrosio, 2004; Konijn, 2013). The aim of this badge is to show how players can manipulate basic emotions in order to rile up their followers and make their content shared more readily.

This is the first badge where players produce content for their fictional news site. They are prompted to browse news headlines for a topic that they can publish about on their site, with a choice between climate change and genetically modified organisms (GMOs). Players are then asked for their opinion on their topic of choice. The game prompts them to say that their topic will either bring about the apocalypse (in the case of GMOs) or is a complete hoax (in the case of climate change), as this is the easiest way to gain followers. The game asks them to choose an approach to the topic at hand: attack scientists, post an emotional story, or talk about the science. The latter option returns a negative response, as players are encouraged to use reactionary content to rile up their followers. They can then either create a meme (a humorous piece of media, usually an image or GIF, that spreads from person to person on the internet) or write an article that reflects their choice. Each choice comes with numerous options, of which one is always bad (because it misses the point). Some of their followers will react to their post on Twitter in an emotional, angry way, which is exactly the player's goal.

Polarization

Polarization involves deliberate attempts to expand the gap between the political left and the political right and drive people away from the political center (Bessi et al., 2016; Groenendyk, 2018; Melki & Pickering, 2014; Prior, 2013; Twenge, Honeycutt, Prislin, & Sherman, 2016). In order to gain followers, young news sites often use polarization as a way to stake out a niche in the online media landscape. This badge also covers the concept of "false amplification" or the idea that it is not necessary to create a completely fake story in order to get a point across. Instead, one can also amplify existing grievances and make them look more popular than they really are (Bertolin et al., 2017).

At the start of this badge, players are asked if they want to publish something fake or something real. Choosing "fake" tells them that they do not always have to invent fake news in order to make headlines, but that they can also find a real story and blow it out of proportion. They can then drive left and right further apart by choosing between three local news stories as reported by random citizens on Twitter: a chemical spill, a small-town bribery scandal, or the heavy-handed arrest of a criminal. Players first pick a target: in two cases, they can attack either big corporations or the government, and in one case either the police or violent criminals. They try to give voice to the story by talking about it on their news site's Twitter account from their chosen perspective, but this fails. They are asked to make the story look bigger than it is by writing an article about it or by posting a meme. This gets them more followers, as people are beginning to pick up on the story. Next, the game asks players if they want to purchase Twitter bots that can amplify the story for them. If they repeatedly refuse, the game ends, but if they accept, they gain 4,000 robot followers. They are shown examples of bots amplifying their chosen story. Their target determines if they are polarizing their chosen topic toward the left (by focusing on big corporations or police brutality) or the right (by focusing on the government or crime-related issues). The key lesson is that it doesn't matter what side they ultimately choose: the aim is simply to polarize.

Conspiracy

Conspiracy theories are part and parcel of fringe online news sites. Conspiracies can be defined as the belief that unexplained events are orchestrated by a covert group or organization with sinister intentions (Goertzel, 1994; Lewandowsky, Gignac, & Oberauer, 2013; van der Linden, 2015).

In this badge, players are first encouraged to come up with an interesting new theory and post it on their news site. However, since all options are overtly ridiculous (e.g., public schools no longer teach cursive writing so that people stop reading the Communist Manifesto), their theory is too far removed from reality to be believable. Some followers call the player out for their strange theory. To save their credibility, players then look for a more believable conspiracy. They can either choose between Agenda 21, a non-binding United Nations treaty on sustainable development, or the so-called vaccine conspiracy (the idea that the World Health Organization uses vaccinations to indoctrinate people). Players score points if they cast doubt on the official narrative and ask questions that point people in the direction of conspiratorial thinking, and lose points for going off the rails by publishing content that is considered too weird. Followers react more positively this time, and the player is encouraged to write a serious news article about their topic of choice. If they do well, they gain a cult following, with people trusting their news site more and more and becoming more skeptical of the so-called mainstream media.

Discrediting opponents

When misleading news sites are accused of bad journalism, they can deflect attention away from the accusation by attacking the source of the criticism ("you are fake news!", see van der Linden, Panagopoulos, & Roozenbeek, 2020) or denying that the problem exists (A'Beckett, 2013; Lischka, 2017). In this badge, players are confronted with a fact checker who debunks the conspiracy theory from the previous badge. They are given three options: either apologize, do nothing, or take revenge. The first option costs them points, and the game moderator explains that apologizing is never a good idea. "Do nothing" prompts a response from one of their news site's followers asking why they are not responding to the fact check. Eventually, all three choices lead to the same point where players have to choose between either denying the allegations or attacking the fact checker. Their vehement denial or ruthless ad hominem attack on the fact checker triggers a supportive response in the player's followers, and their reputation remains intact.

Trolling

Trolling is a fishing term, originally referring to the process of slowly dragging a lure or baited hook from the back of a fishing boat. On the internet, it means deliberately evoking a response by using bait (Griffiths, 2014; McCosker, 2014; Thacker & Griffiths, 2012).

In this badge, players put together the techniques they learned in the other five badges. This time, they can only choose one topic. At the beginning of the badge, they are asked to talk about one of three topics (the 25 most romantic cities in Europe; a passenger plane crash; and a newly discovered species of starfish), of which only the second one leads to the next stage. Choosing one of the other two provokes a scolding from the game's moderator. After this, players are given two options: either pay respects to the victims of the plane crash or start sowing doubt about its cause. The first option prompts a response from their followers asking why they are not investigating the story in more detail. Both options eventually lead to the player to ask whether the crash was a cover-up. Due to their higher credibility and number of followers, their post attracts the attention of other news sites as well, and the story begins to escalate. Players can then throw fuel onto the fire by either impersonating a crash victim's family member or photoshopping evidence of a cover-up. Both choices then lead to even more emotional responses, and now the mainstream media is also beginning to weigh in on the story. Players are instructed to keep increasing the pressure, either by discrediting the investigation further or by using another army of Twitter bots to spread the hashtag #InvestigateNow. Depending on their initial choice between impersonating a victim's family member or photoshopping evidence, they can then deliver the final blow by fabricating another news article about the crash. The Aviation Disaster Committee, the (fictional) agency responsible for the investigation, then responds to the manufactured controversy on Twitter. Players then attack this response either by calling for the resignation of the chairman of the Committee or by using the Twitter bot army again. The game ends with the Committee chairman resigning over the handling of the investigation.

Launch and survey results

Following its launch in February 2018, international media around the world covered the game's release both online and in print (BBC, 2017; Reuters, 2018; CNN, 2019). The game included a voluntary pre-post survey, which tested people's ability to recognize disinformation techniques. Over the course of two months, hundreds of thousands of people played the game (mostly from the UK and US). In total, about $N = 15,000$ people opted in for scientific research and completed all of the (pre-post) survey tests. Each survey question came in the form of a fabricated tweet that represented a specific disinformation strategy. Specifically, as an initial evaluation, we tested participants' ability to recognize impersonation (by way of an account impersonating HBO saying that "The 8th season of Game of Thrones will be postponed due to a salary dispute"), conspiracy (a tweet stating that "The Bitcoin exchange rate is being manipulated by a small group of rich bankers"), discrediting opponents (another tweet claiming that "The mainstream media has been caught in so many lies that it can't be trusted as a reliable news source") and polarization (we showed participants an invented news headline that was randomized to state either that a "New study shows that left-wing people lie far more than right-wing people" or the reverse "New study shows that right-wing people lie far more than left-wing people"). Participants were asked to rate the reliability of each of these tweets on a scale between one and seven, plus two "real" control tweets that did not contain any disinformation strategies (e.g., #Brexit, the United Kingdom's exit from the European Union, will officially happen in 2019). We used fictional headlines inspired by "real" fake news for two key reasons; namely (1) to be able to isolate the specific disinformation techniques and (2) to avoid familiarity confounds with real "fake" content (Roozenbeek & van der Linden, 2019). An example of the testing environment is provided in Figure 9.6.

The results are displayed in Figures 9.7 and 9.8. In Figure 9.7, the leftmost bar of the pair is the response people gave before playing (light gray), and the bar on the right is from after playing (dark gray). Some initial concerns about the game were that it could simply make players more skeptical about news media across the board. This is not what we found. "Control_1" and "Control_2"

FIGURE 9.6 Bad News game survey

Notes: The top panel illustrates how a technique [impersonation] is used in the game, and the bottom panel shows how the same technique is used in a different example on which participants were evaluated before and after playing.

represent the control questions. We expected these to be rated quite reliably by participants, both before and after playing. This is also borne out by the results: in both cases, the pre- and the post-measure are almost identical and rated highly reliable. The other questions represent techniques commonly used in disinformation that also appear in the game: impersonation, conspiracy, and discrediting opponents. The figure shows that participants rated the "fake news" questions significantly lower after playing the game, indicating a significant inoculation effect for impersonation ($d = .36$), conspiracy ($d = .35$), deflection ($d = .30$), and polarization ($d = 0.16$). These effect sizes are in line with resistance to persuasion research (Walter & Murphy, 2018) and can be considered meaningful, especially when scaled across a population (Funder & Ozer, 2019). Importantly, the learning effects did not differ significantly by political ideology, age, gender, or education (Figure 9.8) and were greater for those who proved most susceptible on the pre-test, bolstering the potential for broad-spectrum immunization. In other words, by actively inoculating people against the strategies that underpin the creation of fake news – through weakened exposure – broad-scale resistance against misinformation can be conferred.

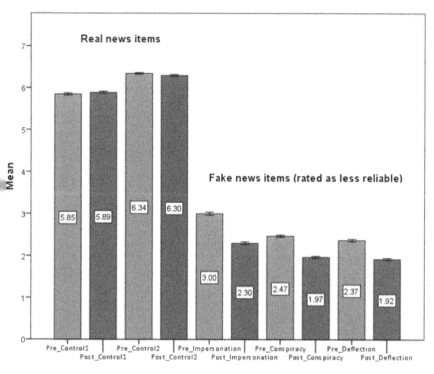

Real news items

Fake news items (rated as less reliable)

5.85 5.89 6.34 6.30 3.00 2.30 2.47 1.97 2.37 1.92

Pre_Control1   Pre_Control2   Pre_Impersonation   Pre_Conspiracy   Pre_Deflection
Post_Control1   Post_Control2   Post_Impersonation   Post_Conspiracy   Post_Deflection

FIGURE 9.7   Results from the Bad News game

Note: Paired bars represent judgments before (light grey) and after (dark grey) playing the game. Participants rated the reliability of all real (control) and fake news items on a 1–7 scale

Limitations and conclusion

In this chapter, we have looked at why disinformation is a problem and what types of solutions are being explored to combat it. In our view, a large part of the solution lies in empowering individuals with evidence-based tools from psychology and behavioral science. We have argued that it is especially important to focus on *preventing* disinformation from going viral in the first place. In fact, the spread of fake news can be modelled much like the spread of a viral contagion. As such, inoculation theory offers an intuitive framework to help develop broad-spectrum immunization against fake news.

In three studies, we have shown how the inoculation metaphor can be extended from the realm of cultural truisms to contested issues, and how we can move from narrow-spectrum vaccines targeting single instances of fake news to a broad-spectrum approach that inoculates people against the very strategies that underlie the production of most disinformation. Of course, these studies are not without their limitations. First, although the samples were diverse, they were either based on students, Mturkers, or a large but self-selected convenience

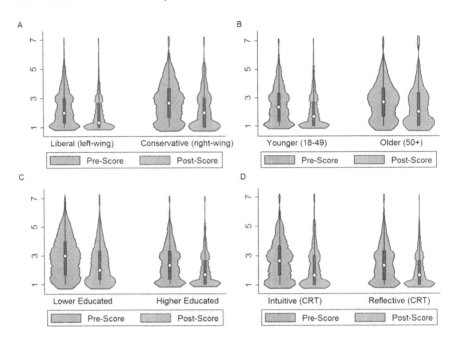

FIGURE 9.8 Violin plots adopted from Roozenbeek & van der Linden (2019) displaying mean pre-post fake news reliability judgments (aggregated) by political ideology (A), age (B), education (C), and a 1-item cognitive reflection measure (D)

sample. Accordingly, these results are not representative of the population. In addition, study 3 used single-item measures and lacked a randomized control group. As such, its causal effects should therefore be interpreted with caution. In addition, although the inoculation treatments proved effective across the ideological spectrum, participants in the game could still branch scenarios in a manner relatively congenial to their ideology. Nonetheless, by documenting the translational process of how to move from a theoretical finding in the lab to a real-world intervention, we highlight the educational potential of novel interactive game-based interventions. The value of intervention science can also be seen in many of its applications. For example, in partnership with the UK government, we have translated the game into 12 new languages, which allows for large-scale cross-cultural evaluations of the game's effectiveness (Roozenbeek, van der Linden, & Nygren, 2020). We have also partnered with WhatsApp to create a special version of the game to help inoculate people against the spread of fake news on direct messaging platforms. We are working with the U.S. government and Behavioral Insights Team in the UK and Lebanon to conduct larger randomized trials to continue to evaluate and improve the success of the intervention. In short, if the new science of *prebunking* is as effective as it appears, there are many open and important questions that future social and behavioral science research can answer to help cultivate societal immunity against fake news.

Note

1 Though later research has not always found this (see Banas & Rains, 2010), possibly due to the higher cognitive load associated with participants' having to generate their own counterarguments.

References

A'Beckett, L. (2013). Strategies to discredit opponents: Russian representations of events in countries of the former Soviet Union. *Psychology of Language and Communication*, 17(2). https://doi.org/10.2478/plc-2013-0009

Aday, S. (2010). Leading the charge: Media, elites, and the use of emotion in stimulating rally effects in wartime. *Journal of Communication*, 60(3), 440–465. https://doi.org/10.1111/j.1460-2466.2010.01489.x

Adl-Tabatabai, S. (2016). Australia to forcibly vaccinate citizens via Chemtrails. Retrieved August 8, 2018, from https://yournewswire.com/australia-to-forcibly-vaccinate-citizens-via-chemtrails/

Bakir, V., & McStay, A. (2017). Fake news and the economy of emotions: Problems, causes, solutions. *Digital Journalism*, 1–22. https://doi.org/10.1080/21670811.2017.1345645

Banas, J. A., & Rains, S. A. (2010). A meta-analysis of research on inoculation theory. *Communication Monographs*, 77(3), 281–311. https://doi.org/10.1080/03637751003758193

Barthel, M., Mitchell, A., & Holcomb, J. (2016, December). Many Americans believe fake news is sowing confusion. *Pew Research Center*. Retrieved from www.journalism.org/2016/12/15/many-americans-believe-fake-news-is-sowing-confusion/

Baxter, D. (2018). Melania Trump bans white house staff from taking flu shot. Retrieved August 8, 2018, from http://archive.is/F0vor

BBC. (2017). Cambridge scientists consider fake news "vaccine". Retrieved August 29, 2017, from www.bbc.co.uk/news/uk-38714404

BBC News. (2018a, July 19). How WhatsApp helped turn an Indian village into a lynch mob. Retrieved from www.bbc.co.uk/news/world-asia-india-44856910

BBC News. (2018b). Government announces anti-fake news unit. Retrieved August 8, 2018, from www.bbc.co.uk/news/uk-politics-42791218

BBC News. (2018c, August 28). A fake billionaire is fooling people on Twitter. Retrieved from www.bbc.co.uk/news/world-us-canada-45331781

Bertolin, G., Agarwal, N., Bandeli, K., Biteniece, N., & Sedova, K. (2017). Digital Hydra: Security implications of false information online. Retrieved from www.stratcomcoe.org/digital-hydra-security-implications-false-information-online

Bessi, A., Zollo, F., Del Vicario, M., Puliga, M., Scala, A., Caldarelli, G., . . . Quattrociocchi, W. (2016). Users polarization on Facebook and Youtube. *PLoS One*, 11(8), 1–24. https://doi.org/10.1371/journal.pone.0159641

Bremner, C. (2018). France aims to ban fake news at election time. Retrieved from www.thetimes.co.uk/article/france-aims-to-ban-fake-news-at-election-time-jwspzjx83

Calfas, J. (2017). Google is changing its search algorithm to combat fake news. Retrieved August 8, 2018, from http://fortune.com/2017/04/25/google-search-algorithm-fake-news/

Channel 4. (2017). C4 study reveals only 4% surveyed can identify true or fake news. Retrieved August 29, 2017, from www.channel4.com/info/press/news/c4-study-reveals-only-4-surveyed-can-identify-true-or-fake-news

CNN. (2019). Researchers have created a "vaccine" for fake news: It's a game. Retrieved from https://edition.cnn.com/2019/07/04/media/fake-news-game-vaccine/index. html?utm_medium=social&utm_content=2019-07-04T13%3A46%3A03&utm_source=twCNN&utm_term=link

Compton, J. (2013). Inoculation theory. In J. P. Dillard & L. Shen (Eds.), *The SAGE handbook of persuasion: Developments in theory and practice* (2nd ed., pp. 220–236). Thousand Oaks: Sage Publications. https://doi.org/10.4135/9781452218410

Compton, J. (2019). Prophylactic versus therapeutic inoculation treatments for resistance to influence. *Communication Theory*, qtz004.

Compton, J., Jackson, B., & Dimmock, J. A. (2016). Persuading others to avoid persuasion: Inoculation theory and resistant health attitudes. *Frontiers in Psychology*, 7, 122.

Cook, J., Lewandowsky, S., & Ecker, U. K. (2017). Neutralizing misinformation through inoculation: Exposing misleading argumentation techniques reduces their influence. *PloS One*, 12(5), e0175799. https://doi.org/10.1371/journal.pone.0175799

Cook, J., Oreskes, N., Doran, P. T., Anderegg, W. R. L., Verheggen, B., Maibach, E. W., . . . Rice, K. (2016). Consensus on consensus: A synthesis of consensus estimates on human-caused global warming. *Environmental Research Letters*, 11(4), 48002. Retrieved from http://stacks.iop.org/1748-9326/11/i=4/a=048002

Del Vicario, M., Bessi, A., Zollo, F., Petroni, F., Scala, A., Caldarelli, G., . . . Quattrociocchi, W. (2016). The spreading of misinformation online. *Proceedings of the National Academy of Sciences*, 113(3), 554–559. https://doi.org/10.1073/pnas.1517441113

Eagly, A. H., & Chaiken, S. (1993). *The psychology of attitudes.* Orlando, FL: Harcourt Brace Jovanovich.

Elgin, B., & Wang, S. (2018). Facebook's battle against fake news Notches an Uneven scorecard. Retrieved August 8, 2018, from www.bloomberg.com/news/articles/2018-04-24/facebook-s-battle-against-fake-news-notches-an-uneven-scorecard

Eurobarometer (2018). *Final results of the Eurobarometer on fake news and online disinformation.* Directorate-General CONNECT, European Commission. Retrieved from https://ec.europa.eu/digital-single-market/en/news/final-results-eurobarometer-fake-news-and-online-disinformation

European Commission. (2018). Final report of the high level expert group on fake news and online disinformation. Retrieved from https://ec.europa.eu/digital-single-market/en/news/final-report-high-level-expert-group-fake-news-and-online-disinformation

FastCompany. (2018). Innovation by design awards: University of Cambridge/DROG. Retrieved from www.fastcompany.com/innovation-by-design/2018/company/university-of-cambridge-drog

Ferrara, E. (2017). Disinformation and social bot operations in the run up to the 2017 French presidential election. *First Monday*, 22(8). Retrieved from https://papers.ssrn.com/sol3/papers.cfm?abstract_id=2995809

Funder, D. C., & Ozer, D. J. (2019). Evaluating effect size in psychological research: Sense and nonsense. *Advances in Methods and Practices in Psychological Science*, 2(2), 156–168.

Goertzel, T. (1994). Belief in conspiracy theories. *Political Psychology*, 15(4), 731–742. https://doi.org/10.2307/3791630

Goga, O., Venkatadri, G., & Gummadi, K. P. (2015). The doppelgänger bot attack: Exploring identity impersonation in online social networks. In *Proceedings of the 2015 internet measurement conference* (pp. 141–153). New York, NY, USA: ACM. https://doi.org/10.1145/2815675.2815699

Griffiths, M. D. (2014). Adolescent trolling in online environments: A brief overview. *Education and Health*, 32(3), 85–87. Retrieved from http://irep.ntu.ac.uk/id/eprint/25950/

Groenendyk, E. (2018). Competing motives in a polarized electorate: Political responsiveness, identity defensiveness, and the rise of partisan antipathy. *Political Psychology*, *39*, 159–171. https://doi.org/10.1111/pops.12481

Gross, K., & D'Ambrosio, L. (2004). Framing emotional response. *Political Psychology*, *25*(1), 1–29. Retrieved from www.jstor.org/stable/3792521

Hovland, C. I., Lumsdaine, A. A., & Sheffield, F. D. (1949). *Experiments on mass communication.* (Studies in social psychology in World War II) (Vol. 3). Princeton, NJ: Princeton University Press.

Huddy, L., Sears, D. O., & Levy, J. S. (2013). *The Oxford handbook of political psychology.* Oxford: Oxford University Press.

Konijn, E. A. (2013). The role of emotion in media use and effects. *The Oxford Handbook of Media Psychology*, 186–211.

Kragh, M., & Åsberg, S. (2017). Russia's strategy for influence through public diplomacy and active measures: The Swedish case. *Journal of Strategic Studies*, *40*(6), 773–816. https://doi.org/10.1080/01402390.2016.1273830

Kurtzleben, D. (2016). Do fact checks matter? Retrieved August 8, 2018, from www.npr.org/2016/09/27/495233627/do-fact-checks-matter

Lazer, D. M. J., Baum, M. A., Benkler, Y., Berinsky, A. J., Greenhill, K. M., Menczer, F., . . . Zittrain, J. L. (2018). The science of fake news. *Science*, *359*(6380), 1094–1096. https://doi.org/10.1126/science.aao2998

Le Pen, M. (2018, March 19). Twitter post. Retrieved August 30, 2018, from https://twitter.com/mlp_officiel/status/975808872802856960?lang=en

Lewandowsky, S., Ecker, U. K. H., & Cook, J. (2017). Beyond misinformation: Understanding and coping with the "post-truth" era. *Journal of Applied Research in Memory and Cognition*, *6*(4), 353–369. https://doi.org/10.1016/j.jarmac.2017.07.008

Lewandowsky, S., Ecker, U. K. H., Seifert, C. M., Schwarz, N., & Cook, J. (2012). Misinformation and its correction: Continued influence and successful debiasing. *Psychological Science in the Public Interest*, *13*(3), 106–131. https://doi.org/10.1177/1529100612451018

Lewandowsky, S., Gignac, G. E., & Oberauer, K. (2013). The role of conspiracist ideation and worldviews in predicting rejection of science. *PLoS One*, *8*(10), 1–11. https://doi.org/10.1371/journal.pone.0075637

Lischka, J. A. (2017). A badge of honor? How the New York Times discredits President Trump's fake news accusations. *Journalism Studies*, 1–18. https://doi.org/10.1080/1461670X.2017.1375385

McCosker, A. (2014). Trolling as provocation: YouTube's agonistic publics. *Convergence*, *20*(2), 201–217. https://doi.org/10.1177/1354856513501413

McGuire, W. J. (1970). A vaccine for brainwash. *Psychology Today*, *3*(9), 36–64.

McGuire, W. J., & Papageorgis, D. (1961). The relative efficacy of various types of prior belief-defense in producing immunity against persuasion. *Journal of Abnormal and Social Psychology*, *62*, 327–337.

McGuire, W. J., & Papageorgis, D. (1962). Effectiveness of forewarning in developing resistance to persuasion. *Public Opinion Quarterly*, *26*(1), 24–34. https://doi.org/10.1086/267068

Melki, M., & Pickering, A. (2014). Ideological polarization and the media. *Economics Letters*, *125*(1), 36–39. https://doi.org/10.1016/j.econlet.2014.08.008

Nyhan, B., Porter, E., Reifler, J., & Wood, T. J. (2019). Taking fact-checks literally but not seriously? The effects of journalistic fact-checking on factual beliefs and candidate favorability. *Political Behavior*, 1–22.

Orita, A., & Hada, H. (2009). Is that really you? An approach to assure identity without revealing real-name online. In *Proceedings of the 5th ACM workshop on digital identity management* (pp. 17–20). New York, NY, USA: ACM. https://doi.org/10.1145/1655028.1655034

Papageorgis, D., & McGuire, W. J. (1961). The generality of immunity to persuasion produced by pre-exposure to weakened counterarguments. *Journal of Abnormal and Social Psychology, 62*, 475–481.

Patriot United. (2018). Muslim doctor refuses to save a Christian man's life on flight from New York to Las Vegas. Retrieved August 8, 2018, from https://web.archive.org/web/20180108183412/http:/patriotunited.club/2018/01/03/muslim-doctor-refuses-to-save-a-christian-mans-life-on-flight-from-new-york-to-las-vegas/

Pfau, M., Park, D., Holbert, R. L., & Cho, J. (2001). The effects of party-and PAC-sponsored issue advertising and the potential of inoculation to combat its impact on the democratic process. *American Behavioral Scientist, 44*(12), 2379–2397.

Pieters, J. (2018). Dutch politicians want EU anti-fake news watchdog scrapped. Retrieved August 8, 2018, from https://nltimes.nl/2018/03/06/dutch-politicians-want-eu-anti-fake-news-watchdog-scrapped

Poland, G. A., & Spier, R. (2010). Fear, misinformation, and innumerates: How the Wakefield paper, the press, and advocacy groups damaged the public health. *Vaccine, 28*(12), 2361–2362.

Prior, M. (2013). Media and political polarization. *Annual Review of Political Science, 16*(1), 101–127. https://doi.org/10.1146/annurev-polisci-100711-135242

Readfearn, G. (2016). Revealed: Most popular climate story on social media told half a million people the science was a Hoax. Retrieved August 8, 2018, from www.desmogblog.com/2016/11/29/revealed-most-popular-climate-story-social-media-told-half-million-people-science-was-hoax

Reuters. (2018). Fake news "vaccine" teaches you to spot disinformation. Retrieved January 15, 2019, from https://uk.reuters.com/video/2018/03/20/fake-news-vaccine-teaches-you-to-spot-di?videoId=410596269

Reznik, M. (2013). Identity theft on social networking sites: Developing issues of internet impersonation. *Touro Law Review, 29*(2), 12.

Roozenbeek, J., & van der Linden, S. (2018). The fake news game: Actively inoculating against the risk of misinformation. *Journal of Risk Research, 22*(5), 570–580. https://doi.org/10.1080/13669877.2018.1443491

Roozenbeek, J., & van der Linden, S. (2019). Fake news game confers psychological resistance against online misinformation. *Nature Palgrave Communications, 5*(65). https://doi.org/10.1057/s41599-019-027

Roozenbeek, J., van der Linden, S., & Nygren, T. (2020). Prebunking interventions based on "inoculation" theory can reduce susceptibility to misinformation across cultures. *Harvard Kennedy School Misinformation Review, 1*(2). https://doi.org/10.37016//mr-2020-008

Shao, C., Ciampaglia, G. L., Varol, O., Yang, K. C., Flammini, A., & Menczer, F. (2018). The spread of low-credibility content by social bots. *Nature Communications, 9*(1), 4787.

Snopes. (2018). Did "Muslim migrants" attack a Catholic Church during mass in France? Retrieved August 30, 2018, from www.snopes.com/fact-check/muslim-migrants-attack-catholic-church-mass-france/

Tandoc, E. C., Jr., Lim, Z. W., & Ling, R. (2018). Defining "fake news" a typology of scholarly definitions. *Digital Journalism, 6*(2), 137–153.

Thacker, S., & Griffiths, M. D. (2012). An exploratory study of trolling in online video gaming. *International Journal of Cyber Behavior, Psychology and Learning, 2*(4). https://doi.org/10.4018/ijcbpl.2012100102

Twenge, J. M., Honeycutt, N., Prislin, R., & Sherman, R. A. (2016). More polarized but more independent: Political party identification and ideological self-categorization among U.S. adults, college students, and late adolescents, 1970–2015. *Personality and Social Psychology Bulletin, 42*(10), 1364–1383. https://doi.org/10.1177/0146167216660058

van der Linden, S. (2015). The conspiracy-effect: Exposure to conspiracy theories (about global warming) decreases pro-social behavior and science acceptance. *Personality and Individual Differences, 87,* 171–173. Retrieved from www.sciencedirect.com/science/article/pii/S0191886915005024

van der Linden, S. (2017). Beating the hell out of fake news. *Ethical Record: Proceedings of the Conway Hall Ethical Society, 122*(6), 4–7. Retrieved from https://ssrn.com/abstract=3089590

van der Linden, S., Leiserowitz, A., Rosenthal, S., & Maibach, E. (2017). Inoculating the public against misinformation about climate change. *Global Challenges, 1*(2), 1600008. https://doi.org/10.1002/gch2.201600008

van der Linden, S., Maibach, E., Cook, J., Leiserowitz, A., & Lewandowsky, S. (2017). Inoculating against misinformation. *Science, 358*(6367), 1141–1142. https://doi.org/10.1126/science.aar4533

van der Linden, S., Panagopoulos, C., & Roozenbeek, J. (2020). You are fake news: political bias in perceptions of fake news. *Media, Culture & Society, 42*(3), 460–470.

van der Linden, S., Roozenbeek, J., Oosterwoud, R., Compton, J., & Lewandowsky, S. (2018). *The science of prebunking: Inoculating the public against fake news.* Written evidence submitted to the Parliamentary Inquiry on Fake News. House of Commons, UK Parliament, London: UK. Retrieved from http://data.parliament.uk/writtenevidence/committeeevidence.svc/evidencedocument/digital-culture-media-and-sport-committee/fake-news/written/79482.html

Varol, O., Ferrara, E., Davis, C. A., Menczer, F., & Flammini, A. (2017). *Online human-bot interactions: Detection, estimation, and characterization.* Proceedings of the Eleventh International AAAI Conference on Web and Social Media. Retrieved from www.aaai.org/ocs/index.php/ICWSM/ICWSM17/paper/viewPaper/15587

Vosoughi, S., Roy, D., & Aral, S. (2018). The spread of true and false news online. *Science, 359*(6380), 1146–1151. https://doi.org/10.1126/science.aap9559

Wakabayashi, D. (2017). As Google fights fake news, voices on the margins raise alarm. Retrieved February 15, 2018, from www.nytimes.com/2017/09/26/technology/google-search-bias-claims.html

Wakefield, J. (2017). Facebook's fake news experiment backfires. Retrieved August 8, 2018, from www.bbc.co.uk/news/technology-41900877

Walter, N., & Murphy, S. T. (2018). How to unring the bell: A meta-analytic approach to correction of misinformation. *Communication Monographs, 85*(3), 423–441.

PART III

Motivational processes in accepting, sharing, and correcting misinformation

10

YOUR FAKE NEWS, OUR FACTS

Identity-based motivation shapes what we believe, share, and accept

Daphna Oyserman and Andrew Dawson

Introduction

On June 23, 2016, British voters went to the polls, or rather, seven in ten British voters went to the polls; the others refrained (The Guardian, 2016). The less than full turnout was surprising because what was at stake was whether or not Britain (England, Northern Ireland, Scotland, and Wales) would remain part of the European Union (EU) as they had been since 1973. The EU was built on the assumption that members were safer, stronger, and freer together – their countries less likely to face war; their economies more prosperous; their citizens more able to choose their own path. A British generation had grown up with London as an EU financial center (Brush & Weber, 2019), with EU research funds flowing into British universities (UK Research and Innovation, 2019) and British products flowing seamlessly through the EU, Britain's largest trading partner, dwarfing trade with its next three largest trading partners combined (McCrae, 2018). This generation had grown up assuming that they could flow too – be educated, get jobs, raise families anywhere in the EU. As noted by the Stay campaign website (www.strongerin.co.uk/), voting to leave would undermine all of that.[1] It would leave Britain alone in a connected world and, by creating borders with Ireland, an EU member, would undermine a central element of the 1999 Good Friday peace accord with Northern Ireland that ended a long and bloody history of strife. Not only that, but the leave campaign provided no plan for how borders, trade, and already signed commitments would be handled if Britain exited the EU (Cooper, 2016).

Yet, the "exit" vote won at 51.9%. Not only that, but 18-to-24-year-olds, those with the most time at stake in the future, overwhelmingly voted "stay" but were also much less likely to vote at all than pensioners who came out in force and voted "exit" overwhelmingly (The Guardian, 2016). The same was true for

Northern Ireland, where only six in ten voters went to the polls (the majority of those who did vote, voted stay (BBC, 2016). Why did so many young voters and so many Northern Irish voters fail to vote on a referendum on what their future would be? Why might pensioners set Britain up to renege on the Good Friday agreement and undermine their financial certainty? One possibility is that this happened because people did not use the information just described in making their choice and instead reframed their choice (attribute substitution, Kahneman & Frederick, 2002). Instead of addressing the question of how leaving would address the problems in British society or the question of how it would provide alternatives to the benefits of being part of the EU, people addressed a different question. Rather than attempting to synthesize complex information regarding which choice would be better for Britain's economic and security future, people asked which choice felt like an "us" thing to do. If they could not decide, they stayed at home (Douthat, 2015; Massie, 2015).

How did this reframing occur? That is our focus in the current chapter. We suggest that people shifted from a complicated-to-answer information-based question to a simple-to-answer identity-based question. An information-based approach would require considering the relevance of large quantities of estimated data on costs (how much Britain paid into the EU), benefits (what Britain received from the EU), and alternatives (changes required to maintain trade, peace, and secure borders). To do so, for example, they would have to read reports to figure out if being in the EU lengthened wait times at the National Health Service (Giuntella, Nicodemo, & Vargas-Silva, 2015). They would have to read reports to figure out if unwanted people living and working in Britain were due more to being in the EU or too lax British policies on employment, on tracking people who overstayed visas, and of not having national identity cards (Blinder & Markaki, 2018; Goodwin, 2015). In contrast, an identity-based approach required simply that people ask themselves what "stay" or "leave" implied for who they were and might become – whether "stay" or "leave" felt more like an "us" thing to do.

In the current chapter, we focus on persuasive attempts to shift people from information-based to identity-based reasoning. To do so, we distinguish between *disinformation* and *information*. Disinformation is content shared to produce a particular judgment or course of action in message recipients, irrespective of the veracity, or bias of what is shared. In contrast, information is content shared to inform message recipients, what is shared is assumed to be true. As we detail, the persuasive power of a disinformer's call to action comes from weaponizing people's cultural expertise to efficiently channel them from information-based to identity-based processing.

We outline the steps in making this happen – creating the appearance of a culturally relevant "legitimate" question, framing the issue as an identity-based rather than an information-based concern, presenting a clear identity-based choice, and framing alternative choices as identity threatening. At step 1, disinformation campaigns use people's cultural expertise to reframe topics as questions, taking what would otherwise be considered an "illegitimate" question, because the answer goes without saying, and reframing it as a "legitimate" question – one in which the answer does not go without saying. At step 2, disinformation campaigns capitalize on people's cultural expertise so that the topic is framed in culturally fluent terms by using culturally recognizable icons, phrasing, embodied, and sensory cues. Having set the stage, disinformation campaigns frame a specific course of action as identity-relevant (what "we" do) and for good measure, suggest that failure to take the identity-relevant action threatens the identity itself – in the case of leaving the EU, that staying would result in a loss of British identity. Thus, as we outline in this chapter, there is more to the story than simply the lack of information or the presence of misinformation. It is how persuasive messages channel people to use their identities to make sense of what information implies for action that matters.

We use Britain and the 2016 British referendum on whether to stay in or secede from the EU as our concretizing example to frame our discussion of these three steps. The referendum was nicknamed Brexit, a mashup of the words "British" and "exit." This nickname helped frame the question of whether to stay or secede as being about exiting the EU. Alternative nicknames, for example, Brit-in, a mashup of the words "Britain" and "in" would have shifted framing to be about staying in the EU. In the next section, we operationalize what we mean by cultural expertise and why it matters for reasoning.

Cultural expertise, cultural fluency, and cultural disfluency

From an ecological perspective, group living is a survival necessity and human culture is essential to adapting to group living (Boyd & Richerson, 2005; Cohen, 2001; Haidle et al., 2015; Kurzban & Neuberg, 2005). Group living requires that people develop "social tuning" (sensitivity to others' perspectives) and "self-regulation" (the ability to control the focus of one's attention) skill (Chiu et al., 2015; Oyserman, 2011, 2017; Shteynberg, 2015). These culturally necessary skills are the basis of cultural practices evolved to create "good enough" solutions to the survival problems of coordinating, fitting in, and sharing. These solutions are "good enough", rather than optimal, but, once developed, they become "sticky" by virtue of being the way "we" do things – "our" structures, practices, norms, and values (Cohen, 2001; Oyserman, 2015a). They permeate all aspects of behavior, constrain and enable perception and reasoning, and provide a shared blueprint or outline for meaning-making across a variety of situations (Chiu, et al., 2010; Nisbett & Norenzayan, 2002; Oyserman, 2017; Shweder & LeVine, 1984; Triandis, 2007).

In this way, culture is in part a set of associative knowledge networks, tacit operating codes, or meaning-making frameworks through which people make sense of their world, understand what they want, and how they go about getting it. These culture-rooted associative knowledge networks provide mental models, affording people the cultural expertise to predict how situations will likely unfold. Each of a culture's "good enough" solutions entails a knowledge network including the content, procedures, and goals related to its overarching theme – individualism, collectivism, and honor. The same is the case for each of a culture's practices. Each practice entails knowledge networks, including specific, often implicit, knowledge about how things work – what brides wear, what breakfast entails, and so on. Immediate contexts make some subset of available cultural knowledge networks accessible in the moment.

Cultural mindsets shape accessible mental procedures

People use the subset of their available culture-based knowledge that is accessible at the moment of judgment to make an automatic prediction about what will happen next. People use the mental procedure associated with an accessible cultural mindset. For example, after an individualistic mindset is primed, people are better at quickly naming a distinct object in a visual array (Oyserman, Sorensen, Reber, & Chen, 2009, Study 3). This response suggests that they are using a pull-apart-and-separate procedure. In contrast, after a collectivistic mindset is primed, people are better at recalling where objects were in a visual array (Oyserman et al., 2009, Studies 1, 2) and have more trouble ignoring extraneous visual (Oyserman et al., 2009, Studies 4, 5) or auditory (Oyserman et al., 2009, Studies 6, 7) information. This response suggests that they are using a connect-and-relate procedure. Other studies support these procedure-based predictions of an accessible collectivistic mindset (e.g., Mourey, Oyserman, & Yoon, 2013; Oyserman et al., 2009). After this happens, people are willing to pay more to complete a set (Mourey et al., 2013, Study 1b). They are willing to accept previously undesired options if a set cannot be completed (Mourey et al., 2013, Studies 2 to 4). They have more difficulty finding the best match and ignoring other plausible but not as good matches in a standardized antonym and analogies task (Oyserman, et al., 2009, Study 8). People from different countries (the United States, Norway, Hong Kong, Korea) and different racial-ethnic groups (e.g., Latino, African American, Asian, or Asian American) shifted to using or not using a collectivistic mindset, depending on momentary cues. Across experiments, the mental procedure people used depended on the cultural mindset accessible in the moment. Anything that makes people's group-based identities (e.g., being British, being rural, being patriotic) salient at the moment should trigger their use of a collectivistic mindset (Oyserman, 2007). Once a collectivistic mindset is triggered, people are more willing to focus on how things connect and that can make it harder to see flaws in logic (Oyserman, 2019a).

Cultural knowledge shapes what is fluent and disfluent and hence reasoning style

Cultural knowledge sets up implicit expectations as to how things will unfold. It is easier for people to make sense of a situation that unfolds as they expect that it will and more difficult for them to make sense of a situation if the way it unfolds violates their implicit expectations. A classic example comes from Bruner and Postman (1949). They showed that American college students were slower to recognize shapes when they saw shapes (hearts, diamonds, clubs, spades) in colors that mismatched (e.g., a red spade) their culture-based knowledge about the color of these shapes on playing cards (they are supposed to be black). Students in this study applied their culture-based knowledge automatically. They did so even though the experimenters never said that the task was a playing card shape task and never told them that they should use their knowledge of the colors of shapes on playing cards. They applied their knowledge automatically. As a result, people had trouble discerning shape when the shape was a club but the color was red. People were particularly likely to apply their culture-based knowledge on the first card they saw and seemed to continue to use their culture-based knowledge unless multiple trials showed it was irrelevant. Culture, of course, is dynamic, and that experiment will only replicate among current American college students if playing cards are as common a pursuit now as it seems to have been when the experiment was originally conducted in the 1940s.

Cultural knowledge not only makes it easier to process culturally fluent information, but it also helps people know when something is not right, triggering a shift from associative, gut-based reasoning to systematic, rule-based reasoning when the unexpected occurs (Oyserman, 2011). As an example, consider four experiments conducted by Mourey, Lam, and Oyserman (2015). In each experiment, the cultural cue (independent variable) was being exposed to a culturally fluent (matched cultural expectation) or culturally disfluent (mismatched cultural expectation) situation or product. The first experiment involved having or not having the color pink as a border on Valentine's Day or after Valentine's Day, the second and third involved first rating the quality of photographs of weddings, the fourth involved first choosing among formats of an obituary for a family and then engaging in the cognitive task. The prediction was that cultural expertise would make the match easier to process than the mismatch and that this cultural expertise-driven processing difficulty would trigger a shift to systematic reasoning.

The effect on reasoning (dependent variable) was assessed with a cognitive task that was specifically devised to have both a gut-based and a rule-based answer. Though gut-based responses are not always wrong, they lead people astray in situations in which applying a processing rule does not come naturally but is the correct way to proceed. Here is an example from the original task (taken from Frederick, 2005): "A fishing rod and fishing bait cost $1.1 in total. The fishing rod costs $1.0 more than the bait. How much does the bait cost?" The gut-based but incorrect response is $.10 based on the gist focus on the "$1.0" piece of information resulting in simply subtracting $1.0 from $1.1 ($1.1 − $1.0 = $.10). The rule-based and correct response is $.05 based on the rule-based focus on the "$1.0 more" as a piece of information resulting in the equation: $1.1= n + (n + $1.0). People give the $.10 gut-based or $.05 rule-based response, only a few people give answers that cannot be coded as gut or rule-based (answers other than $.10 or $0.05).

The first experiment took place in Ann Arbor, Michigan (United States), and in Hong Kong, S.A.R. China. In each location, people were randomly assigned to one of four groups – groups varied as to the day (Valentine's Day or a week later) they were approached and the screen border color (pink, not pink) they saw. One group (cultural fluency group) did the task on Valentine's Day and worked on a screen that displayed a pink-colored border. The other three groups were control groups. They did the task on Valentine's Day but without a pink-colored border, or a week after Valentine's Day with or without the pink-colored border. People who were randomly assigned to the cultural fluency group saw a pink border on Valentine's Day (the "right" color at the "right" time). This match to culture-based expectation preserved "gut"-based reasoning even when rule-based reasoning was needed. Indeed, people in the cultural fluency group were more likely to give the wrong answer than people in the other three groups (who did not differ). The rule was not hard to apply, it just required that people notice that it should be applied. The time people took to respond did not differ for those who used a rule compared to those who used their gut.

This finding – that even in situations calling for rule-based, systematic reasoning, people stuck to associative gut-based reasoning after receiving culturally fluent cues, was replicated in three follow-up experiments. Tellingly, in these experiments, effects were found even though exposure to the cultural cue that triggered cultural fluency and disfluency was separate from the subsequent reasoning task. In two experiments, cultural expertise about weddings was triggered. In these wedding studies, half of the participants were randomly assigned to rate eight culturally fluent wedding photographs and the other half were randomly assigned to rate eight culturally disfluent photographs. In the culturally fluent photographs, the bride was in white, the groom in black, their tiered wedding cake had white fondant icing, and their wedding party had bridesmaids and groomsmen. In the culturally disfluent photographs, the bridal dress included some green and purple, the groom's tuxedo also had some purple, their tiered wedding cake was decorated with colorful cogs, and there was no wedding party. In the final experiment, cultural expertise about funerals and mourning was triggered. In this obituary study, half of the participants were randomly assigned to a culturally fluent obituary set and the other half to a culturally disfluent obituary set. In the culturally fluent condition, they saw two versions of the same sad in tone, praising the deceased, obituary. In the culturally disfluent condition, they saw two versions of the same not sad in tone, not praising the deceased obituary. The researchers found the not sad, not praising obituary and created a parallel sad, praising obituary. Thus, "had no hobbies . . . will not be missed" in the original was edited to "had numerous hobbies . . . will be missed". The researchers made two versions of each obituary by rearranging paragraph order.

Across experiments, the people who were randomly assigned to the culturally fluent condition were more likely to use gut-based reasoning than those randomly assigned to the cultural disfluent condition. As these experiments demonstrate, experiences of cultural fluency and of cultural disfluency are the result of the interface between what observers' cultural expertise leads them to (implicitly) expect, what they actually observe, and the meaning they draw from their ensuing metacognitive experiences of ease or difficulty (Oyserman, 2011, 2017). What makes for a metacognitive experience of ease or difficulty is not the observation itself but the match or mismatch between observation and culture-based expectation. Experiencing match or mismatch requires having the cultural expertise to know (implicitly) what to expect. These expectations are rooted in one's culture – what one has learned explicitly or picked up implicitly through observation and socialization practices. When messages appear in culturally fluent terms, people may be more susceptible to disinformation simply because the message does not trigger a shift to systematic reasoning (Oyserman, 2019a).

Cultural expertise and persuasive messages

Prior research on cultural fluency and disfluency has not directly assessed the effects of cultural expertise on the people's processing of persuasive messages (for a review, Oyserman & Yan, 2019). The reasoning strategy people use matters for which kind of message people find persuasive (Petty & Cacioppo, 1981, 1984). If they are using an associative reasoning approach, they are less likely to notice differences in message quality than if they are using a systematic reasoning approach. Messages that use some mix of the images, phrasing, sounds, and content people tacitly expect are more culturally fluent. In this section, we consider how a message's cultural fluency might matter.

Recall that people are less likely to use systematic reasoning in culturally fluent situations. We infer from this that people may be less likely to reason systematically when they are confronted with culturally fluent persuasion attempts. Because they are not reasoning systematically, the quality of the persuasive argument may not matter as much. As a result of not paying attention to message quality, people may fail to distinguish information from misinformation – messages meant to convey facts as known at the time, from factually incorrect or biased information. They may fail to distinguish between informational messages meant to inform choice and judgment, and disinformational messages meant to yield a particular course of action. For a message to be culturally fluent, a message needs to contain some mix of the images, phrasing, and content that people tacitly expect to see or hear in a situation.

As we articulate next, cultural fluency activates identity-based, rather than information-based, reasoning. When people are using information-based reasoning, they have access to both associative and systematic strategies. In contrast, when they are using identity-based reasoning, their access to systematic reasoning strategies is effectively blocked. We apply the logic of communication, described next, to explain why.

The logic of communication

Following conventions of language use, people typically assume that message sharers have a goal of informing (Grice's maxims of communication or "logic of communication", Schwarz, 2014). That is, people assume that message sharers share content they believe to be factually true, unbiased, and potentially useful in informing judgment and decision making, even if sometimes message sharers get it wrong and, unbeknownst to themselves, misinform – share factually untrue or biased content. According to these conventions of language use, unless they have reason to be suspicious, people start with the assumption that communicators are attempting to be informative – to clearly tell them something that is relevant, something that their audience does not already know (Schwarz, 2014).

The logic of communication and communicative intent

The logic of communication serves people well when sender and receiver share a mutual goal of informing. Because their reasoning is shaped by the logic of communication, people make (often implicit) assumptions about information from how it is communicated (Gilbert, 1991; Gilbert, Krull, & Malone, 1990; Schwarz, Strack, Hilton, & Naderer, 1991; Schwarz, 2014; Schwarz & Sudman, 2012; Sudman, Bradburn, & Schwarz, 1996). They do so whether or not the communicator intended them to make these inferences and often without awareness of the source of their inference (Schwarz et al., 1991).

The logic of communication, however, can also shield the intentions of those message senders who do not have a goal of informing judgment and choice but instead have a goal of shaping judgment and producing a particular outcome (a judgment, a choice). Although message veracity and bias are relevant when message senders have a goal of informing, they are irrelevant when message senders have a goal of shaping judgment and producing a particular choice. As we noted in our opening paragraphs, we use the term "disinformation" to describe this latter form of message content shared by senders who do not have the intent to inform but the intent to shape recipient judgment and decision making independently of the probative content of the messages they send. Veracity and bias are irrelevant to disinformation messaging, it does not matter if the content is true or unbiased; it only matters if the intended response is produced (Weedon, Nuland, & Stamos, 2017). What we are proposing is that people are particularly unlikely to notice disinformation if it is presented in a culturally fluent way because, in these situations, they are less likely to feel suspicious, notice something is off, and shift to systematic reasoning.

The logic of communication and "legitimate" (versus "illegitimate") questions

Because people make assumptions based on how information is communicated, communicators can raise doubt by simply asking a question. Following the logic of communication, question recipients typically assume cooperative intent. Regarding questions, cooperative intent implies that the communicator is posing a question because more than one option is possible. Having more than one possible answer is what makes a question legitimate. If there is only one possible answer, the question is not a legitimate one. But the possibility that the question is not legitimate is typically overlooked when people assume cooperative intent. That is why asking "who is buried in Grant's tomb?" (a question that includes its answer, Grant) is puzzling; if this is a legitimate question then that means that there is more than one possible answer option. That implies that Grant is not buried in Grant's tomb, that what seems to be the only possible answer (General Grant) is not. When the goal is not to inform but to disinform – to change judgment rather than to inform it, then raising a question can be a first step in changing judgment. Having been asked "who is buried in Grant's tomb?" people often respond by saying "I don't know, who?" having ruled out that it is Grant. But of course, this is not a legitimate question – Grant *is* buried in Grant's tomb. We propose that such *illegitimate* questions, ones not based on lack of a single answer, have the intention of sowing doubt and leading people to be open to being told any possible alternative.

In 2016, the question "should Britain exit the EU?" was not, at least initially, a clearly legitimate question. After all, if whether to leave the EU could be considered a legitimate question, it would imply that what was assumed to be true might not be so, that maybe being in the EU is a problem, otherwise, why ask the question? By getting the question on the ballot, the secession campaign succeeded in making the question seem as if it might be legitimate. Beyond getting the question on the ballot, the exit campaign could have used informational or disinformation messaging, as of course, could the stay campaign. In the next section, we outline what identity-based motivation is. Then we use identity-based motivation to explain the appeal of disinformation campaigns, using examples from the Brexit campaign (we looked for but did not find examples in the Stay campaign).

Identity-based motivation

Dynamic construction, interpretation of experience, and action readiness

Identity-based motivation (IBM) theory is a situated cognition theory of self-regulation that predicts that people prefer to make sense of situations and act in ways that feel congruent with their important social and personal identities (Oyserman, 2007, 2009, 2015b). Social identities are identities linked to group membership – being patriotic, nationalistic, British, a Londoner, a European, male, a parent, a taxpayer. These identities may be linked to a variety of content and in this way, overlap with personal identities – as fiscally prudent, proud, loyal. Social identities may reference both semantic content (what we value, our beliefs) and sensory content – what we look like, what we sound like, the tastes we like. People have many past, current, and future possible social and personal identities available to them in memory and these identities have no preset organizational structure (Oyserman, Elmore, & Smith, 2012). Instead, people are affected by the particular identities that are accessible ("on their mind") at the moment of judgment, if these identities feel relevant to the task at hand.

Dynamic construction

To paraphrase William James (1890), thinking (about the self) is for doing. Because doing requires sensitivity to the affordances and constraints in the situation, which identities come to mind, and what these "on-the-mind" identities seem to mean, is sensitively attuned to momentary and chronic features of context (for a review, Oyserman et al., 2012). People not only pull from memory what an identity means, they also infer from context what an identity must mean given features of the immediate situation. In that sense, identities are dynamically constructed in the moment – the seemingly same identity may imply different actions in different contexts. Thus, in the moment, being British may be part of being European – when traveling without need of visas, but it could also be in contrast to being European – when people from other countries register their children in your local school. That people are sensitive to the implications of their immediate situation is a design feature, not a design flaw. Sensitivity to social context allows people to make inferences about what people like themselves likely do, which strategies work for them, and what inferences to draw when they progress smoothly as well as when they run into difficulties (Oyserman et al., 2017).

Using the logic that we outlined in the section on the evolution of culture, messages from in-groups should feel more credible – in-group members share values and are less likely to be harmful than out-group members. From an evolutionary perspective, being able to recognize who is in the in-group is critical. The in-group is safe, can be approached. The in-group is unlikely to deceive or pose a threat, reducing the need to be wary, suspicious, and guarded (Brewer, 1979; Platow, Foddy, Yamagishi, Lim, & Chow, 2012). With the in-group, one's guard can be let down, but how can one tell who is providing the message? The senses can be a cue – people like "me" sound a certain way, use certain turns of phrase, have certain accents, and people like me "look" a certain way, wear certain styles, focus on certain iconic images, people like "me" share tastes, values, and desires. Thus, in-group messages are more likely to "ring true" and to "sound right"; they are more likely to feel familiar and be culturally fluent.

Procedural readiness

Sense-making or "procedural readiness" is the readiness to make sense of new situations in the ways afforded by the cued identities. For example, when collectivistic "we" social identities are cued, people are more likely to use connecting and relating mental procedures, whereas when individualistic "I" personal dentities are cued, people are more likely to use separating and distinguishing mental procedures (Oyserman, 2007). This implies that if disinformation campaign message content includes social identities, the campaign message carries a trigger to think in terms of connections and associations rather than to focus on a main point. We show examples of this process in the section labeled Disinformation Campaigns and Identity-based Motivation.

Action readiness

The readiness to act in new or ambiguous situations in identity-congruent ways is referred to as "action-readiness". If taking a particular action is identity-congruent, "for me" or "for us", that implies the importance of persisting when difficulties starting or staying on course arise. In contrast, if taking a particular action is identity-irrelevant or even identity-incongruent, people are likely to interpret difficulties starting or staying going differently. In these cases, difficulty implies that the action is not for "me" anyway (Elmore & Oyserman, 2012; Oyserman, 2019b). Prior research has focused on the interplay of social identities with taking school-focused action – studying, engaging in class discussion, paying attention, asking for help, going to the library (e.g., for reviews, Oyserman et al., 2012; Oyserman, 2019b). Though not directly assessed, the implication is that taking identity-congruent action is identity affirming and failing to do so is identity threatening. For example, if good students study, studying should affirm that one is a good student; failing to study implies that one is something else. In the case of the Brexit campaign, social identities, including being British and being an environmentalist, were linked to the particular action of voting "leave". The implication is that if that is what "we" do, a person who fails to vote "leave" might not really be a part of the identity group and worse, might be contributing to the demise of the group and what the group stands for.

As illustrated in Figure 10.1, each of the three identity-based motivation components (dynamic construction of identity, readiness to act, and meaning-making in identity-congruent ways) operates in tandem. This mutuality means that cues to action not only trigger action but also cascade to meaning-making and identity. Hence, if in context, an identity comes to mind, its implications for meaning-making and action are also afforded. The same holds if an action comes to mind (actions' implications for identity and meaning-making are afforded) or if a way of making sense of experience comes to mind (meaning-making's implications for identity and meaning-making are afforded).

Identity stability is a useful fiction

Though dynamic construction is a key feature of the functioning of identity-based motivation, people do not necessarily experience their identities or their motivational processes in this flexible way. Instead, people typically experience their identities as stable across time and space (Oyserman, 2019b). This belief is useful for

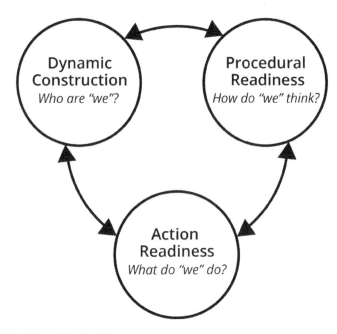

FIGURE 10.1 Three interlocking components

several reasons. First, it allows people to make predictions about their future preferences given what they prefer now by experiencing current "me" and future "me" as essentially the same "me" (Oyserman, 2019b). Second, it facilitates choice among action alternatives. That is, taking current action for the sake of future "me" – doing schoolwork (Nurra & Oyserman, 2018) or saving for retirement (Lewis & Oyserman, 2015) – makes sense if current and future "me" are essentially the same. Third, by increasing certainty, it minimizes the extent that people need to seek out supporting information for identity-based choices and sense making.

Consequential yet difficult: shifting from information-based to identity-based reasoning

Of course, people do not have to use identity-based reasoning; they can (and do) engage in information-based reasoning. Information-based reasoning entails using the information at hand to guide judgment and inform choice. People are likely to use information-based processing when the information to be used is easy to access, clear, and limited; in these cases, computational processing (e.g., trading off risks and rewards) is possible (Reyna, 2004). Information-based reasoning can be quick. For example, which navigation route is faster can be answered by searching a web-based traffic application; which product costs more can be answered by price comparisons. Yet, the information to be used in making choices and forming judgments is often none of these things, particularly

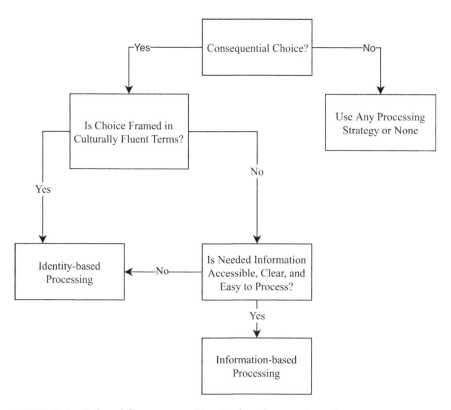

FIGURE 10.2   Cultural fluency as an identity-based processing trigger

when choice is consequential for the long run, but long-run outcomes are complex, uncertain, and difficult to process. Attempting to use a computational rule to process information in these cases is not only difficult, it may not be possible, requiring that people need to use another strategy. We propose that culturally fluent framing of information facilitates a shift from a difficult to address information-based question to an easy to address identity-based one. We summarize this process in Figure 10.2.

Social media and the dissemination of disinformation

Social media platforms are designed for people to come together and share identity-relevant content. These platforms seem free and friendly – people feel that they are choosing what to engage with, that their choices are not being constrained, and that they can choose whom to affiliate with. Yet by engaging freely in what appears to be a friendly, safe, in-group setting, people also provide platform organizers with a large pool of rich data on themselves and their networks. They, and their data, become a product that platform organizers can sell. This combination – a flow of information through personal "friend" or "follower" connections and the availability of rich data – make social platforms ideal for campaigns seeking to spread culturally fluent disinformation messages targeted to important social identities. Users willingly or unwittingly turn over their data and other high-resolution behavioral insights to corporations in exchange for the ability to connect and share information (Redazione, 2018). Much of these data can readily be turned into targeting demographics for advertising. Facebook, for example, generates a vast majority of its revenue from advertising, over $55 billion USD in 2018 (Facebook, 2019). Facebook has admitted to allowing Cambridge Analytica to harvest an estimated 87 million Facebook user's information including their networks (Kang & Frenkel, 2018).

At their core, social media platforms are highly efficient advertising networks. Their algorithms aim to increase content engagement and time spent on the platform by directing attention to stimulating content personalized for an individual, by providing content that fits a user's worldview or content that is emotion-based (Barberá, Jost, Nagler, Tucker, & Bonneau, 2015; Kramer, Guillory, & Hancock, 2014). Facebook produces detailed data profiles on users, including facial recognition data, location information, interests, demographics, behaviors, and social network maps; by allowing for interactivity, it can harvest the information people contribute, the specific content users engage with, and what they do with this content (Facebook, n.d.). All of these data can be used to tailor and disseminate disinformation effectively (Facebook, 2019; Shochat, Shniberg, Hirsch, & Tagiman, 2009). Big data techniques allow abstraction of specific metrics – demographics, psychological abstractions such as personality traits and more – from these data (Kosinski, Stillwell, & Graepel, 2013).

Identity-based motivation and disinformation campaigns

We illustrate how this disinformation process works by returning to the example of the Brexit campaign. To succeed, the secession campaign needed to do two things: it needed to persuade some voters to vote "leave" and it needed to persuade other voters to stay home and not vote at all. To do so, the Brexit campaign used targeted disinformation (false or manipulated content meant not to inform but to produce a particular action). The campaign reduced the chances that voters would notice that messages were disinformational by using culturally fluent materials (reducing likelihood of shift to systematic reasoning) and social identities (increase likelihood of collectivistic mental procedures, that is, reasoning in terms of connections and associations). The campaign increased chances that disinformational messages would be accepted by framing judgment and choice in terms of social identities (how "we" think, the choices "we" make), likely triggering both action-readiness and a collectivistic frame (which should increase sensitivity to the communicative intent of the message sender, e.g., Haberstroh, Oyserman, Schwarz, Kühnen, & Ji, 2002). Having done so, the Brexit campaign then framed a particular action (vote "exit") as the identity-relevant one for some voters. For other voters, the Brexit campaign focused instead on undermining confidence in the triggered identity or in what that identity implied for behavior. This culturally luent identity-based reformulation succeeded in two ways. First, it made Brexit a legitimate question. Second, it freed people from having to digest complex, competing, and uncertain estimates of the financial cost of staying or leaving and allowed them to ask instead what a "stay" or "leave" vote (or voting at all) felt like in terms of who they were. Of course, this reformulation from information-based to identity-based choice could not have worked if people did not already have a preference for making identity-congruent choices, taking identity-congruent action, and making sense of their experiences in identity-congruent ways.

To attain these outcomes, two different secession campaigns, the "BeLeave" campaign and the "Vote Leave" campaign hired a digital firm to run their media-based persuasion (House of Commons, 2019). The firm, Aggregate IQ (AIQ), is a North American firm whose founders specialize in persuasive power on digital platform-based social media, including Facebook. The firm was an established player in the domain of digital mass persuasion, specifically in the political arena. AIQ developed software products for the SCL group, a large "global election management agency" more commonly known by their subsidiary Cambridge Analytica. AIQ's tools were also used in North American elections by the SCL group, working for the Republican Party (House of Commons, 2018).

To persuade British voters in the Brexit referendum, AIQ used their knowledge of how Facebook operates to generate thousands of different content pieces for Facebook (Facebook, n.d.). The firm took an identity-targeting strategy to disinformation. The chief architect of the information operation framed the underlying thesis as: "We use data to capture and identify a person's identity . . . we design personalized interventions – informational or communications interventions – that will change their behavior in a way that is bespoke to that person" (Cadwalladr, 2018; Redazione, 2018). AIQ both consulted with the campaigns on the efficacy of preexisting content and independently created large quantities of new content. They served this content using internal dissemination teams, leveraging advanced demographic targeting and profiling – that is, they knew who exactly they were targeting with which content pieces, and selected specific pieces for each individual and their personal susceptibilities (House of Commons, 2018). In this way, British citizens were delivered content that looked "right", "rang true", or "spoke" to them, in clear and visceral terms. But what appeared to unsuspecting social media users as simply catchy visuals and tag lines were actually carefully designed culturally fluent frames to deliver an identity-based call to action.

Effects of culturally fluent identity-based motivational framing: the Brexit campaign

Leveraging culturally fluent identity-based motivation to increase "leave" voting

Figure 10.3 (teacup) and Figure 10.4 (polar bear) provide two examples of what content pieces meant to propel "leave" voting looked like. The teacup message takes an identity "British" and dynamically constructs particular content from

FIGURE 10.3 A culturally fluent nostalgic British identity framing EU secession as necessary for maintenance of British identity

Source: Reprinted from *House of Commons* under the Open Parliament License v3.0

FIGURE 10.4 A culturally fluent environmentalist identity framing EU secession as necessary for maintenance of an environmentalist identity

Source: Reprinted from *House of Commons* under the Open Parliament License v3.0

this identity. It takes culturally fluent visual (Big Ben, red phone booth) and sensory cues (implied taste of British tea and sound of "cuppa") of "British" and creates a novel meaning that being "British" is best attained by voting the leave the EU. This message is targeted at people for whom Britishness of a certain nostalgic nature might easily come to mind and is multifaceted. That is, not only does cuppa informally mean "cup of tea", linguistically cuing Britishness in everyday speech, but the saying "not my cuppa [tea]", means "not for me", adding more cultural fluency. Not only does the teacup message frame a particular course of action for its targeted audience, but it is also so clearly nostalgic that it is unlikely to be experienced as relevant to other audiences. Hence, it is unlikely to mobilize action among a potential "stay" audience.

The polar bear message frames a different identity, environmentalist, and suggests that having that identity requires a specific action – exit the EU. It is targeted at people for whom social identities other than nostalgic Britishness might more easily come to mind. Much like the teacup message, people who are unlikely to have an environmentalist identity triggered are unlikely to process this information as relevant – if anything it might seem just silly. Lacking a framework to make sense of the polar bear, they are unlikely to respond at all to the message.

Leveraging culturally fluent identity-based motivation to undermine "stay" voting

To persuade potential "stay" voters to just stay home, the Brexit campaign had two options. It could increase doubt that voting "leave" really was a "we" thing to do or increase doubt that voting at all was something that "we" do. Figure 10.5 (jet travel) provides an example of what content pieces meant to undermine certainty that voting was a "me" or "us" thing to do looked like. The jet travel message frames two possible identities, a sensible, frugal British identity

FIGURE 10.5 Culturally fluent framing of EU support as support for corruption resulting in undermined confidence in EU and British identities fitting together

Source: Reprinted from *House of Commons* under the Open Parliament License v3.0

and an environmental identity. The British identity frame is in some ways similar to the nostalgic teacup frame; in this case, recalling the postwar austerity years. Like the teacup frame, there is no ambiguity to the call for action – vote "exit". In contrast, the environmental identity frame poses the question of whether staying or leaving is the better environmental choice. Like many environmental choices – is it better to wash the recyclable plastic (wasting water) or to throw it into a landfill (wasting energy)? Or is it simpler not to choose? For the environmentalist, the jet travel message undermines certainty as to whether voting "stay" or "leave" is the identity-congruent action. Moreover, with its whiff of potential corruption, the jet travel message undermines certainty that political leaders have anything but their own interests at heart. The message produces a lack of clarity as to which action to take and reduces the likelihood of acting at all. Exposure to this message should reduce the likelihood that environmentalists see voting as clearly identity-congruent while at the same time increasing the likelihood that nostalgic pensioners did. It should undermine certainty that voting at all is identity congruent, given that messages from a corrupt source are unlikely to be providing useful information as to what people like "me" should do.

After the vote: long-term effects

Because they trigger culturally fluent identity-based reasoning, the effects of disinformation campaigns are likely to be long-lasting. By engaging with culturally fluent social identity-based cues, people are likely to actively produce an identity. This identity triggers immediate action and carries over to frame subsequent judgments. In the case of the Brexit campaign, the immediate action is a shift in voting behavior. Being British is not necessarily antagonistic to being a European, but once framed in this way, people are likely having this association whenever the linked British identity cues come to mind. By linking action to identity-based processing, disinformation triggers, and maintains an associative reasoning style. Because social identities trigger a collectivistic connecting and relating mental procedure, people experience the engineered action as identity-relevant thing to do. It becomes the way "we" act, with the implication that it fits "our" values. As we describe in the section on dynamic construction, disinformation does not need to rely on already available identity-to-action associations. These associations can be constructed in context. However, once they are constructed and repeatedly engaged, whenever the identity is triggered, the associated actions and implied values will be triggered as well (as portrayed in Figure 10.1). Once linked to identity, it is neither necessary nor useful to recall where information came from since disinformation is agnostic as to the veracity of information.

Comparing effectiveness of information, misinformation, and disinformation: a culturally infused IBM perspective

The conventions of language use lead people to assume that message sharers typically have a goal of informing (Grice's maxims of communication or 'logic of communication', Schwarz, 2014). Informing entails sharing content one believes to be factually true, unbiased, and potentially useful for making a decision. This logic holds even if sometimes message sharers get it wrong and, unbeknownst to themselves, misinform by sharing factually untrue or biased content. However, disinformation may be more potent because it focuses directly on shaping judgment and engineering behavior. Hence, misinformation is more likely to affect action. Other informational messaging techniques such as narrative building may effectively change opinion and this may translate the change into action if linked to social identities (Murphy, Frank, Moran, & Patnoe-Woodley, 2011). That is, rather than change attitudes, narrative techniques may take an identity-based route to persuasion (e.g., via social norms, Paluck, 2009). The implication is that identity-based persuasion techniques can improve an information campaign's likelihood of affecting judgment and behavior, whether or not the information can be accurately recalled. The challenge in correcting misinformation and disinformation is that once a question has been framed as "how do we think about this?", it is unlikely that people will switch to a different question of "what is the probative value of this information?" Worse yet, once people come to believe that "we" think and act in a certain way, they are more unlikely to consider other information as other than "alternative facts". Correction attempts that do not focus on triggering the construction of alternative identity-based reasoning are unlikely to succeed. Future research addressing when identity-based persuasive framing works, when it backfires, and how to address their potential for abuse are sorely needed.

Note

1 This set of information-based arguments, including job figures, consumer goods prices, and returns on EU investments, was the focus of Britain Stronger in Europe, the leading remain campaign, with the slogan "More Jobs, Lower Prices, and Workers Rights" (www.strongerin.co.uk/).

References

Barberá, P., Jost, J., Nagler, J., Tucker, J., & Bonneau, R. (2015). Tweeting from left to right: Is online political communication more than an echo chamber? *Psychological Science, 26*(10), 1531–1542.

BBC. (2016). Interactive map with regional voter results June 23, 2016. *EU Referendum Results.* Retrieved September 9, 2019, from www.bbc.com/news/politics/eu_referendum/results

Blinder, S., & Markaki, Y. (2018). *Public attitudes toward EU mobility and Non-EU immigration: A distinction with little difference* (No. WP-18-141). COMPAS, School of Anthropology, University of Oxford. Retrieved September 9, 2019, from www.compas.ox.ac.uk/2015/the-effects-of-immigration-on-nhs-waiting-times/

Boyd, R., & Richerson, P. J. (2005). *The origin and evolution of cultures.* New York, NY: Oxford University Press.

Brewer, M. B. (1979). In-group bias in the minimal intergroup situation: A cognitive-motivational analysis. *Psychological Bulletin, 86*(2), 307–324.

Britain Stronger in Europe. (n.d.). Britain stronger in Europe. Retrieved September 15, 2019, from www.strongerin.co.uk/get_the_facts. Declared as the official "Remain" campaign for the referendum by the Electoral Commission on 13 April 2016.

Bruner, J. S., & Postman, L. (1949). On the perception of incongruity: A paradigm. *Journal of Personality*, *18*, 206–223.

Brush, S., & Weber, A. (2019, July 2). London's fight to remain a financial hub after Brexit. *Bloomberg*. Retrieved September 9, 2019, from www.bloomberg.com/news/articles/2019-07-03/london-s-fight-to-remain-a-financial-hub-after-brexit-quicktake

Cadwalladr, C. (2018, March 18). "I made Steve Bannon's psychological warfare tool": Meet the data war whistleblower. *The Guardian*. Retrieved September 9, 2019, from www.theguardian.com/news/2018/mar/17/data-war-whistleblower-christopher-wylie-faceook-nix-bannon-trump

Chiu, C.-Y., Gelfand, M., Harrington, J. R., Leung, A., Liu, Z., Morris, M., . . . Zou, X. (2015). A conclusion, yet an opening to enriching the normative approach of culture. *Journal of Cross-Cultural Psychology*, *46*(10), 1361–1371.

Chiu, C.-Y., Gelfand, M., Yamagishi, T., Shteynberg, G., & Wan, C. (2010). Intersubjective culture: The role of intersubjective perceptions in cross-cultural research. *Perspectives on Psychological Science*, *5*(4), 482–493.

Cohen, D. (2001). Cultural variation: Considerations and implications. *Psychological Bulletin*, *127*, 451–471.

Cooper, C. (2016, June 26). Brexit campaigners admit "there is no plan" for what comes next as rivals plan Tory leadership bids. Retrieved September 8, 2019, from www.independent.co.uk/news/uk/politics/brexit-eu-referendum-campaigners-there-is-no-plan-next-pm-tory-leadership-contest-a7104711.html

Douthat, R. (2015, May 9). The suicide of Britain. *The New York Times*. Retrieved September 9, 2019, from www.nytimes.com/2015/05/10/opinion/sunday/ross-douthat-the-suicide-of-britain.html?searchResultPosition=4

Elmore, K., & Oyserman, D. (2012). If "we" can succeed, "I" can too: Identity-based motivation and gender in the classroom. *Contemporary Educational Psychology*, *37*(3), 176–185.

Facebook. (n.d.). Facebook advertising targeting options. Retrieved April 15, 2019, from www.facebook.com/business/ads/ad-targeting#

Facebook. (2019, January 30). Facebook reports fourth quarter and full year 2018 results. Retrieved April 15, 2019, from https://investor.fb.com/investor-news/press-release-details/2019/Facebook-Reports-Fourth-Quarter-and-Full-Year-2018-Results/default.aspx

Frederick, S. (2005). Cognitive reflection and decision making. *Journal of Economic Perspectives*, *19*(4), 25–42.

Gilbert, D. (1991). How mental systems believe. *American Psychologist*, *46*(2), 107–119.

Gilbert, D., Krull, D., & Malone, P. (1990). Unbelieving the unbelievable: Some problems in the rejection of false information. *Journal of Personality and Social Psychology*, *59*(4), 601–613.

Giuntella, O., Nicodemo, C., & Vargas-Silva, C. (2018). *The effects of immigration on NHS waiting Times* (No. Working Paper No. 124). COMPAS, School of Anthropology, University of Oxford. Retrieved from www.compas.ox.ac.uk/2015/the-effects-of-immigration-on-nhs-waiting-times/

Goodwin, M. (2015, September 21). Why a "Brexit" looms large. *The New York Times*. Retrieved September 9, 2019, from www.nytimes.com/2015/09/22/opinion/why-a-brexit-looms-large.html?searchResultPosition=20

The Guardian. (2016). Interactive map with regional results 06/23/2016. *EU Referendum: Full Results and Analysis*. Retrieved September 9, 2019, from www.theguardian.com/

politics/ng-interactive/2016/jun/23/eu-referendum-live-results-and-analysis?
CMP=twt_b-gdndata

Haberstroh, S., Oyserman, D., Schwarz, N., Kühnen, U., & Ji, L. J. (2002). Is the inter-
dependent self more sensitive to question context than the independent self? *Journal of
Experimental Social Psychology, 38*(3), 323–329.

Haidle, M., Bolus, M., Collard, M., Conard, N., Garofoli, D., Lombard, M., . . . Whiten,
A. (2015). The nature of culture: An eight-grade model for the evolution and expan-
sion of cultural capacities in hominins and other animals. *Journal of Anthropological
Sciences, 93*, 43–70.

House of Commons, Digital, Culture, Media and Sport Committee, United Kingdom.
(2018). Disinformation and "fake news": Interim Report: Government Response to
the Committee's Fifth Report of Session 2017–19.

House of Commons, Digital, Culture, Media and Sport Committee, United Kingdom.
(2019). Disinformation and "fake news": Final Report (Eighth Report of Session
2017–19 ed.).

James, W. (1890). *The principles of psychology.* New York, NY: Dover.

Kahneman, D., & Frederick, S. (2002). Representativeness revisited: Attribute substi-
tution in intuitive judgment. In T. Gilovich, D. Griffin, & D. Kahneman (Eds.),
Heuristics and biases: The psychology of intuitive judgment (pp. 49–81). New York, NY:
Cambridge University Press.

Kang, C., & Frenkel, S. (2018, April 4). Facebook says Cambridge Analytica harvested
data of up to 87 million users. *The New York Times.* Retrieved September 9, 2019, from
www.nytimes.com/2018/04/04/technology/mark-zuckerberg-testify-congress.html

Kosinski, M., Stillwell, D., & Graepel, T. (2013). Private traits and attributes are predictable from digital records of human behavior. *Proceedings of the National Academy of
Sciences, 110*(15), 5802–5805.

Kramer, A., Guillory, J., & Hancock, J. (2014). Experimental evidence of massive-scale
emotional contagion through social networks. *Proceedings of the National Academy of
Sciences, 111*(24), 8788–8790.

Kurzban, R., & Neuberg, S. (2005). Managing ingroup and outgroup relationships. In D.
Buss (Ed.), *The handbook of evolutionary psychology* (pp. 653–675). Hoboken, NJ: John
Wiley & Sons.

Lewis, N., Jr., & Oyserman, D. (2015). When does the future begin? Time metrics matter, connecting present and future selves. *Psychological Science, 26*(6), 816–825.

Massie, A. (2015, May 9). Reflections on the revolution in Scotland. *The Spectator.*
Retrieved September 9, 2019, from www.spectator.co.uk/2015/05/this-election-has-
been-all-about-scotland/

McCrae, R. (2018, July 31). Geographical breakdown of the current account. *The Pink Book.*
Retrieved September 9, 2019, from www.ons.gov.uk/economy/nationalaccounts/
balanceofpayments/datasets/9geographicalbreakdownofthecurrentaccountthepink
book2016

Mourey, J., Lam, B., & Oyserman, D. (2015). Consequences of cultural fluency. *Social
Cognition, 33*(4), 308–344.

Mourey, J., Oyserman, D., & Yoon, C. (2013). One without the other: Seeing relationships in everyday objects. *Psychological Science, 24*(9), 1615–1622.

Murphy, S., Frank, L., Moran, M., & Patnoe-Woodley, P. (2011). Involved, transported,
or emotional? Exploring the determinants of change in knowledge, attitudes, and
behavior in entertainment-education. *Journal of Communication, 61*(3), 407–431.

Nisbett, R., & Norenzayan, A. (2002). Culture and cognition. In D. Medin (Ed.), *Ste-
vens' handbook of experimental psychology* (pp. 561–597). New York, NY: Wiley.

Nurra, C., & Oyserman, D. (2018). From future self to current action: An identity-based motivation perspective. *Self and Identity*, *17*(3), 343–364.

Oyserman, D. (2007). Social identity and self-regulation. In A. Kruglanski & E. T. Higgins (Eds.), *Social psychology: Handbook of basic principles* (pp. 432–453). New York, NY: Guilford Press.

Oyserman, D. (2009). Identity-based motivation: Implications for action-readiness, procedural-readiness, and consumer behavior. *Journal of Consumer Psychology*, *19*, 250–260.

Oyserman, D. (2011). Culture as situated cognition: Cultural mindsets, cultural fluency, and meaning making. *European Review of Social Psychology*, *22*(1), 164–214.

Oyserman, D. (2015a). Culture as situated cognition. In R. Scott & S. Kosslyn (Eds.), *Emerging trends in the behavioral and social sciences* (pp. 1–11). Hoboken, NJ: John Wiley and Sons.

Oyserman, D. (2015b). *Pathways to success through identity-based motivation*. New York, NY: Oxford University Press.

Oyserman, D. (2017). Culture three ways: Culture and subcultures within countries. *Annual Review of Psychology*, *68*, 435–463.

Oyserman, D. (2019a). Cultural fluency, mindlessness, and gullibility. In R. Baumeister & J. Forgas (Eds.), *The social psychology of gullibility*. New York, NY: Routledge.

Oyserman, D. (2019b). The essentialized self: Implications for motivation and self-regulation. *Journal of Consumer Psychology*, *29*(2), 336–343.

Oyserman, D., Elmore, K., & Smith, G. (2012). Self, self-concept, and identity. In M. Leary & J. Tangney (Eds.), *Handbook of self and identity* (pp. 69–104). New York, NY: Guilford Press.

Oyserman, D., Lewis, N., Jr., Yan, V., Fisher, O., O'Donnell, S. C., & Horowitz, E. (2017). An identity-based motivation framework for self-regulation. *Psychological Inquiry*, *28*, 139–147.

Oyserman, D., Sorensen, N., Reber, R., & Chen, S. (2009). Connecting and separating mind-sets: Culture as situated cognition. *Journal of Personality and Social Psychology*, *97*(2), 217–235.

Oyserman, D., & Yan, V. X. (2019). Making meaning: A culture-as-situated cognition approach to the consequences of cultural fluency and disfluency. In S. Kitayama & D. Cohen (Eds.), *Handbook of cultural psychology* (pp. 536–565). New York, NY: Guilford Press.

Petty, R., & Cacioppo, J. T. (1981). *Attitudes and persuasion: Classic and contemporary approaches*. Dubuque, IA: Wm. C Brown.

Petty, R., & Cacioppo, J. T. (1984). Source factors and the elaboration likelihood model of persuasion. *Advances in Consumer Research*, *11*, 668–672.

Paluck, E. L. (2009). Reducing intergroup prejudice and conflict using the media: A field experiment in Rwanda. *Journal of Personality and Social Psychology*, *96*(3), 574–587.

Platow, M., Foddy, M., Yamagishi, T., Lim, L., & Chow, A. (2012). Two experimental tests of trust in in-group strangers: The moderating role of common knowledge of group membership. *European Journal of Social Psychology*, *42*(1), 30–35.

Redazione. (2018, May 9). Exclusive interview with Christopher Wylie, the Cambridge Analytica whistleblower. *Vogue Italia*. Retrieved September 9, 2019, from www.vogue.it/en/news/daily-news/2018/05/09/interview-with-christopher-wylie-cambridge-analytica/

Reyna, V. (2004). How people make decisions that involve risk: A dual-processes approach. *Current Directions in Psychological Science*, *13*(2), 60–66.

Schwarz, N. (2014). *Cognition and communication: Judgmental biases, research methods, and the logic of conversation.* New York, NY: Psychology Press.

Schwarz, N., Strack, F., Hilton, D., & Naderer, G. (1991). Base rates, representativeness, and the logic of conversation: The contextual relevance of "irrelevant" information. *Social Cognition, 9*(1), 67–84.

Schwarz, N., & Sudman, S. (Eds.). (2012). *Context effects in social and psychological research.* Berlin and Heidelberg, Germany: Springer Science & Business Media.

Shochat, E., Shniberg, M., Hirsch, G., & Tagiman, Y. (2009). U.S. Patent No. US8666198B2. Washington, DC: U.S. Patent & Trademark Office. Relationship mapping employing multi-dimensional context including facial recognition.

Shteynberg, G. (2015). Shared attention. *Perspectives on Psychological Science, 10*(5), 579–590.

Shweder, R., & LeVine, R. (Eds.). (1984). *Culture theory: Essays on mind, self and emotion.* New York, NY: Cambridge University Press.

Sudman, S., Bradburn, N. M., & Schwarz, N. (1996). *Thinking about answers: The application of cognitive processes to survey methodology.* San Francisco, CA: Jossey-Bass.

Triandis, H. (2007). Culture and psychology. In S. Kitayama & D. Cohen (Eds.), *Handbook of cultural psychology* (pp. 59–76). New York, NY: Guilford Press.

UK Research and Innovation (2019, August 9) Government pledges to protect science and research post Brexit [Press Release]. Retrieved from www.gov.uk/government/news/government-pledges-to-protect-science-and-research-post-brexit?utm_source=3aa9d710-efe1-4eea-b45f-043b81d05c9d

Weedon, J., Nuland, W., & Stamos, A. (2017). *Information operations and Facebook.* Retrieved September 9, 2019, from https://fbnewsroomus.files.wordpress.com/2017/04/facebook-and-information-operations-v1.pdf

11

CONSPIRACY BELIEFS

Knowledge, ego defense, and social integration in the processing of fake news

Dolores Albarracín

Fake news must not be difficult to come across because it took me six minutes to find this quote:

> It has been 15 months since a senior CDC scientist, Dr. William Thompson, became a whistleblower when he admitted that a 2004 CDC study was falsified in order to show that there was no link between the MMR vaccine and autism. In August of 2014 Dr. Thompson stated, "I regret that my coauthors and I omitted statistically significant information in our 2004 article published in the Journal of Pediatrics".
>
> Folks, we have a whistleblower at the CDC who has admitted, under oath that the CDC falsified data in order to deny a link between vaccinations and autism. Furthermore, Dr. Thompson has stated that senior CDC researchers tried to destroy all documents related to this cover-up. Dr. Thompson has saved these documents. It is nearly 15 months later and nothing has happened.
>
> *(https://healthimpactnews.com/2015/*
> *cdc-cover-up-of-autism-and-vaccine-link-continues/)*

Should we really believe that there is evidence that the MMR (Measles, Mumps, and Rubella) vaccine causes autism and also that this evidence has been covered up? Conspiracy beliefs such as those promoted in "fake news" set a double bind in which we are told to both (1) believe the information on the basis of evidence and (2) be satisfied with imperfect verification because the evidence has been covered up. Because of this double bind, conspiracy theories propose a pseudoreality that is plausible or nearly scientific while retaining the appeal of magical thinking and anticipating that *the truth* may never come to light. The model I present in this chapter describes how such conspiratorial arguments and

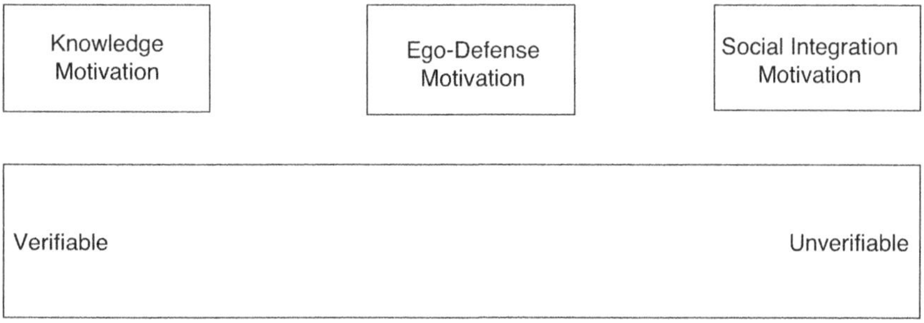

Knowledge Motivation	Ego-Defense Motivation	Social Integration Motivation

Verifiable	Unverifiable

FIGURE 11.1 The verifiability continuum and human motivations

related misinformation acquire plausibility and unfalsifiability in relation to the needs for knowledge, ego defense, and social integration. The knowledge motivation is the goal to form accurate and complete representations of the world. The ego defense motivation is the goal to defend the self from unpleasant emotional feelings such as fear. The social integration motivation is the goal to get along with and be valued by other people.

I first classify beliefs in terms of verifiability and place conspiracy beliefs and theories on this verifiability continuum. I then proceed to review how conspiracy theories and other propositions common in fake news connect with (1) the need for knowledge, (2) the need for ego defense, and (3) the need for social integration. If only one of these motivations was implicated, these beliefs would probably not be nearly as seductive. However, conspiracy theories allow news recipients to "have their cake and eat it too" by feeling "informed" while also indulging in convenient lies that appeal to their ego or keep them socially connected at the expense of accuracy. The framework guiding the chapter appears in Figure 11.1.

Belief verifiability

Beliefs can be (1) verifiable or (2) unverifiable. The verifiable end includes propositions based on direct observation through the senses and the scientific method. Scientific groups, for example, are bound together by a shared, explicit method of verification. Investigative journalism has similar principles in areas of political, educational, or financial concern. Within verifiable beliefs, *misconception* refers to a belief that is purported to be correct but has no correspondence with reality (Chan, Jones, & Albarracín, 2017). Many misconceptions are at the center of social groups (e.g., "anti-vaxers") that reinforce the misconceptions. A theory is an organized set of assumptions that guide predictions about reality in a systematic way. Scientific theories use the scientific method of systematic observation, obtaining replications of the observations, comparing conditions, and debating conclusions in the open.

The unverifiable end includes (1) conspiratorial theories and (2) religious theories that involve nonsystematic and indirect forms of evidence gathering. A *conspiracy theory* of the type that abounds in fake news is a structure of beliefs stating that powerful hidden forces are responsible for events covered up by these forces (Douglas, Sutton, Jolley, & Wood, 2015; Enster, 1999; Groh, 1987; Pratt, 2003; van Prooijen & Krouwel, 2015). Conspiracy theories have devices that inoculate members against potential attacks, namely instilling distrust in information coming from external sources. These belief structures are strong and resistant to verification.

Religious beliefs are supported by a supernatural entity and can have either a weak structure or a strong structure. Weak systems have several interrelated beliefs but are typically simpler and/or less organized, and lack mechanisms to block disconfirming information. For example, *universalism* describes a number of "new age" beliefs, paganism, and tribal religions in which the universe or the earth are the deity. Universalism also involves systems in which God is perceived to be in all objects, or in all people. Universalist systems are generally loose and do not exist as a written code of behavior, nor do they prescribe all outside beliefs to be wrong.

Strong religious systems, such as *sects* are offshoots from a larger religious system and emphasize the *unique* legitimacy of the group's beliefs and practices (Meagher & O'Brien, 1979). Sects maintain firm boundaries with the rest of society and the larger group from which the sect is separated. The Boko Haram group in Nigeria is an example of a sect because it defined itself as a dissident group, rejected traditional education, and increased secrecy and reliance on privileged knowledge. Second, *fundamentalism* entails strict and literal adherence to religious texts. For example, Billy Graham's Evangelistic Association supports a literal interpretation of the bible (e.g., the story of creation) through a mass media empire. Islamic extremism is of course common as well. Examples include the Kharijites from the seventh century and the Wahhabi fundamentalism presumably promoted by Saudi Arabia, Pakistan, and Qatar (Braswell, 2000; Delong-Bas, 2008; Huff, 1995; Nasir, 2009). All of these belief systems are strong in terms of unverifiability because they involve revealed truths but also discourage followers from seeking change.

Verifiability continuum and human motivations

The verifiability continuum appears in Figure 11.1 and provides an interesting framework to understand how beliefs can serve different types of motivations. On the left end, the most verifiable beliefs serve primarily a knowledge function because they can be aligned with reality. On the right end, the least verifiable beliefs should serve primarily social-integration functions because we need others to tell us stories about secret or spiritual worlds. At the center, both verifiable and unverifiable beliefs serve ego-defense functions, the verifiable because of the action-control functions of the ego (i.e., the need for effective action and outcome control) and the unverifiable because of purely defensive functions of the ego. Verifiable beliefs benefit action control when navigating reality, and unverifiable ones sustain us in our convenient illusions.

Given the considerations in Figure 11.1, conspiracy theories may serve any of these functions and are located, as we suggest, at the midpoint between verifiability and unverifiability. They are close enough to verifiability to be plausible, but also unfalsifiable enough to be unverifiable. In an analysis of tweets with vaccination contents, we (Palmer & Albarracín, 2018) classified the tweets in terms of anti- and pro-vaccination across two domains: MMR and HPV (Human Papilloma Virus) vaccines. As shown, the level of scientific content was quite prevalent and only slightly less so in the anti- than pro-vaccine posts. These data are presented in Table 11.1 and indicate that some conspiracy theories are argued in a way that makes them appear scientifically plausible, and thus closer to the left end of verifiability in Figure 11.1. At the same time, however, the prevalence of contents denouncing a cover-up demonstrate that "anti-vax" contents were also unverifiable because belief of a cover-up removes an audience's ability to judge information. The subterfuge is to place conspiratorial messages in limbo by making them both verifiable and unverifiable at the same time.

We gathered additional data showing that conspiracy theories are different from true conspiracies in both plausibility and unfalsifiability. In a series of studies, we asked participants to rate the theories, some true, some false, by judging their beliefs, as well as the perceived plausibility and unfalsifiability of each theory. The false theories included:

(1) Barak Obama was not born in the US; he faked his birth certificate to become president.

(Politico, 2011)

(2) Illegal immigrants voting illegally prevented Republicans from winning the popular vote in 2016.

(Business Insider, 2018)

(3) The US government created the HIV epidemic by experimentally injecting the virus in people of African descent.

(Heller, 2015)

TABLE 11.1 Features of vaccine-relevant tweets

Feature	*MMR vaccine* N = 857		*HPV vaccine* N = 737	
	Anti	Pro	Anti	Pro
Scientific content	16%	18%	14%	16%
Denouncing a cover-up	18%	0%	8%	0%

(4) The MMR vaccine causes autism but this has been covered up by the US government.

(Eggertson, 2010)

(5) Hillary Clinton ran a pizza-parlor child-sex ring in Washington, D.C.

(Rolling Stone, 2017)

(6) Lizard aliens hybridized with humans who now occupy positions of power.

(goo.gl/T79SzH)

Each of these theories had a true counterpart. For example, the pizza-parlor theory has Clinton using her private server for classified communications as its corresponding true event. Overall, although there was great variability in belief in the presented theories, participants believed in true theories more than false ones. Furthermore, we were able to study the correlations of beliefs with plausibility and unfalsifiability. Plausibility was defined as understanding why the type of situation would happen and remembering other historical examples of the situation. Unfalsifiability was defined as belief that contradictory evidence was the product of a cover-up or was false. Analyses showed overall healthy associations of beliefs with each dimension, although unfalsifiability correlated more positively with beliefs in conspiracies theories than with other beliefs. As predicted from the fact that conspiratorial beliefs are partly verifiable and partly unverifiable, both dimensions were important.

In the upcoming sections, I explain how conspiracy theories are sustained by the knowledge, ego defense, and social integration motives. Consider first the importance of the knowledge motivation. We build theories because they are useful explanations of our observations about reality. The stars in the sky have held a strong grip on lay people, philosophers, and scientists, all of whom have attempted to explain disconcerting observations: astronomical objects disappearing, growing larger, changing the way in which they move, etc. "Retrograde movement", for example, is the observation that planets occasionally appear to move backwards in the firmament. Ptolomeo had to create an elaborate explanation of retrograde movement because his model asserted that planets and stars move forward around the earth. His explanation involved a complicated arrangement of circles, in which a planet would rotate around the earth following a circular orbit. At some point, however, the planet would enter a small loop before resuming its trajectory around the main orbit. In entering this loop, the planet, which was always moving forward, would "appear" to be moving backwards when somebody observed it from earth.

Complicated explanatory models like Ptolomeo's are often abandoned in favor of a more parsimonious explanation. A case in point is Copernicus's explanation of retrograde movement. He revolutionized the scientific and religious understanding of the universe by proposing that the earth orbits around the sun. The velocity of rotation and the orbits themselves, however, differ, creating the *illusion* of retrograde movement as the earth moves at a faster speed than other bodies. In this case, a more straightforward explanation replaced the prior one.

Of course, Ptolomeo's theory was a perfectly useful explanation of the movement of celestial bodies in the sky. Explaining why the theory was replaced even though it was useful and well accepted socially requires a consideration of the concept termed *epistemic motivation* (Kruglanski, 1989, 1990; Kruglanski, Dechesne, Orehek, & Pierro, 2009; Kruglanski, Orehek, Dechesne, & Pierro, 2010), which many others have labeled as *accuracy motivation* (Hart et al., 2009). According to the concept, humans seek knowledge for the sake of knowledge, even if it has no practical use. The *knowledge motivation* is at the basis of both accurate beliefs and misconceptions. *Knowledge motivation* seems more appropriate a term than *accuracy motivation* because knowledge and information span the spectrum from inaccurate to accurate. The *New York Times* writer William Davies (2016) titled a description of the 2016 presidential campaign in the United States as "The Age of Post-Truth Politics". In his view, the tendency to represent society in terms of facts began with the introduction of accounting at the end of the medieval age. Before that time, however, facts were not as important because knowledge and truth were revealed in nonliteral fashion, which superseded the more trivial realm of facts.

In addition to knowledge, we are driven by ego-defense motivation, which is the goal to defend the self from unpleasant feelings, such as the disappointment, shame, or sadness that may arise from behaving in incompetent or socially reproachable ways. A vast literature centered on self-enhancement and motivated reasoning suggests that people accommodate their beliefs to their psychological need of self-enhancement (Baumeister, 1997; Eagly & Chaiken, 1993; Kunda, 1990; Tesser, 2001). For example, they self-defend by rejecting or modifying information that diminishes their perceived self-worth. But the ego is also concerned with action and adaptation to reality. From that point of view, the motivation to act also balances the motivation to know, such as when we are forced to make decisions with necessarily incomplete information.

The knowledge and ego-defense needs trigger goals that set several critical psychological processes in motion, including bringing concepts into focus, employing rudimentary reasoning tools like heuristics and mindsets, and deploying more effortful analysis of information. In turn, progress through these stages depends on the level of confidence people seek, or what Shelly Chaiken (see Chaiken & Maheswaran, 1994; Chen & Chaiken, 1999; Chen, Duckworth, & Chaiken, 1999) termed "confidence thresholds". A relatively low desired level of confidence should lead to concept activation and rudimentary reasoning processes. A higher level of desired confidence will cause people to engage in deeper analytical reasoning until actual confidence reaches the desired confidence threshold.

Confidence thresholds are important for both knowledge and ego-defense motivation. People who seek to gain a thorough understanding of a problem will first activate concepts and attempt to apply heuristics. If the heuristics satisfy their desired level of confidence, people are likely to arrive at a judgment based on the heuristic. In contrast, if the desired level of confidence is not met, people are likely to continue with more effortful analysis of information, ending when they reach their desired confidence threshold. Even though these mechanisms follow from both knowledge and ego-defense motivation, additional processing has different effects depending on the motivation type. When knowledge is sought, higher processing produces a more complete, unbiased understanding. However, when ego defense is sought, higher processing simply rationalizes a desired conclusion.

People also strive to be integrated socially, and this need also influences their beliefs. For example, believing that our ancestors protect us from the afterlife may strengthen our ego but also may give us a spiritual form of social integration. Moreover, many conspiracy beliefs, and most scientific beliefs, create automatic social connections with a community of fellow believers.

Conspiracy theories and need for knowledge

Understanding reality involves constructing knowledge and making judgments that are inherently subjective. *Knowledge* is what we believe to exist independently of ourselves: we write with the certainty that the keyboard in front of us exists, and we are similarly certain that we need the correct password to gain access to our computer. In addition to this knowledge, we can make *judgments* with awareness that they are subjective. Beliefs in God or beliefs quitting smoking is healthy are examples. These beliefs position each person in relation to others but do not describe reality or the absolute probability that a statement is true.

Knowledge, beliefs, and attitudes play a number of key roles, including representing reality, understanding objective features of the world, and comparing those features with subjective standards. For example, a carpenter may measure a future table top as having a three-foot diameter. Whether three feet is large or small, however, cannot be ascertained with a tape measure. Rather, it involves an observer equipped with a mental standard making a judgment that is likely to differ from that of others. Naturally, correct representations of reality allow us to navigate the world outside of ourselves. In this context, the convenience of having beliefs is less clear and brings us to an important point: we form beliefs when we need to predict the unknown to realize a goal ("I believe that Mary will attend the conference so I will try to set up a time to talk with her then"). We are looking for an approximation that will allow us to act and pursue goals with the recognition that we lack exact knowledge in a particular case. Attitudes allow us to understand that a house cat is safer than a lion, that certain objects are edible whereas others are not, and that some people will reward us whereas others will punish us.

But do conspiracy theories also facilitate our understanding of the world? Yes, considerable research suggests that this is the case. There are three predictors of conspiracy theories that point to that conclusion, including (1) the tendency to perceive patterns, (2) uncertainty, and (3) the need to reduce uncertainty.

Tendency to perceive patterns

Tying the dots when no clear map exists is an important characteristic of conspiracy theories. Thus, factors such as the tendency to perceive patterns has received the attention of researchers. For example, research by Moulding et al. (2016) included various measures of conspiracy theories as well as the Intolerance for Uncertainty Scale (Buhr & Dugas, 2002) and the Need for Cognitive Closure (Webster & Kruglanski, 1994). This study also measured the tendency to perceive a pattern of social relations and just distribution of pain. Specifically, the authors included the *World Assumptions Scale* (WAS; Janoff-Bulman, 1989), which, among other dimensions, assesses perceptions of randomness ("bad events are distributed to people at random"). The measures of belief in conspiracy theories included the Belief in Conspiracy Theories Inventory (Swami, Chamorro-Premuzic, & Furnham, 2010). This scale involves 1 (*completely false*) to 10 (*completely true*) ratings of such items as "The Apollo moon landings never happened and were staged in a Hollywood film studio". The study also included several other conspiratorial measures, all of which had moderate positive correlations with need for closure and the tendency to perceive patterns. More recent research has reached similar conclusions (Van der Wal, Sutton, Lange, & Braga, 2018; van Prooijen, Douglas, & De Inocencio, 2018).

Uncertainty

Conspiracy theories serve a knowledge function because they allow people to perceive the world as organized and predictable (Bale, 2007; Clarke, 2002; Hofstadter, 1964; Miller, 2002; van Prooijen & Jostmann, 2013). Although any form of explanation serves the knowledge function, conspiracy theories excel in this function because of their monolithic system structure. This type of structure, which I term "strong system", renders a set of explanations unfalsifiable by casting doubt on any evidence against the theory. For example, the theory that alien lizards occupy powerful positions on earth contains mechanisms of evidence invalidation by which aliens are able to *shape shift* and cover-up any evidence about their existence. This mechanism introduces suspicion concerning any data offered by potential debunkers of the theory and thus prioritize the validity of the conspiratorial advocacy.

Psychologically, uncertainty is defined as a feeling of doubt, which is generally assumed to be at least mildly unpleasant (Wichman et al., 2010). Uncertainty is produced by a discrepancy between the actual level of understanding of an event or phenomenon and the desired level of understanding (Park, 2010). Work conducted by van Prooijen and Jostmann (2013) revealed how uncertainty propels belief in conspiracy theories without affecting other beliefs. In the first experiment reported in this paper, participants were induced to experience uncertainty by having them write about either an experience of uncertainty or the experience of watching television. They then read one or two excerpts, one about the personnel policies of oil companies being unethical (labeled "immoral" in the article) and the other about the policies being ethical (labeled "moral" in the article). Even though the excerpts did not specifically discuss a conspiracy, one can expect that an actor described as immoral provides the ideal terrain for a conspiracy theory to fill in the blanks. Thus, after reading the information about oil companies, participants were asked to answer three questions: "Do you believe that oil companies had a vested interest in the war in Iraq?", "Do you believe that oil companies helped to cause the war in Iraq?", and "To what extent do you believe that people who are associated with oil companies gave the order to start the war in Iraq?" Responses to these items had high internal consistency and were averaged as a measure of belief in conspiracy theories.

The hypothesis that guided van Prooijen and Jostmann's (2013) first experiment was that states of uncertainty will lead to spontaneously believing in conspiracies for unethical (vs. ethical) actors even though no conspiratorial information was presented. However, in the absence of uncertainty, the researchers expected no difference between the unethical and ethical conditions. In this experiment, participants were more likely to *deduce* a conspiracy when an actor was perceived as generally unethical (vs. ethical), but this effect was only present when uncertainty was made accessible.

The results of Experiment 1 were reproduced in a second experiment with the same uncertainty manipulation but describing the government of an African city to be corrupt or law-abiding. After this description, participants learned that a candidate for presidential elections opposed the government and had died in a car accident. Again, if people who feel uncertain construct a conspiracy theory as a way of reducing uncertainty, unethical actors should lead to greater endorsement of conspiratorial interpretations than ethical ones. As shown by the findings, this was in fact the case.

More indirect evidence of the effect of uncertainty comes from research on the effects of ambivalence on endorsement of conspiracy beliefs. Van Harreveld, Rutjens, Schneider, Nohlen, and Keskinis (2014) manipulated ambivalence by asking research participants to describe an issue or opinion that personally elicited ambivalence or unequivocal points of view. Participants then rated the degree to which work or financial outcomes described in a vignette were related to the actions of others. Findings indicated that the ambivalence manipulation indeed produced ambivalence as well as negative affect in relation to the ambivalence. Moreover, the unpleasant feelings associated with doubt in turn increased conspiracy beliefs.

Need to reduce uncertainty

Uncertainty alone would have little effect if humans could be content without certainty, and individuals certainly vary in their need to reduce uncertainty.

Thus, not surprisingly, a number of studies has examined the relation between this individual difference and misconceptions. The need to reduce uncertainty is often measured with the Intolerance of Uncertainty Scale (Carleton, Norton, & Asmundson, 2007; Freeston, Rhéaume, Letarte, Dugas, & Ladouceur, 1994) with statements like "I can't stand being taken by surprise" on a 5-point Likert scale (1 = *not at all characteristic of me* to 5 = *entirely characteristic of me*). Another popular measure is the Need for Cognitive Closure Scale (Roets & Van Hiel, 2011; Webster & Kruglanski, 1994), with statements such as "I dislike unpredictable situations" measured on a 6-point Likert-type scale (1= *Strongly Disagree* to 6 = *Strongly Agree*). The latter scale has a close relative, the Uncertainty Orientation Scale (Sorrentino & Short, 1986), which was apparently the result of a close collaboration by teams that eventually parted ways. Any of these measures could be predicted to show a positive association with conspiracy theories.

Contrary to expectations though, the scientific data have shown only tenuous support for a direct association between conspiracy theories and the need to reduce uncertainty. Recall that van Prooijen and Jostmann's (2013) study included five measures of conspiracy theory endorsement. With this level of thoroughness, the study provides excellent data to determine the degree to which belief in conspiracy theories correlate with need for closure and intolerance of uncertainty. However, the data were disappointing as only the association between the Conspiracy Mentality Questionnaire and the Intolerance for Uncertainty Scale was significant.

Weak associations between need for cognitive closure and conspiracy theory endorsement could be attributed to either a lack of true link between the two or to nonlinear associations. A likely candidate for such a nonlinear association is an interaction between need for cognitive closure, a chronic predisposition to make conspiratorial attributions, and available evidence at the time of making a judgment. Leman and Cinnirella (2013) investigated exactly this question by administering Swami et al.'s (2010) Belief in Conspiracy Theories Inventory as a measure of chronic conspiracy disposition and the Need for Closure Scale to college students in the United Kingdom. In addition, the authors presented ostensible evidence about a plane crash leading to five fatalities, one of whom was a political figure the opposition wanted to block. The evidence either did or did not imply a conspiracy.

If need for cognitive closure is high, one would expect the audience to want to reach a definitive conclusion by using the available evidence. Thus, chronically high conspiracy endorsers who are also high in need for closure should be more likely to attribute the accident to the conspiracy than low endorsers. Furthermore, high-need for cognitive closure participants who received no evidence of cause for the crash and of suspicious travel-plan changes should assume that a conspiracy took place, whereas high-need for cognitive closure recipients of information that all parties had been satisfied that the crash was an accident should assume that an accident took place. However, people whose need for closure is low may be less quick to reach conclusions and may thus be unaffected by either the information that was supplied to them or their chronic conspiratorial thoughts.

The results from Leman and Cinnirella's (2013) experiment conformed to expectations about chronic conspiracy endorsement. Overall, both habitually suspecting conspiracies and receiving information favoring a conspiracy increased the probability of participants suspecting foul play. However, need for cognitive closure moderated the influence of the chronic endorsement of conspiracy theories. People high in need for cognitive closure were more likely to make conspiracy attributions when they scored high (vs. low) on Belief in Conspiracy Theories Inventory (approximately $Ms = 34$ vs. 30 on a scale of 0–50). In contrast, people with low need for cognitive closure were insensitive to the information presented to them (approximately $M = 28$ in both cases). This study may thus suggest that need for closure makes people follow their habitual hunches to explain ambiguous information but has little effect when the information is compelling.

In research conducted by Marchlewska, Cichocka, and Kossowska (2017), Polish participants underwent procedures similar to those used by Leman and Cinnirella's (2013). In Experiment 1, participants read information about the arrival of refugees into Poland. Generally, need for closure correlated with the belief that the arrival of refugees was part of a conspiracy against Poland ($r = .22$). Furthermore, the effect of need for closure was stronger when participants were presented with an ostensible internet conversation suggesting that the refugee arrival was part of a conspiracy by the European Union to harm Poland. Importantly, these effects were replicated in a second experiment in which, similar to Leman and Cinnirella's (2013) work, participants were exposed to information about a plane accident.

Conspiracy theories as a form of support for the ego

A central motivation for believing in conspiracy theories within our conceptualization is the need to bolster the ego. This motivation entails defending the ego from unpleasant thoughts about the self, such as avoiding perceptions that one is malevolent, deceptive, or incompetent. But strengthening the ego also involves ensuring the executive capacities that are necessary for successful action and management of the challenges of life.

Ego defense

Personality traits associated with schizotypal personality and paranoia dominated the literature on conspiracy theories for decades. From the point of view of psychodynamic theory, schizotypal personality is characterized by omnipotence, idealization, devaluation, denial, primitive projection or projective identification, and splitting. Schizotypal personality also involves autistic fantasy and an absence of repression (Perry, Presniak, & Olson, 2013). These mechanisms allow individuals to believe that the self is all-powerful and to protect themselves from shame or fear by imagining that others have these thoughts and emotions. Through autistic fantasy, the self can be protected by imagining the world just as hey would like it to be. When people with schizotypal personality lose contact with reality, delusions of persecution, unwarranted jealousy, or exaggerated self-importance are common. One can thus speculate that schizotypy and paranoia are the result of the same type of defense mechanisms.

If paranoia is to be the cause of conspiracy theorizing, it is first necessary to demonstrate that the two factors are separate. In an excellent article of this question, Imhoff and Lamberty (2018) synthesized correlations between conspiracy theories and paranoia stemming from 11 studies. These correlations appear in Table 11.2 and are suggestive of separate constructs, which Imhoff and Lamberty confirmed via factor analyses in two additional primary studies.

In one of the studies included in Imhoff and Lamberty's meta-analysis, Darwin et al. (2011) measured adherence to conspiracy theories with an ad-hoc questionnaire containing items like "There are specialized government services who attempt to harass UFO witnesses into silence". They used the Paranormal Belief Scale (PBS; Tobacyk & Milford, 1983) to measure traditional religious belief, psi beliefs, witchcraft, superstition, spiritualism, extraordinary life forms, and precognition. They also measured paranoid tendencies with the Paranoid Ideation Scale (Fenigstein & Vanable, 1992), which consists of 20 statements rated from 1 (*not at all applicable to me*) to 5 (*extremely applicable to me*) measuring thoughts that others want to harm the respondent. They also administered the Schizotypal Personality Questionnaire (SPQ), which includes 22 items and subscales for cognitive-perceptual deficits, interpersonal deficit, and disorganization. An inspection of these data in Table 11.3 suggests considerable shared variance between conspiracy theorizing and each of these scales, particularly parapsychology and paranoid ideation. Causal modeling analyses revealed that the best fitting model was one in which the overall schizotypy score influenced conspiracy theorizing, both directly and via

TABLE 11.2 Correlations between conspiracy theories and paranoia

Study	r
Barron, Morgan, Towell, Altemeyer, and Swami (2014)	0.24
Brotherton and Eser (2015)	0.52
Bruder, Haffke, Neave, Nouripanah, and Imhoff (2013), Study 2	0.45
Bruder et al. (2013), Study 3	0.5
Cichocka, Marchlewska, and Golec de Zavala (2016)	0.37
Darwin, Neave, and Holmes (2011)	0.47
Grzesiak-Feldman and Ejsmont (2008)	0.62
Grzesiak-Feldman (2015)	0.3
Wilson and Rose (2014), Study 1	0.27
Wilson and Rose (2014), Study 2	0.27
Wilson and Rose (2014), Study 3	0.29
Wilson and Rose (2014), Study 4	0.3

Source: Adapted from Imhoff & Lamberty, 2018

TABLE 11.3 Correlations between conspiracy beliefs, religious beliefs, various paranormal beliefs and abnormal perceptions

	Conspiracy score *(N = 120)*
Religious belief	.26*
PSI (Parapsychology)	.53**
Witchcraft	.40**
Spiritualism	.43**
Superstition	.22*
Extraordinary life forms	.30*
Precognition	.22**
Total paranormal belief score	.47**
Paranoid ideation	.47**
Cognitive-perceptual deficits	.31**
Interpersonal deficit	.19*
Disorganization	.27*
Total schizotypy score	.34**

*: $p < .05$, **: $p < .01$

Source: Adapted from Darwin et al., 2011

mediating influences on paranoid ideation. This model, however, did not include the Paranormal Belief Scale.

Anxiety and support for action

The need to exercise control over one's environment has been outlined as a key factor in conspiracy theory endorsement. The hypothesis of control states that people's tendency to introduce purpose and order into their worlds stems from the need to exercise control and facilitates beliefs in conspiracy theories. Hofstadter (1964) pointed out that conspiracy beliefs help powerless or voiceless individuals to understand their disadvantaged social reality (see also Bale, 2007). Consistently, past findings indicate that the motivation to make sense of threatening events within a community increases belief in conspiracy theories (van Prooijen & van Dijk, 2014; see also van Prooijen & van Lange, 2014). Control applies to social threats but also to a general desire to retain control over any aspects of the world and has led to research on meaning-making (Heine, Proulx, & Vohs, 2006; Park, 2010; van den Bos, 2009) and compensatory control (Kay, Whitson, Gaucher, & Galinsky, 2009; Rutjens, van Harreveld, & van der Pligt, 2013). The more disturbing an event is, or the greater the loss of control, the more likely that people will endorse conspiratorial interpretations of the event (Mccauley & Jacques, 1979; Pipes, 1997; Robins & Post, 1997; Shermer, 2011; J. van Prooijen & van Dijk, 2014).

Perceptions of personal control protect us from the disorienting randomness of our lives (Lerner, 1980). According to Kay et al. (2009), humans have an arsenal of compensatory psychological mechanisms to preserve a sense of order even when actual control is not possible (see also Axt, Landau, & Kay, this volume). A compensatory perceptual reorganization of the world as orderly seems a consequence of the experience of anxiety associated with decreases in control. To test this possibility, Whitson and Galinsky (2008) had research participants recall experiences of feeling out of control and crossed this manipulation with self-affirmation. Self-affirmation (Steele, 1988) is often achieved by recalling one's important values and is expected to reduce anxiety and cognitive dissonance. Thus, in the case of activating the feelings associated with control challenges, self-affirmation should restore a sense of control. In this study, participants who were not self-affirmed had stronger beliefs in conspiratorial explanations than did those that recalled non-self-affirming material or nothing at all. In other words, reestablishing one's self-confidence reduced anxiety and eliminated the need to see order in ambiguous events.

One limitation with Whitson and Galinsky's data is the lack of a baseline for the control manipulation. Fortunately, however, van Prooijen and Acker (2015) conducted a similar experiment in which participants wrote about a time when they had felt out of control, in control, or neither. Participants then read some information about the construction of a subway line in Amsterdam and were asked questions about corruption in the construction contract. As in Whitson and Galinsky, participants with low control had stronger conspiracy beliefs than participants with high control. Extending prior findings, baseline participants did not differ significantly from participants with low control but did differ from participants with high control. All in all, threats to control increase the tendency to introduce purpose, meaning, and order into the world at the expense of believing in conspiracies.

Interestingly, van Prooijen and Acker (2015) also reanalyzed prior survey data about suspected Y2K conspiracies. The survey contained measures about the threat of the Y2K bug for the smooth functioning of computer systems around the world as well as a range of conspiracy beliefs about the Kennedy assassination and the cover-up of evidence for the existence of extraterrestrial life, among other conspiracies. The degree to which respondents felt threatened by Y2K correlated with their beliefs in various conspiracy theories that were completely unrelated to Y2K, suggesting that *any* perceived threat is likely to ignite conspiratorial explanations of events. Interestingly, a perceived Y2K threat was negatively correlated with the belief that a conspiracy surrounded the Y2K bug. This negative association may suggest that people who felt a greater threat were also better informed about the causes of Y2K. Alternatively, the obvious connection between the two measured could have led participants to alter their judgment about the conspiracy in an effort to correct for the influence of their emotions.

A more general demonstration of associations between conspiracy theory endorsement and stress was provided in a correlational study by Swami and colleagues (2016). The researchers collected data from US adults who participated in Amazon Mechanical Turk. Participants filled out the Belief in Conspiracy Theories Inventory, as well as the Perceived Stress Scale (Cohen, Kamarck, & Mermelstein, 1983), the List of Threatening Experiences Questionnaire (Brugha, Bebbington, Tennant, & Hurry, 1985), Form Y-1 of the State-Trait Anxiety Inventory (Spielberger, Gorsuch, Lushene, Vagg, & Jacobs, 1983) as a measure of state anxiety, Y-2 of the State-Trait Anxiety Inventory (Spielberger et al., 1983) as a measure of trait anxiety, and the Profile of Mood States (Shacham, 1983). Perceived stress, stressful life events, and trait anxiety correlated positively with conspiracy theory endorsement (rs = .10 to .29).

One form of anxiety that has received attention in the literature has been insecure attachment. People with secure (vs. insecure) attachment seek instrumental and emotional support from others (Florian, Mikulincer, & Taubman, 1995; Larose, Bernier, Soucy, & Duchesne, 1999). People with insecure attachment may avoid (avoidant attachment) or intensely seek proximity with others. Anxious individuals tend to exaggerate the threats they encounter as a form of gaining support from others and are hypervigilant in interpersonal domains (Cassidy & Berlin, 1994; Cassidy & Kobak, 1988; Mikulincer, Shaver, & Pereg, 2003). Green and Douglas (2018) investigated the possibility that the hypervigilance associated with anxious attachment may be associated with conspiracy theories as an attempt to reduce anxiety (Douglas, Sutton, & Cichocka, 2017). To test this hypothesis, Green and Douglas administered questionnaires measuring beliefs in conspiracy theories and in the general tendency for powerful groups to conspire, as well as attachment. As predicted, anxious attachment predicted conspiratorial thinking even after controlling other interpersonal and political variables.

The effects of reduced control, anxiety, stress, and attachment style on conspiracy theories are likely to not only be unpleasant but also problematic for the enactment of action. In fact, cognitive dissonance has been proposed to exert effects not because of the experience of anxiety but because of the action disruption produced by those feelings (Harmon-Jones, Harmon-Jones, & Levy, 2015). As beliefs and attitudes automatically promote actions, conflict arises if those beliefs and attitudes have opposing implications. Thus, sustaining actions in a relatively orderly way is likely to be the factor that underlies many of the findings associated with reductions in perceived control.

Self-esteem and narcissism

Self-esteem maintenance has been argued to be at the basis of conspiracy theories, assuming that explanations and seeing the negatives outside of the self is comforting (Robins & Post, 1997). A number of studies have measured self-esteem and correlated it with measures of conspiracy theories. In a study conducted in the

UK and Austria (Swami et al., 2011), for example, participants completed measures of conspiracy theory and self-esteem. Belief in a 7/7 conspiracy and a general conspiracy theory inventory correlated with self-esteem $r = -.16$ and $-.20$, supporting the hypothesis that people with low self-esteem endorse conspiratorial ideas more than people with high self-esteem, which replicated in a second study with a fictitious conspiracy theory as well as in other research (Galliford & Furnham, 2017). This seemingly robust finding, however, has two possible explanations. On the one hand, low self-esteem may increase these beliefs as an attempt to improve positive feelings about the self. On the other, low self-esteem may simply color people's views of the world in a negative way.

Research conducted by Cichocka, Marchlewska, De, and Olechowski (2016) illuminated the processes by which self-esteem influences conspiratorial ideas. Even though the zero-order correlations between self-esteem and conspiracy theories were not statistically significant, self-esteem predicted belief in them when controlling for narcissism. Interestingly, however, narcissism had a consistent positive association with conspiracy theories. Specifically, narcissists are more likely than non-narcissists to see themselves as envied and conspired against by others, a paranoia that in turn predicts beliefs in conspiracy theories.

The three studies reported by Cichocka et al. (2016) supported the idea that narcissism correlated positively with conspiracy theories (e.g., $r = .25$ in Study 2) and paranoia (e.g., $r = .18$ in Study 2), and that some of the influence of narcissism on conspiracy theories is mediated by paranoia. In contrast, low self-esteem is associated with lower paranoia, possibly because seeing oneself as the center of a conspiracy requires perceiving that one is valuable. Moreover, self-esteem correlated with esteem for humanity, implying that a person's self-value predicts general positivity toward others.

All of the research on self-esteem and narcissism is naturally correlational but the related variable of need for uniqueness has been varied using experimental procedures. Need for uniqueness is the desire to be different from others and stand out for unique characteristics and ideas (Lynn & Snyder, 2002). Conspiracy theories are ideal markers of uniqueness because they are relatively unconventional and suggest access to privileged knowledge (Lantian, Muller, Nurra, & Douglas, 2017). Participants who wrote about a past instance of individuality, as opposed to conformity, reported stronger conspiratorial interpretations of an accident (Lantian et al., 2017). In this light, it seems possible that the positive association between narcissism and conspiracy theories is also due to many narcissists' tendency to see themselves as intellectually superior and thus better able to perceive difficult-to-detect plots (for research in the area of collective narcissism, see Golec de Zavala & Federico, 2018).

Conspiracy theories as a form of social integration

Conspiracy theories are a social phenomenon, whereas paranoia comprises individual ideas. As other social phenomena then, we should consider the social motives that strengthen conspiratorial thought, many of which have been investigated in the literature. Of course, many of the social factors implicated in conspiracy theories are political, but the effects of isolation and exclusion are generally related to the need to be integrated socially in informal networks.

Isolation and social exclusion have been prime explanatory variables in the study of conspiracy theories but the evidence is not without ambiguities. On the one hand, isolation and social exclusion appears to strengthen beliefs in conspiracy theories by increasing anxiety and need to simplify the world. Graeupner and Coman (2017) investigated this possibility in two studies, one correlational and the other experimental. The correlation between feelings of exclusion and endorsement of conspiracy theories was $r = .19$. On the other hand, connections and concern with groups can increase consideration of such social threats as those depicted in conspiracy theories. In fact, Graeupner and Coman's second study showed that being ostensibly selected as a partner for an experimental task (the manipulation of exclusion) led to higher conspiratorial attributions than not being selected, an effect equal to $r = .25$.

Summary

The review presented in this chapter suggests that the scholarship on how arguments acquire plausibility and unfalsifiability is nascent and that research attention is warranted. In particular, the literature is populated with studies based on college students and nonrepresentative samples. Moreover, research has not paid sufficient attention to the degree to which social media and other digital technologies contribute to the dissemination of conspiracy theories and other pernicious forms of fake news. In the future, more diverse national samples and research different technologies should shed further light on the post-truth era in which we live.

In this chapter, I proposed that conspiracy theories are a fascinating case of an argument that is predicated on the basis of both verifiability and unverifiability. These two poles connect conspiracy theories with all fundamental human needs: the need for knowledge, the need for ego defense, and the need for social integration. In so doing, conspiracy theories provide a pseudo-reality that is plausible or nearly scientific but retains the mystery of cover-ups. This marriage makes these beliefs quite enduring and challenging to correct.

References

Bale, J. M. (2007). *Political paranoia v. political realism: On distinguishing between bogus conspiracy theories and genuine conspiratorial politics: Patterns of prejudice* (Vol. 41). Graduate School of International Policy Studies, Monterey Institute of International Studies. Monterey, CA, US: Taylor & Francis. http://dx.doi.org/10.1080/00313220601118751

Barron, D., Morgan, K., Towell, T., Altemeyer, B., & Swami, V. (2014). *Associations between schizotypy and belief in conspiracist ideation: Personality and individual differences* (Vol. 70). Department of Psychology, University of Westminster. London, United

Kingdom david.barron@my.westminster.ac.uk; Barron, David, 309 Regent Street, London, United Kingdom, W1B 2UW: Department of Psychology, University of Westminster, david.barron@my.westminster.ac: Elsevier Science. http://dx.doi. org/10.1016/j.paid.2014.06.040

Baumeister, R. F. (1997). Identity, self-concept, and self-esteem: The self lost and found. In *Handbook of personality psychology* (pp. 681–710). San Diego, CA, US: Academic Press.

Braswell, G. W. (2000). *What you need to know about Islam & Muslims.* Nashville, TN: B&H Publishing Group.

Brotherton, R., & Eser, S. (2015). Bored to fears: Boredom proneness, paranoia, and conspiracy theories. *Personality and Individual Differences, 80,* 1–5. https://doi.org/10.1016/j. paid.2015.02.011

Bruder, M., Haffke, P., Neave, N., Nouripanah, N., & Imhoff, R. (2013, April). Measuring individual differences in generic beliefs in conspiracy theories across cultures: Conspiracy mentality questionnaire. *Frontiers in Psychology, 4,* 225. https://doi. org/10.3389/fpsyg.2013.00225

Brugha, T., Bebbington, P., Tennant, C., & Hurry, J. (1985). The list of threatening experiences: A subset of 12 life event categories with considerable long-term contextual threat. *Psychological Medicine.* https://doi.org/10.1017/S003329170002105X

Buhr, K., & Dugas, M. J. (2002). The intolerance of uncertainty scale: Psychometric properties of the English version. *Behaviour Research and Therapy, 40*(8), 931–945. https://doi.org/10.1016/S0005-7967(01)00092-4

Business Insider. (2018). 19 outlandish conspiracy theories Donald Trump has floated on the campaign trail and in the White House. Retrieved from www.businessinsider. com/donald-trump-conspiracy-theories-2016-5#claims-3000-people-didnt-die-in-puerto-rico-after-hurricane-maria-and-that-democrats-inflated-the-death-toll-19

Carleton, R. N., Norton, M. A. P. J., & Asmundson, G. J. G. (2007). Fearing the unknown: A short version of the Intolerance of Uncertainty Scale. *Journal of Anxiety Disorders.* https://doi.org/10.1016/j.janxdis.2006.03.014

Cassidy, J., & Berlin, L. J. (1994). The insecure/ambivalent pattern of attachment: Theory and research. *Child Development.* https://doi.org/10.1111/j.1467-8624.1994.tb00796.x

Cassidy, J., & Kobak, R. R. (1988). Avoidance and its relation to other defensive process. In J. Belsky & T. Nezworski (Eds.), *Child psychology. Clinical implications of attachment* (pp. 300–323). Mahwah, NJ: Lawrence Erlbaum Associates.

Chaiken, S., & Maheswaran, D. (1994). Heuristic processing can bias systematic processing: Effects of source credibility, argument ambiguity, and task importance on attitude judgment. *Journal of Personality and Social Psychology.* https://doi.org/10.1037/0022-3514.66.3.460

Chan, M. S., Jones, C. R., & Albarracín, D. (2017). Countering false beliefs: An analysis of the evidence and recommendations of best practices for the retraction and correction of scientific misinformation. In *Handbook of the science of science communication.* https://doi.org/10.1093/oxfordhb/9780190497620.013.37

Chen, S., & Chaiken, S. (1999). The heuristic-systematic model in its broader context. In *Dualprocess theories in social psychology.* https://doi.org/10.4319/lo.2013.58.2.0489

Chen, S., Duckworth, K., & Chaiken, S. R. (1999). Motivated heuristic and systematic processing. *Psychological Inquiry.* https://doi.org/10.1207/s15327965pli1001_6

Cichocka, A., Marchlewska, M., De, A. G., & Olechowski, M. (2016). "They will not control us": Ingroup positivity and belief in intergroup conspiracies, 556–576. https:// doi.org/10.1111/bjop.12158

Cichocka, A., Marchlewska, M., & Golec de Zavala, A. (2016). *Does self-love or self-hate predict conspiracy beliefs? Narcissism, self-esteem, and the endorsement of conspiracy theories:*

Social psychological and personality science (Vol. 7). Canterbury, UK: School of Psychology, University of Kent a.k.cichocka@kent.ac.uk; Institute for Social Studies, University of Warsaw, Warsaw, Poland ; Department of Psychology, Goldsmiths, University of London, London, United Kingdom; Cichock: Sage Publications. http://dx.doi.org/10.1177/1948550615616170

Clarke, S. (2002). Conspiracy theories and conspiracy theorizing. *Philosophy of the Social Sciences.* https://doi.org/10.1177/004931032002001

Cohen, S., Kamarck, T., & Mermelstein, R. (1983). A global measure of perceived stress. *Journal of Health and Social Behavior, 24*(4), 385–396.

Darwin, H., Neave, N., & Holmes, J. (2011). Belief in conspiracy theories. The role of paranormal belief, paranoid ideation and schizotypy. *Personality and Individual Differences, 50*(8), 1289–1293. https://doi.org/10.1016/j.paid.2011.02.027

Davies, W. (2016, August 24). The age of post-truth politics. *The New York Times.* Retrieved from www.nytimes.com/

Delong-Bas, N. J. (2008). *Wahhabi Islam: From revival and reform to global jihad.* Oxford: Oxford University Press.

Douglas, K. M., Sutton, R. M., & Cichocka, A. (2017). The psychology of conspiracy theories. *Current Directions in Psychological Science, 26*(6), 538–542. https://doi.org/10.1177/0963721417718261

Douglas, K. M., Sutton, R. M., Jolley, D., & Wood, M. J. (2015). The social, political, environmental, and health-related consequences of conspiracy theories. In M. Bilewicz, A. Cichocka, & W. Soral (Eds.), *The psychology of conspiracy* (pp. 183–200). New York and London: Routledge/Taylor & Francis Group.

Eagly, A. H., & Chaiken, S. (1993). The psychology of attitudes. Fort Worth, TX: Harcourt Brace Jovanovich College Publishers.

Eggertson, L. (2010). Lancet retracts 12-year-old article linking autism to MMR vaccines. *CMAJ : Canadian Medical Association Journal = Journal de l'Association Medicale Canadienne, 182*(4). https://doi.org/10.1503/cmaj.109-3179

Enster, M. (1999). *Conspiracy theories: Secrecy and power in American culture.* St. Paul, MN: University of Minnesota Press.

Fenigstein, A., & Vanable, P. A. (1992). Paranoia and self-consciousness. *Journal of Personality and Social Psychology.* https://doi.org/10.1037/0022-3514.62.1.129

Florian, V., Mikulincer, M., & Taubman, O. (1995). Does hardiness contribute to mental health during a stressful real-life situation? The roles of appraisal and coping. *Journal of Personality and Social Psychology.* https://doi.org/10.1037/0022-3514.68.4.687

Freeston, M. H., Rhéaume, J., Letarte, H., Dugas, M. J., & Ladouceur, R. (1994). Why do people worry? *Personality and Individual Differences.* https://doi.org/10.1016/0191-8869(94)90048-5

Galliford, N., & Furnham, A. (2017). *Individual difference factors and beliefs in medical and political conspiracy theories: Scandinavian journal of psychology* (Vol. 58). Research Department of Clinical, Educational and Health Psychology, University College London. London, UK: Wiley-Blackwell Publishing Ltd. http://dx.doi.org/10.1111/sjop.12382

Golec de Zavala, A., & Federico, C. M. (2018). Collective narcissism and the growth of conspiracy thinking over the course of the 2016 United States presidential election: A longitudinal analysis. *European Journal of Social Psychology.* https://doi.org/10.1002/ejsp.2496

Graeupner, D., & Coman, A. (2017). *The dark side of meaning-making: How social exclusion leads to superstitious thinking: Journal of experimental social psychology* (Vol. 69). Princeton, NJ, US: Department of Psychology, Princeton University acoman@princeton.edu; Coman, Alin, Peretsman-Scully Hall, #529, Princeton, US, 08540, Department of

Psychology, Princeton University, acoman@princeton.edu: Elsevier Science. http://dx.doi.org/10.1016/j.jesp.2016.10.003

Green, R., & Douglas, K. M. (2018). Anxious attachment and belief in conspiracy theories. *Personality and Individual Differences*, *125*, 30–37. https://doi.org/10.1016/j.paid.2017.12.023

Groh, D. (1987). Draft of a theory of conspiracy theories. In *Changing conceptions of conspiracy*. https://doi.org/10.1007/978-1-4612-4618-3

Grzesiak-Feldman, M. (2015). *Are the high authoritarians more prone to adopt conspiracy theories? The role of right-wing authoritarianism in conspiratorial thinking*. (M. Bilewicz, A. Cichocka, & W. Soral, Eds.), *The psychology of conspiracy BT: The psychology of conspiracy*. New York, NY: Routledge and Taylor & Francis Group. Retrieved from https://search.proquest.com/docview/1717508783?accountid=14553

Grzesiak-Feldman, M., & Ejsmont, A. (2008). *Paranoia and conspiracy thinking of Jews, Arabs, Germans, and Russians in a Polish sample: Psychological reports* (Vol. 102). Warsaw, Poland: University of Warsaw ika@psych.uw.edu.pl; Grzesiak-Feldman, Monika, Stawki 5/7, Warsaw, Poland, 00–183, Faculty of Psychology, University of Warsaw, ika@psych.uw.edu.pl: Psychological Reports Sage Publications. http://dx.doi.org/10.2466/PR0.102.3.884-886

Harmon-Jones, E., Harmon-Jones, C., & Levy, N. (2015). An action-based model of cognitive-dissonance processes. *Current Directions in Psychological Science*. https://doi.org/10.1177/0963721414566449

Hart, W., Albarracín, D., Eagly, A.H., Lindberg, M., Lee, K.H., & Brechan, I. (2009). Feeling validated vs. being correct: A meta-analysis of exposure to information. *Psychological Bulletin*, *135*, 555–588. doi: 10.1037/a0015701. PMID: 19586162

Heine, S. J., Proulx, T., & Vohs, K. D. (2006). The meaning maintenance model: On the coherence of social motivations. *Personality and Social Psychology Review*, *10*(2), 88–110. https://doi.org/10.1207/s15327957pspr1002_1

Heller, J. (2015). Rumors and realities: Making sense of HIV/AIDS conspiracy narratives and contemporary legends. *American Journal of Public Health*, *105*(1), e43–e50. https://doi.org/10.2105/AJPH.2014.302284

Hofstadter, R. (1964, November). The paranoid style in American politics. *Harpers Magazine*.

Huff, T. E. (1995). Rethinking islam and fundamentalism. *Sociological Forum*. https://doi.org/10.1007/BF02095834

Imhoff, R., & Lamberty, P. (2018). *How paranoid are conspiracy believers? Toward a more fine-grained understanding of the connect and disconnect between paranoia and belief in conspiracy theories. European Journal of Social Psychology*. Mainz, Germany: Johannes Gutenberg University of Mainz roland.imhoff@uni-mainz.de: John Wiley & Sons. http://dx.doi.org/10.1002/ejsp.2494

Janoff-Bulman, R. (1989). Assumptive worlds and the stress of traumatic events: Applications of the schema construct. *Social Cognition*. https://doi.org/10.1521/soco.1989.7.2.113

Kay, A. C., Whitson, J. A., Gaucher, D., & Galinsky, A. D. (2009). *Compensatory control: Achieving order through the mind, our institutions, and the heavens: Current directions in psychological science* (Vol. 18). Waterloo, ON, Canada: University of Waterloo ackay@uwaterloo.ca; University of Texas at Austin, Austin, TX, US; Northwestern University, Evanston, IL, US; Kay, Aaron C., 200 University AveWest, Waterloo, Canada, Department of Psychology, University of Water: Wiley-Blackwell Publishing Ltd. Blackwell Publishing Sage Publications. http://dx.doi.org/10.1111/j.1467-8721.2009.01649.x

Kruglanski, A. W. (1989). *Lay epistemics and human knowledge: Cognitive and motivational bases: Perspectives in social psychology*. https://doi.org/10.1007/978-1-4899-0924-4

Kruglanski, A. W. (1990). Lay epistemic theory in social-cognitive psychology. *Psychological Inquiry.* https://doi.org/10.1207/s15327965pli0103_1

Kruglanski, A. W., Dechesne, M., Orehek, E., & Pierro, A. (2009). Three decades of lay epistemics: The why, how, and who of knowledge formation. *European Review of Social Psychology.* https://doi.org/10.1080/10463280902860037

Kruglanski, A. W., Orehek, E., Dechesne, M., & Pierro, A. (2010). Lay epistemic theory: The motivational, cognitive, and social aspects of knowledge formation. *Social and Personality Psychology Compass.* https://doi.org/10.1111/j.1751-9004.2010.00308.x

Kunda, Z. (1990). The case for motivated reasoning. *Psychological Bulletin.* https://doi.org/10.1037/0033-2909.108.3.480

Lantian, A., Muller, D., Nurra, C., & Douglas, K. M. (2017). *"I know things they don't know!": The role of need for uniqueness in belief in conspiracy theories: Social psychology* (Vol. 48). Grenoble, France: University Grenoble Alpes dominique.muller@univ-grenoble-alpes.fr; School of Psychology, University of Kent, United Kingdom; Muller, Dominique, Bâtiment BSHM, Grenoble Cedex 9, France, 38 058, LIP/PC2S, University Grenoble Alpes, dominique.muller@univ-: Hogrefe Publishing Hogrefe & Huber Publishers Verlag Hans Huber. http://dx.doi.org/10.1027/1864-9335/a000306

Larose, S., Bernier, A., Soucy, N., & Duchesne, S. (1999). Attachment style dimensions, network orientation and the process of seeking help from college teachers. *Journal of Social and Personal Relationships.* https://doi.org/10.1177/0265407599162006

Leman, P. J., & Cinnirella, M. (2013). Beliefs in conspiracy theories and the need for cognitive closure. *Frontiers in Psychology, 4.* https://doi.org/10.3389/fpsyg.2013.00378

Lerner, M. J. (1980). The belief in a just world. In *The belief in a just world: A fundamental delusion.* https://doi.org/10.1007/978-1-4899-0448-5_2

Lynn, M., & Snyder, C. R. (2002). *Uniqueness seeking.* In C. R. Snyder & S. J. Lopez (Eds.), *Handbook of positive psychology* (pp. 395–410). New York, NY: Oxford University Press.

Marchlewska, M., Cichocka, A., & Kossowska, M. (2017). *Addicted to answers: Need for cognitive closure and the endorsement of conspiracy beliefs. European journal of social psychology* (Vol. 48). Warsaw, Poland: Institute for Social Studies, University of Warsaw marta.marchlewska@psych.uw.edu.pl; School of Psychology, University of Kent, Canterbury, United Kingdom; Institute of Psychology, Jagiellonian University, Kraków, Poland: John Wiley & Sons. http://dx.doi.org/10.1002/ejsp.2308

Mccauley, C., & Jacques, S. (1979). The popularity of conspiracy theories of presidential assassination: A Bayesian analysis. *Journal of Personality and Social Psychology, 37*(5), 637–644. https://doi.org/10.1037/0022-3514.37.5.637

Meagher, P. K., & O'Brien, T. C. (1979). *Encyclopedic dictionary of religion* (Vol. 3). Sisters of St. Joseph of Philadelphia. Washington, DC: Corpus Publications.

Mikulincer, M., Shaver, P. R., & Pereg, D. (2003). Attachment theory and affect regulation: The dynamics, development, and cognitive consequences of attachment-related strategies. *Motivation and Emotion.* https://doi.org/10.1023/A:1024515519160

Miller, S. (2002). Conspiracy theories: Public arguments as coded social critiques: A Rhetorical analysis of the Twa flight 800 conspiracy theories. *Argumentation and Advocacy.* https://doi.org/10.1080/00028533.2002.11821576

Moulding, R., Nix-Carnell, S., Schnabel, A., Nedeljkovic, M., Burnside, E. E., Lentini, A. F., & Mehzabin, N. (2016). *Better the devil you know than a world you don't? Intolerance of uncertainty and worldview explanations for belief in conspiracy theories: Personality and individual differences* (Vol. 98). Burwood, VIC, Australia: School of Psychology, Deakin University richard.moulding@deakin.edu.au; School of Psychology, Swinburne University of Technology, VIC, Australia; Moulding, Richard, Melbourne Burwood Campus, 221 Burwood Highway, Burwood, Australia, 3: Elsevier Science. http://dx.doi.org/10.1016/j.paid.2016.04.060

Nasir, J. J. (2009). *The status of women under Islamic law and modern Islamic legislation.* Boston, MA: Brill.

Palmer, R., & Albarracín, D. (2018). Trust in science as a deterrent and a facilitator of belief in conspiracy theories: Pseudoscience preys on audiences that trust in science. *University of Illinois at Urbana-Champaign.* https://doi.org/10.13012/B2IDB-4469040_V1

Park, C. L. (2010). Making sense of the meaning literature: An integrative review of meaning making and its effects on adjustment to stressful life events. *Psychological Bulletin.* https://doi.org/10.1037/a0018301

Perry, J. C., Presniak, M. D., & Olson, T. R. (2013). Defense mechanisms in schizotypal, borderline, antisocial, and narcissistic personality disorders. *Psychiatry: Interpersonal and Biological Processes*, 76(1), 32–52. https://doi.org/10.1521/psyc.2013.76.1.32

Pipes, D. (1997). *Conspiracy: How the paranoid style flourishes and where it comes from.* New York: Free Press.

Politico. (2011). Birthersim: Where it all began. *Politico.* In B. Smith, & B. Tau. Retrieved from https://www.politico.com/story/2011/04/birtherism-where-it-all-began-053563

Pratt, R. (2003). Theorizing conspiracy. *Theory and Society.* https://doi.org/10.1023/A:1023996501425

Prooijen, J.-W., & Acker, M. (2015). *The influence of control on belief in conspiracy theories: Conceptual and applied extensions: Applied cognitive psychology* (Vol. 29). Amsterdam, Netherlands: Netherlands Institute for the Study of Crime and Law Enforcement j.w.van.prooijen@vu.nl; Otterbein University, Westerville, OH, US; Prooijen, Jan-Willem, Van der Boechorststraat 1, Amsterdam, Netherlands, 1081 BT, Department of Social: John Wiley & Sons. http://dx.doi.org/10.1002/acp.3161

Robins, R. S., & Post, J. M. (1997). *Political paranoia: The psychopolitics of hatred.* New Haven, CT: Yale University Press.

Roets, A., & Van Hiel, A. (2011). Item selection and validation of a brief, 15-item version of the need for closure scale. *Personality and Individual Differences.* https://doi.org/10.1016/j.paid.2010.09.004

Rolling Stones. (2017). Anatomy-of-a-fake-news-scandal. Retrieved from www.rollingstone.com/politics/politics-news/anatomy-of-a-fake-news-scandal-125877/

Rutjens, B. T., van Harreveld, F., & van der Pligt, J. (2013). Step by step: Finding compensatory order in science. *Current Directions in Psychological Science.* https://doi.org/10.1177/0963721412469810

Shacham, S. (1983). A shortened version of the profile of mood states. *Journal of Personality Assessment.* https://doi.org/10.1207/s15327752jpa4703_14

Shermer, M. (2011). *The believing brain: From ghosts and gods to politics and conspiracies: How we construct beliefs and reinforce them as truths.* New York, NY, USA: Times Books.

Sorrentino, R. M., & Short, J. A. C. (1986). Uncertainty orientation, motivation, and cognition. In R. M. Sorrentino & E. T. Higgins (Eds.), *The handbook of motivation and cognition: Foundations of social behavior* (Vol. 1; pp. 379–403). New York: Guilford Press.

Spielberger, C. D., Gorsuch, R. L., Lushene, R., Vagg, P. R., & Jacobs, G. A. (1983). *Manual for the State-Trait Anxiety Inventory (STAI Form Y): Consulting psychologists Palo Alto.* https://doi.org/10.1002/9780470479216.corpsy0943

Steele, C. M. (1988). The psychology of self-affirmation: Sustaining the integrity of the self. *Advances in Experimental Social Psychology.* https://doi.org/10.1016/S0065-2601(08)60229-4

Swami, V., Chamorro-Premuzic, T., & Furnham, A. (2010). *Unanswered questions: A preliminary investigation of personality and individual difference predictors of 9/11 conspiracist beliefs: Applied cognitive psychology* (Vol. 24). London, UK: Department of Psychology, University of Westminster virenswami@hotmail.com; Department of Psychology, Goldsmiths, University of London, London, United Kingdom; Department of

Psychology, University College London, London, United Ki: John Wiley & Sons. http://dx.doi.org/10.1002/acp.1583

Swami, V., Coles, R., Stieger, S., Pietschnig, J., Furnham, A., Rehim, S., & Voracek, M. (2011). Conspiracist ideation in Britain and Austria: Evidence of a monological belief system and associations between individual psychological differences and real-world and fictitious conspiracy theories. *British Journal of Psychology*, *102*(3), 443–463. https://doi.org/10.1111/j.2044-8295.2010.02004.x

Swami, V., Furnham, A., Smyth, N., Weis, L., Lay, A., & Clow, A. (2016). *Putting the stress on conspiracy theories: Examining associations between psychological stress, anxiety, and belief in conspiracy theories: Personality and individual differences* (Vol. 99). Cambridge, UK: Department of Psychology, Anglia Ruskin University viren.swami@anglia. ac.uk; Department of Clinical, Educational, and Health Psychology, University College London, London, United Kingdom; Department of Psychology, University of: Elsevier Science. http://dx.doi.org/10.1016/j.paid.2016.04.084

Tesser, A. (2001). On the plasticity of self-defense. *Current Directions in Psychological Science.* https://doi.org/10.1111/1467-8721.00117

Tobacyk, J., & Milford, G. (1983). Belief in paranormal phenomena: Assessment instrument development and implications for personality functioning. *Journal of Personality and Social Psychology.* https://doi.org/10.1037/0022-3514.44.5.1029

van den Bos, K. (2009). Making sense of life: The existential self trying to deal with personal uncertainty. *Psychological Inquiry.* https://doi.org/10.1080/10478400903333411

Van der Wal, R., Sutton, R. M., Lange, J., & Braga, J. (2018). Suspicious binds: Conspiracy thinking and tenuous perceptions of causal connections between cooccurring and spuriously correlated events. *European Journal of Social Psychology*, *48*, 970–989.

van Harreveld, F., Rutjens, B. T., Schneider, I. K., Nohlen, H. U., & Keskinis, K. (2014). *In doubt and disorderly: Ambivalence promotes compensatory perceptions of order: Journal of experimental psychology: General* (Vol. 143). Amsterdam, Netherlands: Department of Social Psychology, University of Amsterdam f.vanharreveld@uva.nl; Department of Clinical Psychology, VU University of Amsterdam, Amsterdam, Netherlands; van Harreveld, Frenk, Weesperplein 4, Amsterdam, Netherlands, 1018: American Psychological Association Psychological Review Company. http://dx.doi.org/10.1037/a0036099

van Prooijen, J.-W., Douglas, K., & De Inocencio, C. (2018). Connecting the dots: Illusory pattern perception predicts beliefs in conspiracies and the supernatural. *European Journal of Social Psychology*, *48*, 320–335.

van Prooijen, J.-W., & Jostmann, N. B. (2013). *Belief in conspiracy theories: The influence of uncertainty and perceived morality: European journal of social psychology* (Vol. 43). Amsterdam, Netherlands: Department of Social and Organizational Psychology, VU University Amsterdam jw.van.prooijen@psy.vu.nl; University of Amsterdam, Amsterdam, Netherlands; van Prooijen, Jan-Willem, Van den Boechorststraat 1, Amsterdam, Netherlands, 1081: John Wiley & Sons. http://dx.doi.org/10.1002/ejsp.1922

van Prooijen, J.-W., & Krouwel, A. P. M. (2015). *Mutual suspicion at the political extremes: How ideology predicts belief in conspiracy theories.* In M. Bilewicz, A. Cichocka, & W. Soral (Eds.), *The psychology of conspiracy* (pp. 79–98). New York and London: Routledge/ Taylor & Francis Group.

van Prooijen, J.-W., & van Dijk, E. (2014). When consequence size predicts belief in conspiracy theories: The moderating role of perspective taking. *Journal of Experimental Social Psychology*, *55*, 63–73. https://doi.org/10.1016/j.jesp.2014.06.006

van Prooijen, J.-W., & van Lange, P. A. M. (2014). The social dimension of belief in conspiracy theories. In *Power, politics, and paranoia: Why people are suspicious of their leaders.* https://doi.org/10.1017/CBO9781139565417.017

Webster, D. M., & Kruglanski, A. W. (1994). Individual differences in need for cognitive closure. *Journal of Personality and Social Psychology.* https://doi.org/10.1037/0022-3514. 67.6.1049

Whitson, J. A., & Galinsky, A. D. (2008). Lacking control increases illusory pattern perception. *Science.* https://doi.org/10.1126/science.1159845

Wichman, A. L., Brinol, P., Petty, R. E., Rucker, D. D., Tormala, Z. L., & Weary, G. (2010). Doubting one's doubt: A formula for confidence? *Journal of Experimental Social Psychology, 46*(2), 350–355. https://doi.org/10.1016/j.jesp.2009.10.012

Wilson, M. S., & Rose, C. (2014). *The role of paranoia in a dual-process motivational model of conspiracy belief.* Cambridge: Cambridge University Press. https://doi.org/10.1017/CBO9781139565417.019

12

FAKE NEWS ATTRIBUTIONS AS A SOURCE OF NONSPECIFIC STRUCTURE

Jordan R. Axt, Mark J. Landau, and Aaron C. Kay

Introduction

Over the last several years, claims of "fake news" have become an integral aspect of understanding how individuals perceive the media and participate in the democratic process. Most commonly, the term "fake news" refers to false news stories created by people with the goal of spreading disinformation. In this case, "fake news" refers to knowingly communicating false information with the goal of misleading readers. One example of this form of fake news comes from Russian activists creating Facebook ads that showed doctored images of celebrities (falsely) claiming that Americans could vote from home (Wagner, 2017). Another example comes from the website 70news, whose now-deleted article (falsely) stating that Donald Trump had won the popular vote in the 2016 election briefly became one of the top results for Google News searches of "final election results" (Earl, 2016). In the years since this form of fake news became such a salient force in the 2016 US elections, there has been considerable research on why people believe in such disinformation (e.g., Allcott & Gentzkow, 2017; Lazer et al., 2017; Pennycook, Cannon, & Rand, 2018, Pennycook & Rand, 2019a), who is most likely to do so (e.g., Anthony & Moulding, 2018; Bronstein, Pennycook, Bear, Rand, & Cannon, 2018), and how such beliefs can be reduced (e.g., Pennycook & Rand, 2019b).

However, the term "fake news" has other meanings. In particular, the term "fake news" has also been used as a means of discrediting news stories from more reputable sources with which groups or individuals may disagree. For example, when the Kentucky newspaper *The Courier Journal* published a story noting that governor Matt Bevin had purchased his home for 45% of its market value from a political supporter (Schneider, 2018), Bevin tweeted that the story was "fake news" and the reporter who wrote it a "sick man" (Manchester, 2017).

Here, Bevin is claiming that *The Courier Journal* was intentionally spreading false information in hopes of weakening his governorship, a claim that the reporter responsible for the story would presumably deny. These charges of "fake news" are deployed to undercut likely more legitimate news stories and to shed light on the possibility of a wider, coordinated effort among media members to spread false information with the goal of undermining certain political figures or causes.

These two uses of the term "fake news" have different origins, functions, and implications, so much so that in October 2018, the British government officially decided to no longer use the term "fake news" (Murphy, 2018), as the phrase had become conflated to mean a number of different processes, from genuine human error to intentional foreign interference in the democratic process. While much of the research on "fake news" has centered on political disinformation, we have begun to investigate the psychological function of this other form of "fake news", when individuals make fake news attributions in efforts of discrediting information from more reputable and legitimate sources.

In this chapter, we review how these attributions of fake news build upon prior psychological research on perceptions of bias in the media. Drawing off the tenets of compensatory control theory (CCT; Kay, Gaucher, Napier, Callan, & Laurin, 2008), we then introduce the novel idea that such fake news attributions offer a source of "nonspecific structure" (Landau, Kay, & Whitson, 2015) that allows individuals to preserve a structured (though nefarious) interpretation of reality. We then review both correlational and experimental data we have collected on this topic, before finally discussing some of the practical and theoretical implications for understanding fake news attributions as a source of structure, including possible interventions that may reduce the frequency of such claims.

Prior research on biased media perceptions

Biases in perceptions of the media have been the focus of much prior work in psychological research. For instance, while the primary findings of the classical "They saw a game" study (Hastorf & Cantril, 1954) focuses on the biased perceptions of the Dartmouth and Princeton students, the authors open the work by illustrating how such biases also colored the reporting from each school's student newspaper. After Princeton won the unusually rough football game against their Dartmouth rivals, a writer in the *Daily Princetonian* noted the physical play was clear evidence that the Dartmouth players were "deliberately" attempting to hurt members of the Princeton team. Conversely, a writer in the Dartmouth argued that the Princeton coach had "purposely" instructed his own players to injure their opponents. Comparing across the two reports, it's clear how readers can form the belief that journalists themselves may be a source of bias; surely, many Dartmouth students reading the accounts of the game provided by the Princeton media (or vice versa) would come to the conclusion that the supposedly objective journalists were deliberately misrepresenting the "actual" events that occurred in the game. This suspicion of biases in the media could then generalize such that all stories, no matter their source, have at least the potential to be tainted by journalists' partisan motives.

Similar biases in perceptions of the media were later more fully explored in the "hostile media phenomenon" (Vallone, Ross, & Lepper, 1985). In this work, researchers presented coverage of a prominent international event (the 1982 Beirut massacre) to participants who were either pro-Israeli or pro-Arab. All participants reported their perceptions of the objectivity and fairness of the media team responsible for the coverage. Results revealed that the pro-Israeli and pro-Arab participants saw the media coverage as equally biased *against* their own side. For instance, when using a 1 = *Biased against Israel* to 9 = *Biased in favor of Israel* response scale, pro-Israeli students saw the clip as opposing Israeli sentiment on average ($M = 2.9$) while pro-Arab students saw the same clip as supporting Israeli positions on average ($M = 6.7$). Moreover, participants higher in self-rated knowledge of the topic had *stronger* beliefs that the media were biased rather than objective.

These results shed light on several notable aspects of how individuals perceive the media. For one, participants consistently viewed the news media as opposing versus supporting their existing viewpoints, regardless of what their actual views were. This outcome is somewhat surprising, given various other self-serving biases in the way that people perceive and remember information; for instance, while people are more likely to forget negative information in memory (e.g., Zhang, Pan, Li, & Guo, 2018) or have a widespread need to prioritize self-enhancing information (e.g., Gaertner, Sedikides, & Cai, 2012; Seih, Buhrmester, Lin, Huang, & Swann, 2013), similar processes did not occur in perceptions of the news media. Rather than view the media as a way of affirming their opinions, people appeared to be motivated to accentuate those aspects of the media that were inconsistent with their worldview.

In addition, the fact that greater self-rated knowledge of the topic was associated with larger perceptions of a biased media illustrates how greater investment in a cause or issue is not associated with stronger motivation to settle on an objective truth but rather a stronger motivation to discredit potentially conflicting information As a result, for many beliefs and perhaps especially for political beliefs, even well-informed people do not view the news media as a means of arriving at an unbiased perspective but rather as a source of bias that needs to be discounted. Indeed, this widespread distrust in the media may partly explain the rising polarization in political discourse (Iyengar & Hahn, 2009). As people view the media more suspiciously, they may engage the media primarily as a means of supporting existing ideologies rather as a method for arriving at accurate perceptions of the world. To remain relevant, media organizations are increasingly pressured to cater to their viewers' ideologies, resulting in increased polarization across the media landscape.

This hostile media effect, in which members of opposing viewpoints view the same material as equally biased, is not lost on many journalists themselves.

ndeed, to many public figures, perceptions of their supposed biases are so wide-pread that the best they hope for is to be seen as *equally* biased rather than unbi-sed. For instance, James Comey, the former director of the FBI turned political commentator and author, took pride in noting how another commenter called him a clear "political hack", but simply could not figure out which political party Comey was biased toward (Comey, 2018). Likewise, sports broadcasters Joe Buck and Bob Costas have each said they take solace in knowing that they will nevitably be labeled as biased by fanbases of both teams when calling the World Series (Sandomir, 2009).

However, although there is a long line of work on perceptions of bias in the media, it is a much more recent phenomenon for these biases to evolve into claims of "fake news", which carry the specific accusation that journalists are not merely selectively reporting certain facts but rather knowingly spreading false information to advance a particular viewpoint. This specific attribution of ntentional deception on behalf of the news media carries its own consequences for how individuals perceive both the news media and the social world more generally.

"Fake news": accidental or intentional?

Much of the prior work on perceptions of the news media finds that many people see the media as a source of bias, particularly in the form of biases that oppose or downplay the causes individual readers support. However, claims of "fake news" go a step further in arguing that the news media are not merely biased (i.e., selectively reporting certain facts) but wrong (i.e., reporting information that is factually incorrect). In these cases, reporters can arrive at presenting incor-rect information due to relatively unintentional (e.g., publishing an incorrect story after failing to double-check a timeline offered by a source) or intentional reasons (e.g., attempting to intentionally deceive readers in hopes of spreading a certain political viewpoint or ideology).

In one sense, these two competing attributions (i.e., incorrect news reports arriving from honest mistakes or from intentional deception) serve the same function in that they allow individuals the ability to discredit information that is inconsistent with one's worldview. As a result, such claims of "fake news" may be viewed as another form of motivated reasoning (Kunda, 1990), a process in which people work to discredit information that is threatening to one's world-view. However, these two forms of attributions carry strongly different implica-tions for how one's social reality operates. Claiming instances of "fake news" arise from incompetence and honest mistakes is one means of discrediting them, but carries a perspective that the social world is random and lacks order. A world where journalists routinely spread false information due to simple negligence is one where serious mistakes occur that are largely impossible to predict. On the other hand, attributions that "fake news" occurs because of intentional decep-tion provides an ordered but malicious world, where known actors behave in ways that can be predicted and understood. These attributions of fake news due to willful deception are likely to be especially appealing for understanding the news media, which can be conceptualized as a large group of coordinating agents working with shared goals to undermine the same, repeated targets.

Attributions of fake news due to deception (rather than honest mistakes) is a clear option for individuals seeking to both discredit news sources with which they disagree *and* preserve a conception of the world as an orderly place. This strategy then aligns with prior work arguing that environmental threats to feelings of personal control create greater individual preferences for well-structured explanations of reality (i.e., through *nonspecific structure*; Landau et al., 2015). When experiencing threats to personal control, many individuals may then prioritize a worldview that is high in structure, even if that same worldview implies a reality where other, nefarious actors continually work to oppose one's own interests. Parallel effects have emerged in prior work using various forms of threats to control. In one study, threats to personal control (such as through reading about the risks posed by climate change) resulted in greater endorsement of the notion that large companies were working to willfully destroy the environment (Rothschild, Landau, Sullivan, & Keefer, 2012). Similarly, participants who were shown a list of threats over which they had very little control (e.g., exposure to various diseases) were more likely to think that political opponents were engaging in intentional, unethical behavior (e.g., through voter suppression) than participants whose feelings of control had not been threatened (Sullivan, Landau, & Rothschild, 2010).

In both studies, individuals experiencing lower feelings of personal control were attempting to restore that control by promoting worldviews that were simultaneously more predictable. Prior work then suggests that one effective means of retaining a perception of structure is to see the world as the result of intentional actions rather than random, impersonal forces. Notably, this strategy holds for both positive and negative events. For example, nice weather on one's wedding day may be more likely to be attributed to a benevolent deity than to random luck. However, this work focuses primarily on negative events because we are interested in how people interpret undesired information in the political realm (i.e., negative news stories about preferred political figures). In these instances, people may seek to explain negative events not by random chance but through the malevolent intentions of others.

In the case of "fake news" attributions, survey data strongly suggest that many people believe journalists are spreading false news stories intentionally more so than unintentionally. Although it may be unsettling to believe that we are consistently exposed to reports that have been willfully fabricated, this perspective is quite common among Americans. In one recent survey, 53% of Democrats, 79% of Independents, and 92% of Republicans reported believing that traditional news sources report news that they know to be "fake, false, or purposely misleading" (Fischer, 2018). Mirroring much of the prior work on threats to control, there is a widespread notion that instances of "fake news" are the result of intentional, coordinated efforts made by specific actors. In our work, we explore the individual and environmental factors that make such attributions of fake news as knowing deception psychologically appealing.

Personal need for structure and fake news attributions

One means for studying the relation between fake news attributions and need for structure can come from examining whether individual differences in need for structure, or manipulations that experimentally prompt a greater need for structure, are associated with greater willingness to attribute contested news stories as being a result of intentional deception compared to simple error. In particular, we believe that fake news attributions as being due to intentional deception should be associated with differences in the construct of Personal Need for Structure (PNS), which assesses variation in desire for a predictable and well-ordered world (Thompson, Naccarato, Parker, & Moskowitz, 2001). Prior work on PNS has shown that the construct shows divergent validity from possibly related constructs like authoritarianism, uncertainty orientation, and psychological rigidity (Neuberg & Newsom, 1993).

Much of the earliest work on PNS focused on relatively lower-level questions concerning how PNS was related to more basic social cognitive processes. For instance, individuals higher in PNS showed less complexity when asked to develop taxonomies for both non-social (e.g., colors) and social (e.g., descriptors of elderly people) stimuli, and exhibited greater reliance on gender stereotypes in an impression formation task (Neuberg & Newsom, 1993). However, more recent work has shifted toward understanding the construct as a motivated phenomenon, meaning that individuals higher in PNS see a structured world not merely as a personal preference but as a source of meaning. From this perspective, PNS is not simply a cognitive style or an impartial tendency to think in simple, clear-cut ways. Rather, it describes individual differences in how much structure people desire in the world. This motivational perspective leads to a testable hypothesis: when individuals high in PNS encounter situations that threaten structure – such as complexity, inconsistency, or ambiguity – they will respond with exaggerated cognitive efforts to restore structure. We would not expect this compensatory response to structure threats if PNS were a "cold", unmotivated, cognitive style.

For instance, only individuals high in PNS reported greater meaning in life following a mortality threat, and parallel associations with meaning in life emerged among people high in both PNS and death-thought accessibility (Vess, Routledge, Landau, & Arndt, 2009). In addition, only individuals high in PNS showed greater need to prioritize tradition in response to a terrorism-related threat (Routledge, Juhl, & Vess, 2010). Finally, people high in PNS show lower levels of death-related anxiety after experiencing a mortality salience threat (Routledge, Juhl, & Vess, 2013). In total, these more recent findings suggest that PNS is a partly motivated phenomenon; people naturally high in PNS (or induced to be so) do not simply prefer a more structured world but will rather use this preference for a structured world as a source of meaning (Swanson & Landau, in press).

Drawing from this prior research, we developed several hypotheses concerning the relation between PNS and attributions of fake news as intentional deception. First, at a correlational level, PNS should be associated with belief that "fake news" (i.e., contested news stories) is more a result of willful deception on behalf of journalists than a series of honest but harmful mistakes. Second, this association between PNS and fake news attributions as a result of willful deception should exist for both ideologically consistent news (i.e., when individuals read stories that paint disliked political figured in a negative light) *and* ideologically inconsistent news (i.e., when individuals read stories that paint preferred political figures in a negative light). In other words, since belief that the news media is engaging in intentional deception is related to a larger desire to see the world as an ordered place, the effect should be seen both when news is and is not aligned with one's own political ideology. Such an analysis can then rule out attributions of intentional deception as simply being a form of in-group favoritism (i.e., when negative stories about candidates I like are retracted, it shows intentional bias, but when negative stories about candidates I dislike are retracted, it's just an honest mistake). Rather, attributions of intentional deception may better reflect a desire to retain a perception of structure.

Finally, to provide causal evidence on the connection between PNS and attributions of fake news, individuals randomly assigned to experience a threat to their feelings of personal control should then show a greater tendency to attribute errors in news reporting to intentional deception relative to simple mistakes caused by incompetence. We believe that such work has the potential to advance our understanding of the psychological processes behind the growing appeal of claiming "fake news".

Studying fake news attributions

One unavoidable challenge in studying attributions of fake news is the ultimately subjective nature of belief. To many, there is no difference between Russian instigators knowingly spreading false information – like articles claiming it is possible to vote from home or that Donald Trump had won the popular vote – and contested news stories from more established organizations, such as the report in *The Courier Journal* over the suspiciously low price Kentucky Governor Matt Bevin paid for his home. Similar accusations of fake news have followed some of the most established names in media, such as *The New York Times*, *The Washington Post*, and CNN. However, perceived legitimacy alone is not enough to convince skeptical readers that certain news items do not represent the willful spread of false information.

To avoid this issue, we believe it is productive to focus on cases where news organizations had to correct or retract stories. These retractions and corrections hen provide a clear instance where reporters had made incorrect statements, which then forces readers into evaluating *why* such errors occurred – either as a result of honest mistakes or intentional misleading. For instance, in May of 2017, Fox News published an online article about the 2016 murder of Seth Rich (Grynbaum, 2018), a former employee of the Democratic National Committee (DNC). Among other details, the article speculated that Rich's death was somehow connected to the leak of emails from prominent DNC officials like John Podesta. In particular, the article implied that Rich may have been murdered by people working on behalf of the DNC as a form of payback for his possible role in leaking the sensitive emails.

Soon after the article appeared, several news organizations attacked Fox News for publishing the piece (e.g., Pilkington, 2017). These criticisms highlighted the distinct lack of hard evidence connecting anyone associated with the DNC to Rich's murder. Eventually, Fox News retracted the article and removed the content from their website because it did not meet the "high degree of editorial scrutiny" the site requires (Statement on coverage of Seth Rich, 2017). To Fox News defenders, the retracted story was only the result of an honest but harmful reporting error that occurred as a result of the natural reporting process, for example from failing to confirm accounts provided by anonymous sources. To others, the story was an example of a biased news organizations knowingly spreading false information in the hopes of furthering a specific political cause, such as painting the DNC in a negative light. The public was faced with the same problem: was the retracted report an instance where journalists made natural errors in the reporting process, or had Fox News simply been caught in a larger effort to intentionally deceive their audience? The Seth Rich story, and other retracted reports, force audience members to choose between a less harmful but random explanation based on honest mistakes versus a more malicious but structured explanation of coordinated deception.

In our initial studies on this topic (Axt, Landau, & Kay, in press), we presented participants with descriptions of news stories that were retracted or corrected. For one study, participants only saw ideologically consistent news stories presented across multiple vignettes, which largely entailed retracted stories that depicted members of one's own political party in a negative light (e.g., Democratic participants read about the Fox News Seth Rich story, while Republican participants read about the retracted ABC News story that Michael Flynn was prepared to testify that Donald Trump had instructed him to collude with Russian officials to influence the 2016 presidential election). After reading each vignette, participants responded to a number of items that assessed the degree to which they believed the retracted story was either the result of honest errors in reporting versus a willful desire to spread knowingly false information. For instance, participants reported whether they believed it was more likely that the story's error was due to either a lack of attention or an intentional attack on behalf of the journalist. Responses were made on a six-point Likert scale, so participants could indicate a degree of confidence in their responses ("Extremely more likely to be an honest mistake", "Moderately more likely to be an honest mistake", etc.).

Across items, we then developed an internally reliable measure of the degree to which participants thought retracted news stories were a result of willful deception from the news media. We used this measure and examined the degree to which beliefs that erroneous news was due to willful deceptions was correlated with, and caused by, personal need for structure.

At a descriptive level, results were compatible with the previously mentioned survey finding that many Democrats and Republicans believe traditional the news media are knowingly spreading false information in hopes of furthering their own political agenda. For instance, in our first study, 72.7% of Democrats believed that the Seth Rich story was due to active deception, and 84.9% believed the same to be true over Breitbart's retracted "Pizzagate" story concerning a possible sex-trafficking ring involving several prominent Democrats. Among Republicans, 53.5% believed the ABC News story over Michael Flynn was an instance of journalists engaging in intentional deception, and 55.4% provided the same explanation for a retracted "MSNBC" story alleging that Wikileaks had offered prominent Republican officials special access to DNC emails that would later be posted online. While Democrats appeared to have higher rates of attributions for intentional deception, the differences in study materials makes it difficult to compare rates between Democratic and Republican participants. Finally, though Independents were not included in primary analyses, their results also revealed that perceptions of deception were not limited to partisans; in the same study, 58.3% of Independents believed the Seth Rich Fox News story to be an act of intentional deception, and 40.0% thought the same over the Michael Flynn ABC News story.

Most importantly, across all studies, we observed a consistent, positive relationship between measured PNS (Thompson et al., 2001; example items include: "I become uncomfortable when the rules in a situation are not clear", and "I enjoy having a clear and structured mode of life") and a greater belief that the news media were actively trying to deceive their audience. In later studies, we found that this positive relationship persisted both when people learned about erroneous news reports that conflicted with and supported their political beliefs, and also persisted when individual differences in strength of political orientation was controlled for. These findings suggest that the association between PNS and attributions of intention deception reflect more than just a desire to enhance one's own political in-group or other forms of ideological bias; rather, PNS predicted attributions of intentional deception in news stories that negatively depicted both members of one's own or another political party.

We also sought to provide causal evidence on the influence of PNS on fake news attributions by employing an experimental design. Extant research finds that the most effective manipulations on feelings of structure come from threats to personal control (see Landau et al., 2015). We randomly assigned participants to reflect about aspects of their lives that were either relatively controllable versus uncontrollable (see Kay et al., 2008 for prior uses of this manipulation). Results found that those participants asked to reflect upon the uncontrollable aspects of life reported greater belief that news errors were the result of intentional deception versus honest mistakes. We also observed that responding to control threats via increased attributions of bias in news reporting helps buffer feelings that the world is structured.

In sum, then, our work highlights both a correlational and causal relationship between PNS and belief that the media are engaging in intentional deception through "fake news" stories. Across studies, this project illustrates one of the potential functions of fake news and provides groundwork for more general considerations into how claims of fake news can be best understood and even reduced.

Technological progress and lessening the influence of fake news

We believe our work establishes a connection between PNS and attributions of deception in the news media (i.e., claims of "fake news"). While finding such an association is important, it naturally leads to more practical questions concerning how we may apply prior findings related to PNS to the issue of mitigating the problem of fake news. Fortunately, past work on the need for nonspecific structure suggests several ways that attributions of intentional deception in the news media could be mitigated. Perhaps the most straightforward implication comes from research on the benefits of affirming feelings of structure, which is similar to the manipulation we used of asking participants to reflect on a time in their lives where they experienced control. Just as depriving participants of feelings of structure leads to a greater need to attribute order to external systems (e.g., Kay, Shepherd, Blatz, Chua, & Galinsky, 2010; Wang, Whitson, & Menon, 2012), providing participants with feelings of control or structure lessens this need. For example, participants who wrote about a time in their lives when they had high levels of control later showed reduced perceptions of hierarchy in an ambiguous social interaction, and reported less preference for hierarchy (i.e., a system of structure and order) when evaluating various workplace options (Friesen, Kay, Eibach, & Galinsky, 2014).

Drawing from this and our own experimental work, it's clear that affirmation of structure offers one viable means of reducing attributions of fake news; simply put, ascribing malevolent but predictable intent to journalists should be less appealing to those individuals who have higher feelings of personal control. Practical applications of such results may require some creativity; it is not immediately clear how control manipulations can be seamlessly incorporated into the ways in which people receive their news. One possibility comes from social media and new forms of communication. While social media may be the greatest source of fake news – one recent study found that 8.5% of Facebook users had shared at least one story that could be labeled as political disinformation (Guess, Nagler, & Tucker, 2019) – it may also provide the largest opportunity for people to regain feelings of personal control. Interacting with known others, sharing feelings about one's life, or curating one's information stream (e.g., by removing or adding friends) may be some ways in which people can feel some sense of control over their lives, and these features are increasingly common on social media platforms.

One potential prediction from the current work is that participants instructed to engage with social media in a more directed, controlled way may in fact show a lesser need to attribute motives of intentional deception to the news media. That is, instructing people to be more thoughtful with the information they view on social media platforms could lead to greater perceptions of structure in the world. Moreover, the benefits of affirmation of structure will likely not be limited to attributions of fake news, as separate research suggests that increased feelings of control can reduce levels of anxiety (Tullett, Kay, & Inzlicht, 2014) or facilitate goal pursuit (Kay, Laurin, Fitzsimons, & Landau, 2014). Instilling feelings of control has the potential to lessen negative consequences beyond belief in fake news. At the same time, people may experience both beneficial and harmful consequences as social media platforms become more tailored to individual preferences; such changes may create perceptions of a more structured world while also reinforcing partisan bubbles and removing the opportunity to view information not already aligned with one's worldview.

Another possible source of restoring feelings of control may come not from changing individual levels of feelings of control but from altering perceptions of the news media itself. Distrust and misperceptions of journalism are widespread. For instance, a recent survey (Columbia Journalism Review, 2019) found that less than 25% of Democrats and 15% of Republicans report having "a great deal of confidence" in the news media. In fact, among other institutions such as congress, the military, and the supreme court, the media received the highest rate of responses of participants having "hardly any confidence at all". Much of this lack of trust in the news media may stem from false beliefs in how journalism operates. For instance, in that same survey, 60% of respondents believed that journalists pay their sources, and a similar percentage believed that journalists write their articles before learning the facts.

Given the prevailing distrust of the news media and the misperceptions of how journalism operates, attributions of fake news may also be lessened by increasing the transparency of the journalism process. That is, one reason that people may feel free to attribute intentional deception to the news media is that they lack an understanding of the journalistic process, from confirming facts with multiple sources to editing and fact checking. It is plausible that a greater understanding of these processes (and the relatively small rate of errors they produce) could assuage readers' skepticism that the news media is little more than journalists trying to advance their own political agendas. Potentially small changes, such as listing fact checkers and editors in by-lines or putting in headlines the number of sources used to confirm a story, may increase trust in the media and in turn reduce the allure of ascribing intentional deception to journalists. Technological advances in how media is consumed may make more sophisticated changes possible as well; for example, online readers could be shown primary supporting documents when scrolling over relevant passages. These interventions may not change individual levels of PNS, but they may redirect the desire for structure to other sources (e.g., government or religion; Kay et al., 2008; Kay, Gaucher, McGregor, & Nash, 2010) and thereby lessen the potential for structure to be restored through ascribing malevolent intent to journalists.

We anticipate several possibilities for future directions in this area of research. A clear application is in the 2020 US presidential election, where the issue of "fake news" will very likely be relevant again. For instance, the 2020 election opens possibilities for longitudinal data collection, where researchers could track individual changes in personal need for structure and how those changes translate into mistrust of the news media. Similarly, while our experimental evidence suggests that changes to one's sense of structure lead to greater desire to believe in intentional deception, a bi-directional relationship could still exist, where rising mistrust in the news media could lead to later changes in need for structure. Finally, we anticipate that this work may be applied to identifying people who may be most susceptible to claiming "fake news"; for instance, past work has found that individuals lower in social status (e.g., Fiori, Brown, Cortina, & Antonucci, 2006) may have chronically lower levels of personal control, and as a result will find attributions of intentional deception by the news media particularly appealing.

Conclusion

The rise of labeling news stories, often from legitimate outlets, as "fake news" – alleging that journalists are intentionally deceiving the public by spreading false information – poses a serious threat not only for trust in the media but in the democratic process more broadly. Drawing from prior research on compensatory control theory and the personal need for structure, we believe that many fake news attributions are appealing because they offer an avenue for individuals to find sources of nonspecific structure in their environment. A better understanding of the psychological processes that give rise to such claims of fake news will accelerate theoretical and practical progress on how claims of fake news can be understood and potentially reduced.

References

Allcott, H., & Gentzkow, M. (2017). Social media and fake news in the 2016 election. *Journal of Economic Perspectives, 31*, 211–236.

Anthony, A., & Moulding, R. (2018). Breaking the news: Belief in fake news and conspiracist beliefs. *Australian Journal of Psychology*. Advance online publication. https://doi.org/10.1111/ajpy.12233

Axt, J. R., Landau, M. J., & Kay, A. C. (in press). The psychological appeal of fake news attributions. *Psychological Science.*

Bronstein, M. V., Pennycook, G., Bear, A., Rand, D. G., & Cannon, T. D. (2019). Belief in fake news is associated with delusionality, dogmatism, religious fundamentalism, and reduced analytic thinking. *Journal of Applied Research in Memory and Cognition.* Advance online publication. https://doi.org/10.1016/j.jarmac.2018.09.005

Columbia Journalism Review. (2019). Poll: How does the public think journalism happens? Retrieved from www.cjr.org/

Comey, J. (2018, September 30). James Comey: The F.B.I can do this. Retrieved from www.nytimes.com/

Earl, J. (2016, November 14). Google's top search result for "final election numbers" leads to fake news site. Retrieved from www.cbsnews.com

Fiori, K. L., Brown, E. E., Cortina, K. S., & Antonucci, T. C. (2006). Locus of control as a mediator of the relationship between religiosity and life satisfaction: Age, race, and gender differences. *Mental Health, Religion and Culture, 9,* 239–263.

Fischer, S. (2018, June 27). 92% of Republicans think media intentionally reports fake news. Retrieved from www.axios.com/

Friesen, J. P., Kay, A. C., Eibach, R. P., & Galinsky, A. D. (2014). Seeking structure in social organization: Compensatory control and the psychological advantages of hierarchy. *Journal of Personality and Social Psychology, 106,* 590–609.

Gaertner, L., Sedikides, C., & Cai, H. (2012). Wanting to be great and better but not average: On the pancultural desire for self-enhancing and self-improving feedback. *Journal of Cross-Cultural Psychology, 43,* 521–526.

Grynbaum, M. M. (2018, March 13). Family of Seth Rich sues Fox News over retracted article. *The New York Times.* Retrieved from www.nytimes.com/2018/03/13/business/fox-news-seth-rich-lawsuit.html

Guess, A., Nagler, J., & Tucker, J. (2019). Less than you think: Prevalence and predictors of fake news dissemination on Facebook. *Science Advances, 5,* eaau4586.

Hastorf, A. H., & Cantril, H. (1954). They saw a game: A case study. *The Journal of Abnormal and Social Psychology, 49,* 129–134.

Iyengar, S., & Hahn, K. S. (2009). Red media, blue media: Evidence of ideological selectivity in media use. *Journal of Communication, 59,* 19–39.

Kay, A. C., Gaucher, D., McGregor, I., & Nash, K. (2010). Religious belief as compensatory control. *Personality and Social Psychology Review, 14,* 37–48.

Kay, A. C., Gaucher, D., Napier, J. L., Callan, M. J., & Laurin, K. (2008). God and the government: Testing a compensatory control mechanism for the support of external systems. *Journal of Personality and Social Psychology, 95,* 18–35.

Kay, A. C., Laurin, K., Fitzsimons, G. M., & Landau, M. J. (2014). A functional basis for structure-seeking: Exposure to structure promotes willingness to engage in motivated action. *Journal of Experimental Psychology: General, 143,* 486–491.

Kay, A. C., Shepherd, S., Blatz, C. W., Chua, S. N., & Galinsky, A. D. (2010). For God (or) country: The hydraulic relation between government instability and belief in religious sources of control. *Journal of Personality and Social Psychology, 99,* 725–739.

Kunda, Z. (1990). The case for motivated reasoning. *Psychological Bulletin, 108,* 480–498.

Landau, M. J., Kay, A. C., & Whitson, J. A. (2015). Compensatory control and the appeal of a structured world. *Psychological Bulletin, 141,* 694–722.

Lazer, D., Baum, M., Grinberg, N., Friedland, L., Joseph, K., Hobbs, W., & Mattsson, C. (2017). *Combating fake news: An agenda for research and action.* Retrieved from https://shorensteincenter. org/combating-fake-news-agenda-for-research/

Manchester, J. (2017, May 28). Kentucky Governor calls reporter a "sick man". Retrieved from https://thehill.com/homenews/news/335487-kentucky-governor-calls-reporter-a-sick-man

Murphy, M. (2018, October 23). Government bans phrase "fake news". Retrieved from www.telegraph.co.uk/

Neuberg, S. L., & Newsom, J. T. (1993). Personal need for structure: Individual differences in the desire for simpler structure. *Journal of Personality and Social Psychology, 65,* 113–131.

Pennycook, G., Cannon, T. D., & Rand, D. G. (2018). Prior exposure increases perceived accuracy of fake news. *Journal of Experimental Psychology General, 147,* 1865–1880.

Pennycook, G., & Rand, D. G. (2019a). Lazy, not biased: Susceptibility to partisan fake news is better explained by lack of reasoning than by motivated reasoning. *Cognition.* Advance online publication. https://doi.org/10.1016/j.cognition.2018.06.011

Pennycook, G., & Rand, D. G. (2019b). Fighting misinformation on social media using crowdsourced judgments of news source quality. *Proceedings of the National Academy of Sciences,* 201806781.

Pilkington, E. (2017, August 7). The strange case of Fox News, Trump and the death of young Democrat Seth Rich. Retrieved from www.theguardian.com/

Rothschild, Z. K., Landau, M. J., Sullivan, D., & Keefer, L. A. (2012). A dual-motive model of scapegoating: Displacing blame to reduce guilt or increase control. *Journal of Personality and Social Psychology, 102,* 1148–1163.

Routledge, C., Juhl, J., & Vess, M. (2010). Divergent reactions to the terror of terrorism: Personal need for structure moderates the effects of terrorism salience on worldview-related attitudinal rigidity. *Basic and Applied Social Psychology, 32,* 243–249.

Routledge, C., Juhl, J., & Vess, M. (2013). Mortality salience increases death-anxiety for individuals low in personal need for structure. *Motivation and Emotion, 37,* 303–307.

Sandomir, R. (2009, November 2). Some fans see enemies behind every microphone. Retrieved from www.nytimes.com/

Schneider, G. (2018, April 27). Matt Bevin's Anchorage home now valued at almost twice what he paid in controversial deal. Retrieved from www.courier-journal.com/

Seih, Y. T., Buhrmester, M. D., Lin, Y. C., Huang, C. L., & Swann, W. B., Jr. (2013). Do people want to be flattered or understood? The cross-cultural universality of self-verification. *Journal of Experimental Social Psychology, 49,* 169–172.

Statement on coverage of Seth Rich murder investigation. (2017, May 23). Retrieved from www.foxnews.com/

Sullivan, D., Landau, M. J., & Rothschild, Z. K. (2010). An existential function of enemyship: Evidence that people attribute influence to personal and political enemies to compensate for threats to control. *Journal of Personality and Social Psychology, 98,* 434–449.

Swanson, T. J., & Landau, M. J. (in press). Terror management motivation fuels structure-seeking. In C. Routledge & M. Vess (Eds.), *The handbook of terror management theory.* Elsevier.

Thompson, M. M., Naccarato, M. E., Parker, K. C., & Moskowitz, G. B. (2001). The personal need for structure and personal fear of invalidity measures: Historical perspectives, current applications, and future directions. In G. B. Moskowitz (Ed.), *Cognitive social psychology: The Princeton symposium on the legacy and future of social cognition* (pp. 19–39). Mahwah, NJ: Erlbaum.

Tullett, A. M., Kay, A. C., & Inzlicht, M. (2014). Randomness increases self-reported anxiety and neurophysiological correlates of performance monitoring. *Social Cognitive and Affective Neuroscience, 10,* 628–635.

Vallone, R. P., Ross, L., & Lepper, M. R. (1985). The hostile media phenomenon: Biased perception and perceptions of media bias in coverage of the Beirut massacre. *Journal of Personality and Social Psychology, 49*, 577–585.

Vess, M., Routledge, C., Landau, M. J., & Arndt, J. (2009). The dynamics of death and meaning: The effects of death-relevant cognitions and personal need for structure on perceptions of meaning in life. *Journal of Personality and Social Psychology, 97*, 728–744.

Wagner, K. (2017, October 31). These are some of the tweets and Facebook ads Russia used to try and influence the 2016 presidential election. Retrieved from www.recode. net/

Wang, C. S., Whitson, J. A., & Menon, T. (2012). Culture, control, and illusory pattern perception. *Social Psychological and Personality Science, 3*, 630–638.

Zhang, Y., Pan, Z., Li, K., & Guo, Y. (2018). Self-serving bias in memories: Selectively forgetting the connection between negative information and the self. *Experimental Psychology, 65*, 236–244.

INDEX

Made in the USA
Las Vegas, NV
04 May 2022

48399536R00142